Something Other Than God

JENNIFER FULWILER

SOMETHING OTHER THAN GOD

How I Passionately Sought Happiness
and Accidentally Found It

IGNATIUS PRESS   SAN FRANCISCO

Cover detail from *The Holy Spirit* alabaster window
Gian Lorenzo Bernini, St. Peter's Basilica, Rome
Photograph © by Agnus Images

Cover design by John Herreid

To Papaw, who always believed.

All that we call human history . . . [is] the long, terrible story of man trying to find something other than God which will make him happy.

— C. S. Lewis

ACKNOWLEDGMENTS

In the six years that I have been working on this book, God has put some amazing people in my path.

First, of course, is my husband, Joe. He helped shape each draft, watched the kids while I worked, and wasn't afraid to write edits like, "This paragraph makes you seem insane." Everything in life is more fun with him at my side.

Joe's mom, Lou Fulwiler, and my parents, Pam and Don Bishop, bent over backward to help me hit writing deadlines—not to mention the fact that their examples of selfless love lit the path for me to find my way to God in the first place.

My wonderful literary agent, Ted Weinstein, is like the personal trainer who pushes you until you're collapsed and twitching on the gym floor. It's never been so fun to have someone ruin my life. The team at Ignatius Press continually amazes me with their hard work and dedication, and I am profoundly grateful to them for believing in this project. It was also an honor and a pleasure to work with developmental editor Jane Rosenman.

Hallie Lord deserves to have her name somewhere on the cover in recognition of all the hours she put into helping me with this book (many of them in the form of listening to my writer drama). I'm also blessed to have good friends like Nancy Mohn Barnard, Abigail Benjamin, Melanie Casal, Brendan and Cat Hodge, Lori Keckler, Grace Patton, Frank and Patti Scofield, Dorian Speed, Fr. Michael Sullivan, and my cousin, Br. Claude Lane, providing me with prayers, support, and words of wisdom.

I'd still be sketching out Chapter 1 if it weren't for the loving assistance of Rachel Hebert, Irma Campos, Delia Stinson, Ellen and Victoria Hebert, Gabi and Marlena Borrero, Hannah and Katie Villarreal, Annie Scofield, and Abby Brooks.

I think of Nona Aguilar, Cindy Cavnar, Bert Ghezzi, and Patrick Madrid as my writing fairy godparents for all the encouragement and

7

opportunities they sent my way. A special thanks also goes out to Kevin Knight, who helped me find an audience for my writing.

I am deeply grateful to Raymond Arroyo, Fr. James Martin, Tucker Max, and Gretchen Rubin, who were kind enough to offer endorsements of this project early on in the process, as well as to Amy Welborn, Brandon Vogt, Dorian Speed, Arthur Nielsen, Leila Miller, and Nona Aguilar, who took the time to read the manuscript and offer invaluable constructive criticism.

Tom Wehner, Dan Burke, Jeanette DeMelo, and the rest of the team at the *National Catholic Register* have been endlessly supportive as I've needed to take time off to work on the book or have babies (or, sometimes, both).

I love my blog readers, and am humbled and touched by the support they've given me over the years. I wish I could thank each of them by name.

It is one of our family's greatest blessings to be surrounded by the vibrant, faith-filled community of St. William parish, especially Noe Rocha, Fr. Dean Wilhelm, Fr. Uche Andeh, as well as Fr. Alberto Borruel, Fr. Joel McNeil, and Fr. Jonathan Raia.

I thank my children for understanding when mommy spent all that time staring at her computer screen, and for generally being awesome. Being their mother is my life's greatest honor.

And, of course, I thank God, the source of all that is good. He truly never forgets any of his sheep, even the ones who are most lost.

1

My counselor at an East Texas summer camp stepped along the gravel ground, asking us if we wanted to accept the Lord Jesus into our hearts. As she worked her way down the line of girls next to me, I used the time to try to think of a better answer than "no". Luckily, I was at the end of the group, seated on the edge of the picnic table where we'd been lined up like bottles in a carnival game. But our counselor was moving quickly.

She planted herself in front of my friend Jessica, who'd also come to camp with me and a big group of fifth graders from our neighborhood. Jessica was from one of the rare families that didn't go to church every Sunday, so I watched the exchange intently. Surely, she would take one for the team and tell this religious nut to back off.

The counselor, whom we knew only by her nickname, "Tippy", took a deep breath before speaking. She placed her hands on Jessica's bare knees, just below her flowered Jammer shorts. "Jessica", she said. "Jessica, do you want to accept Jesus Christ as your Lord and Savior?"

All the other girls leaned in, their heads cocked. Jessica looked at us, then at Tippy.

She started to say something, but faltered. I nodded in sympathy. This wouldn't be easy. "I ... yes! I'm ready! I want to make Jesus the Lord of my life!" she cried. The other girls erupted into squeals and applause, everyone clobbering Jessica with hugs and pats on the back.

Then they looked at me.

"Jenny", Tippy said. The other girls' celebration died down to wait for their next victory. "Look me in the eyes, Jenny."

I looked up. Her eyeballs glistened with emotion; her chin quivered.

"Jenny, are you 100 percent certain you're going to heaven when you die?"

"That's a big question ..." I tried to buy time. I squirmed and shifted under the pressure of the other girls' gazes.

Though it was of no use to me at that moment, I couldn't help but fixate on the fact that advertisements for Pine Grove summer camp specifically said that you didn't have to be a Christian to attend—which is the only reason my parents let me go in the first place. The slick pamphlets my friends handed me at school boasted color pictures of smiling children water skiing and horseback riding. There were no photos of religious interrogation in the brochure.

"Has the Lord been speaking to your heart?" Tippy wanted to know.

There were so many confusing things about that question that I didn't even know how to begin to answer. I was pretty sure that "the Lord" referred to Jesus, who was a guy who used to live in the Middle East, but then it was also sometimes used to refer to God, who was the invisible ghost who lived in the sky. It was impossible to keep the details of their mythology straight. On top of that, I had no idea how one would go about speaking to a person's heart. I considered suggesting that the Lord speak to my ear in the future, but this was no time for jokes.

"He, umm, I'm not really sure ..." I said. I averted my eyes, looking off toward the towering pecan tree over her shoulder.

"Do you want to get saved?"

"See, I, uhh ..."

She stepped into the path of my gaze. "If you do not get saved, you will not go to heaven. You will end up in hell. Forever. You don't want to go to hell, do you, Jenny?"

Another tough question. I needed more information about this place before I could make an informed decision. I didn't believe in heaven or hell, but even if I were to pretend that I did, I wasn't sure that hell sounded all that bad. Several religious people had assured me that my family and I were going there, and they said it was a terrible place. But so far the only thing I knew about it was that people like them weren't there. For all I knew, I might like it.

I glanced at Jessica, who was leaning against the girl next to her, overcome with the emotion of her big moment. Traitor.

"This is it, Jenny", Tippy said. "Will you accept Jesus Christ as your Lord and Savior?"

I would've been happy to lie and give the answer that would be most likely to increase my popularity within the cabin, but it might backfire. I was afraid she'd start quizzing me about the details of how I'd been communicating with Jesus, and I'd screw it up. My friends seemed to use their imaginations to picture that Jesus gave them detailed instructions about their daily lives, but I didn't know what the boundaries were for those kinds of fantasies. Could I say that Jesus wrote me a note? Or that he left a message on our answering machine? I didn't know. It would be better to try to worm my way out of this one.

"Can I think about it?" I offered hesitantly.

One of the girls gasped. Another shook her head and turned away.

Tippy held her gaze firm. "I've never had a girl in one of my cabins not get saved." She made one more glassy-eyed appeal, assuring me that she was deeply concerned about my burning in hell for eternity.

I could feel blotchy red spots breaking out all over my face. Mostly, it was from embarrassment. But there was something else fueling it as well: an angry certainty that this counselor should be ashamed of her belief system. I was a good person, more or less. Sure, there was that time I snuck into the classroom at recess and poured glue into a classmate's desk, and then let a kid I didn't like take the blame for it. In general, though, I was at least as nice as anyone else sitting on that bench. I might have been only eleven years old, but even I could recognize that worshipping a deity who sends nice people to hell is nothing to be proud of.

Tippy eventually came to the conclusion that I was beyond saving and announced that it was time to go back to the cabin. The next day was Jessica's big moment. She and Tippy left to go do whatever was involved with "getting saved", and when they returned, everyone flooded outside to celebrate the world's newest Christian. I stayed in my bunk. The bedding had been stripped since it was our last day, so I lay on the bare plastic mattress. The racket of the old window air conditioner unit wasn't quite loud enough to drown out my cabinmates' squeals and giggles outside.

Before that moment, I'd never defined myself by my views on religion. I grew up aware of the obvious fact that the physical world around us is all there is, and it never occurred to me that such a normal outlook even needed its own word. But as I listened to the giggles and yelps of the girls through the closed cabin door, I realized that my beliefs differed so radically and fundamentally from other people's beliefs that it would impact every area of my life. For the first time, I assigned to myself a label, a single word that defined me: *atheist*. The concept settled within me as perfectly as puzzle pieces snapping into place, and for the first time in days, I broke into a broad, exuberant smile.

2

"She got what? Got 'saved'? What is that?" my mom said into the phone. It was the Monday after I returned to my home in suburban Dallas, and Jessica's mom had called to report what had happened at camp. After they were finished talking, my mom turned to me. "Did you do it?"

I froze with a forkful of syrup-soaked waffles halfway to my mouth.

I was pretty sure that the correct answer would be "no", but I wasn't positive. My mom could be unpredictable about this kind of thing. On the one hand, she strongly disapproved of people pushing their religion on others. She came from the Northeast, a place where evidently it was not common for people to ask one another to accept Jesus Christ as their Lord and Savior as part of casual conversation. Unlike my dad, my mom wasn't an atheist; agnostic probably wasn't even the right word. She considered spirituality to be a private matter and seemed to see the particulars of religious dogma as irrelevant. She and I didn't talk about religion, but if we did, she probably would have said that what matters most is simply being a good person. Why wait for the rules of a religious belief system to tell you how to treat others with love?

But even though she wasn't religious, and she didn't seem to have a problem with my dad's atheism, I would occasionally find out the hard way that she harbored a certain respect for religion. When our public school invited a Christian group to offer pocket-sized Bibles to students, I grabbed one from the stack to use for arts and crafts projects. At home, I tore out some pages, cut them into little stars and hearts, and glued them to poster board as part of a collage that now hung on the main wall in my room.

When my dad noticed it, he thought it was creative. When my mom walked in with an overflowing basket to put away my clean clothes, she gasped when she saw my artwork, almost dropping the laundry. She stared at it as if I'd spray painted swastikas on my wall and told me in no uncertain terms that I was not to cut up any more Bibles.

So, what was the right answer about getting saved? Was it bad etiquette not to accept someone's religious figure as the Lord of your life? Not able to think of any lie that would guarantee a good response, I just told the truth: "No?" I waited for her response.

"Thank God", she said and shook her head. "I'm sorry they pressured you like that. It's deplorable."

I sighed and resumed chewing my waffles.

After I finished breakfast, my mom whisked my dishes to the sink, slid her watch onto her wrist, and left for the optometry office where she worked part-time as a bookkeeper. We said goodbye, and I went to call one of my friends to see if she wanted to get together. I stopped in mid-stride. All of the kids from the neighborhood were gathering for a Bible study that afternoon, so they wouldn't be available.

We'd only been back from camp for a few days, but a distinct chill had descended on my relationship with my friends. It seemed that summer camp had strengthened all of us in our beliefs: them in their Christianity, and me in my atheism.

For years, I'd strongly suspected that other people's belief in God was preventing me from climbing the elementary school social ladder. When my dad's latest construction project management job took us to Dallas, just before I entered third grade, I'd been certain that this was the place where I would finally take my rightful place as the queen of popularity. I pictured pajama-clad friends packing my couch at sleepovers, all of us giggling at inside jokes while tossing popcorn at one another. At school we would gather in the halls between classes, recognizable by our matching acid-washed blue jean jackets, hushing our conversations when the poor fools in lower social circles walked by, so that they wouldn't hear any confidential in-crowd information.

Things had not gone according to plan, and I was certain that it had nothing to do with the fact that my height left a few inches of white skin perpetually visible between the bottom of my pegged pants and my neon-pink socks. My attempts at teasing my bangs into poofy perfection ended up looking more like I was wearing a failed taxidermy experiment on my forehead, and my self-consciously stooped posture and size 9 shoes inspired my classmates to call me "Bigfoot" so frequently that new students didn't even know my real first name. Still, I saw no reason why any of this would prevent the popular kids from wanting to spend lots of time with me. Other people's religious hang-ups were the only possible explanation for the fact that I could count my friends on one hand.

There had been tension surrounding this issue from the first day we'd moved into the neighborhood, when two families stopped by and asked us where we went to church. My first day at school, I was asked the same question four more times. My excuse that we were "still looking for a church home" had been getting less effective since we hadn't managed to find one in three years. Now, thanks to the camp debacle, it was all out on the table: We didn't go to church. We were never going to church. We were not a Christian family. And now, I had no one to hang out with.

I spent the next couple of weeks roaming through the house, haunted by the absence of my friends who were off at Bible studies. We used to pass hours together while our parents were at work. Our favorite pastime was prank calling the Home Shopping network, and we rejoiced when Jessica's brother convinced the operator to put him on the air so that he could yell "FART ON MY BUTT!" on national television before they disconnected the call. We spent entire afternoons dancing around my living room, flailing our heads and jerking our arms to the *Dirty Dancing* soundtrack. Now my friends had traded all of that wholesome fun for religious brainwashing activities, and I was alone.

* * *

My dad tapped on my open bedroom door and came in for our nightly reading session. He settled onto the bed next to me and picked up our current book from my bedside table, Carl Sagan's *Cosmos*. We'd begun reading it just before I went to camp, the timing of which was probably not a coincidence. He cracked the hardcover book open, smoothed the pages flat, and prepared to read from the chapter about Johannes Kepler's work calculating Mars' orbit. He paused, shifted uncomfortably, then closed it.

"There's something important I want to talk to you about", he said.

Whatever it was must have been big, since he was the king of understatement. My dad lived most of his childhood in the jungles of Mexico, where he and his friends regularly carried guns in their daily wanderings, the threat of running into a bandit or a jaguar ever-present. As an adult he was a Special Forces demolition instructor and high-altitude parachute jumpmaster, and later in life he became an engineer. The man was wired for cool, logical thinking, so the fact that I saw a slight wrinkle in his brow caught my attention.

"I heard you got a lot of pressure from the religious kids at camp. Does that kind of thing happen a lot? At school, or with your friends?"

"Usually they just call me a Satan worshipper."

He nodded slightly and thought for a moment. "Let me tell you a story", he said. He recounted the events of Christopher Columbus' shipwreck of 1503 in what is now Jamaica. The natives had grown tired of the Europeans' constant demands for supplies and had stopped sharing their resources. Columbus saw in an almanac that a lunar eclipse was coming up, and dramatically announced to the natives that his God was so enraged with them that he'd cover the moon with blood and snatch it from the sky. A few nights later, at the exact moment Columbus had predicted, the moon turned red; unbeknownst to the natives, the earth had moved in front of the sun and its atmosphere tinted its rays. Then the earth moved into position to block out the sun's light altogether, and the moon disappeared. Pandemonium ensued, and the panic-stricken natives offered Columbus whatever he wanted if he would please ask his God to forgive them and give the moon back.

"That's kind of awesome", I snickered.

"Not if you're one of the Indians!" my dad said.

"Well, that's true."

"And that's the thing: The Indians weren't stupid; they just didn't have the same knowledge Columbus did." He looked over at me and nudged my leg with his index finger to emphasize: "What happened with Columbus is a nutshell of the whole history of religion. People realized early on that if you fill in the gaps of other people's ignorance by saying it's the work of some god, and then claim that you're in tight with that particular god, you have almost unlimited power as long as people believe it."

"Wow."

He thought for a moment, choosing his words carefully since whatever he said might be repeated with the opener, "Yeah, well, *my dad says ...*" next time I got in a playground spat with my religious friends.

"Belief in gods and angels and stuff like that is a comfort to some people", he continued. "I don't blame them for that. It's okay. It makes them feel good. I just don't like to see them pushing other people into it, especially when it's my kid."

"It's not like I'd—"

"Just make sure you don't fall into that. Make sure you don't start believing things just because someone says it's true, even if it's coming from me. Question everything."

Did my own father really think I was that stupid? My expression must have revealed my thoughts, because he threw up his hands in playful defensiveness. "I know. I know! I'm just telling you that things will change as you get older. When you're an adult, your life won't be easy like it is now. You might be surprised at how tempting it is to believe whatever will make things easier."

"Okay", I said, drawing out the word to indicate that his advice was unnecessary.

He opened *Cosmos* back up and flipped to the previous page to make sure we didn't miss anything. He began reading, his words softened by a touch of a Texas accent. I sunk back into his shoulder, leaned on his arm, and listened to my dad's gentle voice tell me of the wonders of the universe.

3

Thorns scraped my ankles as I ducked under low-hanging branches, and I inhaled notes of wild onion among the pungent aromas of the vegetation. My dad's machete rang like a bell as he hacked at vines and tree limbs. Then, finally, we broke through.

We stood in a cathedral of nature, the tree branches arching toward the sky, the creek lapping quietly below. We checked our equipment to make sure we had the chisel and the hammer. I twisted my hair back into a ponytail, and we headed into the frigid, spring-fed creek like prospectors searching for gold. Only in our case, the treasure we sought was fossils.

This land had been in my family for over a century, and I'd been coming here all eleven years of my life. Every time my parents and I visited my grandparents in central Texas, we always took a trip down to "The Creek", as this land was known in our family. It was a touchstone for me amidst our many moves for my dad's job. I always felt a sense of coming home, a comfort in this landscape that was unchanging except for the color of the leaves.

On my right was the gently sloped bank where my great-grandmother and her best friend once chatted while dangling their feet in the water. Over the cliff to my left was the farmland that my ancestors first saw through the tattered fabric of covered wagons. As we made our way down the creek, I recognized pockets of brushy woods that I'd seen in the background of faded, sepia-toned photographs.

Normally, being surrounded by the history of this place made me feel protected, connected to something larger than myself. This time, I felt the absence of my ancestors more than their presence. I was aware of a creeping realization, and I tried to shake it away—literally giving my head a quick jerk back and forth, as if I had been pestered by a fly.

The waterline inched lower as the pebble-covered creek bed rose beneath our feet, and we stepped up onto a bank. In front of us was our favorite section of rock wall. The water had cut through its hard surface millimeter by millimeter over time, exposing a little more of the wall every few thousand years.

Fallen branches cracked under my feet as I moved toward it. I looked up to the top, which stood as high as a one-story house, but my eyes only briefly lingered there. The good stuff was always lower. The wall was a timeline, the creek's eons of work cutting through the land to reveal the ancient story of one era covered over by another. Just below the grassy farmland at the top was the entombed layer of land that the conquistadors once walked. A few inches below that were the remnants of soil trod by the first humans ever to see this land. Six feet lower, about eye level for me, brought us back tens of millions of years in time. That's where the riches always lay.

Dad said something, maybe a joke about who was going to score the biggest find this time, but I hardly heard him. That formless darkness I'd tried to shoo away earlier grew closer, and my mind raced to pinpoint its source.

I leaned forward and touched a spot on the wall. Eighty million years before that Sunday morning, this spot on earth was the muddy floor of a shallow ocean. My dad had explained with awe that in the time that had passed since then, the continent of Africa had moved across the globe, Mount Everest had risen from flat land, and an entire ocean had receded and left this land dry, with only a creek chuckling through it.

I spotted something: the pattern of a medium-sized ammonite, about the diameter of a small coconut. I pulled the chisel from my pocket and chipped away at the pliable white rock around it.

"Great find!" Dad hopped over rocks to watch me extract it.

It took a few minutes to loosen the wall's grip on my newfound treasure without breaking it, but eventually black cracks shot through the wall around the fossil. The rocks that clutched it were giving way. As I eased it out, Dad thrust his hands under it to catch any pieces that fell, and a complete ammonite emerged.

"Wow. Would you look at that", Dad whispered.

We both gazed at the fossilized form of a round spiral shell, its ripples radiating out from the center with perfect symmetry. This creature had been resting at that spot on earth for so long that, molecule by molecule, its glossy shell had been replaced by stone. A few inches below the indentation left in the wall there was another fossil, one of those simple shells from an entirely different time period, maybe even the late Jurassic. I scanned up and down the space between the two fossils. Millions of years, condensed to inches. To look at that wall of rocks and fossils was to understand that a thousand years is nothing—a century even less—and the span of a human's lifetime is so short that it's not even worth talking about.

My heart pounded faster. I stepped back from the rock wall and made my way over to the water's edge. The fossil in my hands suddenly seemed too heavy to carry, so I dropped down to sit on the rocky bank.

My dad had returned to his own excavation efforts, and the scraping and crunching of his chisel faded away in the noise of my thoughts. The mental gates that had been straining against the dark realization snapped, and it all came roaring into my consciousness.

I looked at the ammonite settled in between my soggy sneakers, and I understood for the first time that my fate was no different than its own.

I had always thought of these creatures as being fundamentally different from me. They were the dead things, I was the alive thing, and that's how it would be forever. Now I wondered what had kept me from understanding that to look at these long-dead life-forms was to look at a crystal ball of what lay in store for me—except that, unless I happened to die by falling into some soft mud, I wouldn't end up a fossil. Ten million years from now, there would be nothing left of me.

I looked over at my dad, who caught my gaze and smiled. He pointed at the wall with an exaggerated expression, joking that he'd found an even better specimen. *Him too?!* I thought. Wasn't he too strong to die? Wasn't he interesting and cool enough that it would carry him past the fate of the old mollusks stuck in the fossil wall? Surely the universe couldn't move on without him.

"You okay?" His voice pulled me out of my thoughts for a moment.

"Yeah. Just thinking." I pulled myself to my feet, the musty smell of creek water wafting up from my wet clothes.

"It's pretty amazing, isn't it? Every time we come here I can't believe how lucky we are to have this place", he said, speaking breathlessly as if The Creek were the Eighth Wonder of the World.

I considered telling him what was troubling me, but it seemed pointless. Either it hadn't occurred to him, in which there was no use in shackling him with this same two-ton ball and chain, or it had occurred to him and there was nothing to talk about. What can you really say when you're having a nice day and the person you're with starts sputtering about how we're all going to die?

Through sheer willpower, I dragged myself back into the present moment. I gathered up all the troubling thoughts and shoved them away, like when I would get sick of cleaning my room and jam all the clutter into my closet, leaning on it to force it shut. We waded to another outcropping thirty yards downstream, but had no luck there. On our way back we stopped by the first bank to pick up the ammonite I'd found, then made our way to the truck.

"You want to drive?" Dad asked when we arrived at the pickup. It was a 1978 blue and white Ford that was built like a tank, and we always borrowed it from my grandfather when we came down here. Since the truck could withstand just about anything and there wasn't much on the property that could be damaged anyway, I was usually allowed to drive to and from the main road.

I slid behind the wheel, my clammy skin welcoming the sun-warmed vinyl seats. I was tall for my eleven years and could reach the pedals easily when I scooted forward. I watched the gear display to make sure that the white line moved over the *D* when I pulled the lever in the steering column, then I eased my left foot off the brake, touched my right foot to the gas, and felt the truck lurch forward.

We bounced along the trail, the trees that lined the creek drifting past the right window. Grasshoppers hopped up in front of the truck like popcorn popping. There was a narrow opening in the fence that divided the wooded area from the fields, and I always had to focus to get the truck through it. My eyes were so locked onto the gate that it took me a moment to register movement on the ground. So close that it was about to disappear behind the hood of the truck, a fat black snake slithered across the path in front of us. My left foot pounded the brake before I had a chance to think about how hard we should stop, and Dad and I slid in unison toward the dashboard as the fossil and the machete flew from the seat between us onto the floor. The snake raced behind a thicket of cacti, flipping wildly as it moved as if it were annoyed by the presence of the truck.

After a beat of silence, Dad and I laughed. And when I laughed, it was a moment of pure, all-encompassing joy. The thoughts that had troubled me earlier dropped so low in my awareness that they effectively ceased to exist, and for a few seconds all I knew was the pleasure of sitting behind the wheel of a big truck with my father at my side.

I put my foot back on the gas and maneuvered the truck through the gate. As we neared the main road, that pleasant burst of distraction began to fade. By the time I scooted over to the passenger seat, the disturbing thoughts floated to the surface once again.

When we returned to my grandparents' house, it was time to start packing so that we could make the three-hour drive back to Dallas before it got too late. I changed into dry clothes and began throwing Garfield comic books and drawing pads into my backpack, and with every move I felt the same sinking sensation I'd had at The Creek.

After a dinner of takeout barbecue, which I barely touched because of a stress–induced nausea that rumbled in my stomach, my parents and I said goodbye to my grandparents and piled into our Oldsmobile. As we backed out of the driveway, the headlights illuminated the pickup truck.

There was no solution to my problem, because it wasn't even a problem; it was just a new awareness of reality. But as I took one last glance at the pickup before it disappeared from view, I felt like there was some answer in that brief flash of happiness I'd experienced while driving the truck. The grim truth I'd uncovered hadn't gone away, but it was somehow rendered less significant when I'd been immersed in the distraction of having fun.

I'd already begun to worry that I'd live the rest of my life with these awful feelings bearing down on me at every second, but now I felt a trickle of hope that some relief could be found if I could amass more experiences like that one. It might not be a solution, but chasing those moments of happiness might be all I had.

4

I didn't forget about my newfound awareness of human mortality after I returned home from my grandfather's house; I hadn't thought I would. I didn't see how anyone could go back to normal life after having a moment of clarity like that one. It seemed like I should *do* something, like the way I approached each day should fundamentally change now that I saw what my life was in the grand scheme of things. Part of me wanted to give up on everything and sit frozen in despair, but another part of me felt like I should do my math homework instead. My mind was split between the side of me that said that nothing ultimately mattered, and another side that felt certain that the little moments of daily life did have lasting significance, even though I couldn't explain why.

Since there were no good solutions, I employed the strategy I'd discovered in my grandfather's pickup truck: I lost myself in fun activities that required a lot of mental energy. Eventually, my struggle settled into an awareness that there was something awful that I was trying not to think about, but I had forgotten what it was. I would be making a Debbie Gibson mix tape, and just as I was wondering whether it would be a betrayal to the concept to include a Tiffany song, I'd feel the unsettling thoughts rumbling nearby. If I hunkered down and focused obsessively about whether "I Saw Him Standing There" could hold its own next to "Foolish Beat", the thoughts would pass by. It was a method of intentional forgetting, and it worked.

The problem was that Christians screwed everything up. I'd be sitting in social studies class, wondering if I could possibly care any less about the difference between the House and the Senate, and some kid in front of me would lean forward and reveal that his T-shirt had a Bible verse printed on the back. The dam that held back another existential crisis would quiver and begin to crack, and it would take a tremendous amount of energy to get my mind back on track. The sheer absurdity of it all—the idea that otherwise normal, reasonable families would cling to fairy tales to avoid facing reality—showed me that the truth was so terrifying that people would do just about anything to avoid it.

The blowup at camp didn't end up being the atom bomb on my social life that I'd originally thought it would be: The memories of what happened began to fade, and my friends eventually found themselves more interested in getting a big enough group together to play Marco Polo in the backyard pool than distancing themselves from heathens. The dismantling of my friendships with Christians ended up being more of a slow process, something that happened little by little, tiny bits of warmth disappearing each time the topic of faith came up.

Usually, it didn't bother me. I was young enough that I hadn't formed deep bonds with very many kids, and it seemed like a waste of everyone's time to force a relationship between people who saw the world completely differently. But sometimes it hurt, and I saw what a tragedy it was that religion could come between people who would otherwise be close. That was the case with my friend Andrea.

Andrea had been in another cabin at the same camp during Tippy's Inquisition, and so she'd heard that I didn't want to get saved (and probably heard that I'd spit on the ground at the name of Jesus and shouted that I hated God, which was the latest from the neighborhood rumor mill). She probably also heard that a week later a friend's mom asked me point blank if I believed in God, and I said no. Before all of that she'd known that my family wasn't religious, but had never asked questions. Now there was palpable tension when the topic of religion came up.

It was around that time that my parents announced that we were moving again for my dad's job, this time to Denver. Anytime Andrea and I hung out, the question of whether we would keep in touch lingered in the air. I'd moved plenty of times before, and between the expense of long distance calls and the hassle of writing letters, I knew that leaving the state was one way to find out who your true friends were.

A few days before the moving van came, I spent the afternoon at Andrea's house. She and I sat on her bed, chatting next to frilly pillows and her favorite stuffed rabbit. The conversation took an unfortunate turn, and Andrea started babbling about church and Jesus. The upheaval from the move had thrown me for a loop, and I'd been having a hard time keeping the dark thoughts at bay. I really, really did not want to hear anything about her religious fairy tales right then.

23

Normally, Andrea was more sensitive to my differing views on this topic, but this time she kept going. An elderly lady who went to her church had died, and Andrea was wondering what it must be like for her in heaven. I shifted on the bed and looked toward the door, trying to make it as obvious as possible that I wasn't engaged. I cleared my throat. I tried to change the subject. But she kept going. Finally, I reached a breaking point.

She said that she and her parents had gone to church to pray for this woman's family, and Andrea had asked her parents if she could stay a while longer. She said that in times like these, she liked to hang out with Jesus. Before I could stop the words from coming out of my mouth, I sneered, "Oh, yeah, Jesus likes to 'hang out' all right." And I held my hands up and cocked my head to the side, in a mockery of the Crucifixion.

It felt good, for a second. It was a release to cause her pain the way she'd caused me pain, like finally hitting someone who's been provoking you. But as soon as I saw the stricken look on her face, I felt sick. My words echoed in my head, and I couldn't believe such a hateful tone had come from my mouth. "I'm sorry. I'm ... I don't know why I said that", I mumbled. Of course, it was too late. The question of whether or not we'd keep in touch after I moved had been answered.

* * *

We lived in Denver for two years, then returned to Texas just in time for my freshman year in high school. We rented a house near where my grandparents lived, just a few miles away from The Creek. Even though the town was semi-rural and predominantly Christian, I managed to find a small group of friends who were all atheist or agnostic. I got straight A's and filled my life with drama that was extreme even by teenage girl standards, which mostly kept my mind off whatever it was I was trying so hard to forget.

When it came time for college, there was never any question of where I would go. All my Texan relatives on my dad's side of the family considered Texas A&M to be the finest university in the world, and there was an assumption that it would be any intelligent person's first choice for higher education. I could have gone to Oxford and my dad's aunts would have whispered with pity, "So she couldn't get in to A&M?" My dad had been a student there before he entered the military, and he told me all about the unique vibe of the campus, which had rigorous academics by day, rowdy hijinks by night, and a whole host of wonderfully bizarre school traditions.

Unfortunately for me, things had changed a lot since Dad was there. Texas A&M still had the wonderfully bizarre traditions, but in recent decades it had become a deeply Christian university. The first semester I was there, a group of professors placed a full-page ad in the student newspaper identifying themselves as believers, inviting students to talk to them about their relationships with Christ. Students would stand and preach from the Bible in front of the Academic Building, entreating passersby to get saved (which always struck me as pointless since, as far as I could tell, I was the only person on campus who wasn't already a Christian). People would chat after Friday classes about which church service they would be attending on Sunday.

It was like elementary school all over again. I had a few friends, and there were plenty of things I liked about where I lived, but I walked around with the constant stress of not fitting in. In anthropology class a guy would raise his hand and suggest that the Amazonian tribe we were studying wouldn't have so many problems if they would embrace the Lord Jesus Christ; in poli-sci a girl would respond to the professor's question with an impromptu speech about how this nation needed to get back to its Christian roots; and at the end of the day, I'd feel drained by all the imaginary arguments I'd had where I totally demolished these people's ridiculous points in my head.

Also like elementary school, being surrounded by vocal Christians made it hard to forget the chilling fact of human mortality. The kids at A&M were smart. The school's engineering and sciences programs were some of the best in the country. To be at the library and see students talking about Jesus like he was sitting next to them, then notice their advanced physics and biomedical engineering books stacked on the table, was to be reminded that the truth about life was bad enough that it could drive even intelligent people to a state of delusional insanity. Every week I was there, I got a little closer to an existential crisis.

By the spring of my sophomore year, I couldn't take it anymore. I applied to transfer to the University of Texas at Austin and withdrew from A&M even before I found out whether I'd been accepted at UT.

I didn't know what I'd do if I got a rejection letter, but staying at A&M was no longer an option.

* * *

I did get into UT, which was a huge relief since I'd already rented an apartment near campus. My mom called one afternoon, only two months before classes were set to begin, and read the acceptance letter that had arrived at our home address. After I hung up the phone, I looked out my window onto Duval Street and watched an orange-and-white campus bus ease to a stop at the corner. Associating myself with those colors felt wrong. I never imagined that I'd graduate from college anywhere other than Texas A&M, and I certainly couldn't have conceived that I would have ended up at its big rival school.

When people asked, I said that I transferred to UT because it had an advertising program that offered a technical track that focused on internet media. There was some truth to that. But I knew the real reason, and it made me feel like an idiot. What was wrong with me that I had to leave a place that I loved in many ways because I couldn't be around religious people? Why was I always so close to an existential crisis that I couldn't function like a normal person? Nobody struggled with that kind of thing. The other atheists I knew didn't seem to have any problem with the fleetingness of human life. I'd never met anyone else who seemed troubled by the insanity of religious fervor, or who had their thoughts constantly drifting in the bleakest directions.

By the time I was done with college, I was determined to pull myself together. I graduated from UT in December, then spent the holidays with my parents. I returned to Austin in time to celebrate the last day of the twentieth century with friends and woke up on January 1, 2000, ready to begin my new life. It felt like I was embarking on a quest that was nothing short of a search for the meaning of life.

5

I sat stiffly in a leather chair at the long meeting table. In front of me was a panel of picture windows that begged me to get lost in the scenic view of the west Austin hill country. Normally, I loved soaking in the atmosphere of working in one of the most beautiful parts of town—sometimes I couldn't believe that I got such an amazing job straight out of college—but today I needed to devote all my focus to the product management meeting. I was the only female in my department and the only person who didn't have a three-page resume that read like an instruction manual called *How to Be the Most Type-A Person on the Face of the Planet*, so sometimes it was hard to make my voice heard in these meetings. I had missed a big deadline for the multimedia piece I was designing for the website. Part of the reason was that I'd been coming in late because our after-work happy hours had begun to stretch past midnight, but part of it was because I didn't have the resources I needed. I was going to ask for more resources.

"Can we start?" a product manager named Ryan asked.

Steve, the twenty-eight-year-old vice president of our department, said no. "We're waiting for Joe."

I looked up from my notes. "Joe? Who's that?"

Ryan rolled his eyes. "The guy the board brought in to babysit us."

"Ryan, he's not babysitting us", Steve said, using a tone that indicated that he and Ryan had discussed this more than once. "The board wants his perspective because he's a B-school grad and he's technical. And since he's friends with the guys who just gave us two million dollars in funding, I think we might want to be cool to him."

Now I knew who they were talking about. Shortly after our twenty-person company threw a forty-thousand-dollar party to celebrate the release of a beta version of our product, the board started asking nosy questions about the way this business was being run. Some bigwig from the venture capital firm that led the last round of funding had flown in from Silicon Valley to personally inspect the office. Unfortunately, on the last day of his visit the IT team hosted an in-office happy hour that got a little out of control, and the investor walked into the bathroom to find a manager passed out in his own vomit next to a urinal. The next Monday, the CEO and three vice presidents walked into a meeting room for a conference call with the board. They walked out as if returning from a wake and announced a whole host of changes, including the impending arrival of a new director of product management named Joe Fulwiler.

I'd heard whispers about this Joe guy's background. It caught my attention that the aggressive, overachieving guys in my department seemed to consider him an aggressive overachiever. He'd recently graduated from Stanford's Graduate School of Business, one of the top business schools in the world. While at Stanford, he'd taken coursework in artificial intelligence in the computer science grad school, rubbing elbows with some of the pioneers of internet technology who were now on the covers of magazines. He'd gone to Yale for undergrad, and someone said something about his going to law school too, though I didn't think that could be right since the guy was only twenty-nine years old.

"Ah, here he comes now", Steve announced pointedly to the meeting room, silencing any further discussion of whether or not we were happy to have the new guy in our department.

Joe walked quickly into the room, but I didn't get the impression that he was hurrying because he was late; he struck me as the type of person who never moved slowly. There were two empty seats: one across from Ryan and one at the head of the long table. Joe took the one at the head of the table.

Steve introduced him to everyone, and after I nodded an obligatory "hello" I returned to my notes. There would inevitably be some introductory small talk, and I planned to use the time to work on my pitch for getting more resources. I tapped my pen on the line where I'd totaled the time estimate for completing my project and thought about whether I should ask to hire an intern to help me. It would be hard to convince the higher-ups to add another employee to our small high-tech startup, so I considered my case carefully. Suddenly, a thought interrupted me, so unexpected that it was like hearing a thunderclap on a clear day.

You are going to marry him.

I froze. The idea was so clear and so unrelated to anything I'd been thinking about that I instinctively looked over my shoulder, as if an unseen person had said it. *Who? That Joe guy?* I replied to whatever part of my brain this crazy notion had come from.

I looked over at Joe, who was engaged in a surprisingly friendly conversation with Ryan. It turned out that they were both members of fraternities at Yale and knew people in common. Ryan even laughed out loud as Joe recounted some antics that had occurred at a fraternity reunion they'd both attended. I almost laughed out loud, too. I couldn't imagine what had prompted that ridiculous thought, since there were few things less likely to happen than my dating this Joe guy, let alone marrying him.

First of all, I wasn't even thinking about marriage. I was barely twenty-two years old, and I was intensely focused on my search to figure out what life was all about (which, in practice, meant working all the time so that I could get ahead in my career). Even if I had been thinking about dating, there was no way this guy and I could be a match. In high school and college I'd been the type of girl who wore ripped fishnet stockings and black lipstick. For a while I dyed my hair green. For fun I attended the concerts of bands like Gwar, a group whose main claim to fame was that they'd have a man dressed up like the pope walk out on stage and they'd pretend to behead him and then spray his fake blood all over the audience.

I'd now traded my black lipstick for a more business-appropriate dark red and had thrown away all my ripped fishnet. These days, I dyed my hair bright red, with black and blonde streaks added by my colorist. I may have smoothed out my appearance to look more normal, but I maintained a distaste for mainstream ideals. In other words: Girls like me had nothing in common with Ivy League frat boys.

I shook my head at the silliness of it all. I tried to get back to my notes for the meeting, but some part of me kept wondering where on earth those words had come from.

* * *

A month later, on a Tuesday afternoon, a new email popped up in my inbox with the subject: *Coffee?* It was from Joe. He wanted to know if I was interested in joining him on his daily Starbucks run.

Our company had an open-office setup designed to promote communication, and so everyone from the executives to the interns sat in the large common room at the center of the building. Joe had been assigned the desk across from mine, and with no cubicle walls to separate us, we couldn't help but interact occasionally.

Over the past few weeks I'd been pleasantly surprised to see that he wasn't the fun-killing automaton we'd all expected him to be. He had long, jocular phone calls with friends where he referenced barbecues and drinking beer at the lake. He smiled easily, and his blue eyes revealed both intensity and sincerity. Sometimes I wanted to talk to him, if for no other reason than to break up the monotony of the twelve-hour days that I usually worked, but he always seemed to be in too much of a hurry. He rarely sat at his desk for more than an hour at a time, and when he did he was so focused on whatever he was doing that he often didn't notice coworkers lined up at his desk, waiting to talk to him. On a few occasions, I was just about to start a conversation when he'd jump up to run into a conference room or to go have lunch with this CEO or that investor.

So when he invited me to get coffee, I was curious. I peeked around my monitor to try to get a glimpse of him, but he was hidden behind his own computer and didn't seem to see me looking at him. "Sure. When?" I typed in reply.

He stood from his chair, grabbed his car keys, and darted out the main door. I looked at my email inbox. His reply said: "Meet me in the parking garage in five minutes."

I wondered why he didn't just lean around his computer and ask me. Then I looked at our coworkers typing away at the desks next to us, and it occurred to me that he must have wanted to invite only me.

We rode to the coffee shop in his car, a maroon Jaguar XJ8 with the glossiest paint job I'd ever seen. The whole way there, I tried to figure out what this meeting was about. We talked about office politics and then drifted into more personal territory. I found out that, like me, he was an only child. He was from Houston, and also came from a family that had been in Texas for generations. He had recently turned down a lead for a job with a Bay Area startup called Google in favor of coming here, mainly because he wanted to come home to Texas.

It also came out that I'd heard correctly that he went to law school. He'd gone to Columbia Law and had worked as an attorney doing corporate finance mergers and acquisitions at one of the top law firms in

Manhattan. He hated the long hours and stifling work environment, so he got a job at a prestigious management consulting firm, then went to business school. He described this transition as if it were an effortless move, the way I might describe my decision to dye my hair a new shade of red.

There was a lull in the conversation after we settled in to a table at the coffee shop, so I thought I'd take the opportunity to get the meeting back on track. I cleared my throat and sat up a little straighter. "Did you want to talk about the new client interface?" I asked. I'd heard that he was now in charge of our main product, for which I was creating a fresh design, so I figured that that's why he invited me here.

"The what?" It was like I'd asked it in a different language. "Oh, the new design? No. Who cares? I'm sure you'll do a great job."

"Oh." I took a sip of my drink, some caffeinated concoction I'd never heard of. I wasn't a coffee drinker and was totally overwhelmed by the Starbucks menu, so I'd waited for Joe to order and exclaimed that that just so happened to be my favorite drink, too. "Was there something else we needed to go over before the next release?"

He seemed to think the question was funny. "No—in fact, let's not talk about that at all."

"Oh", I said. I needed to stop saying "oh." But when he suggested that we talk about something other than my current project at work, I realized that I had become so immersed in my job that my mind went blank when I tried to make conversation about anything else.

Luckily, he took the lead. "Where did you work before this?"

"I did the marketing for a feminist group that promotes girls' involvement in the sciences", I said, hoping that if I made it sound official enough it wouldn't come out that it was a college internship.

He nodded. "So what's next? What do you want to do after this job?"

There was something beyond this job? For the first time in a long while, I thought about my life on a higher level than how I was going to meet the next deadline for the new interface. Into my mind flooded memories of the girl who was depressed at A&M, who ran to UT to escape an existential crisis, who graduated college wondering if she'd always be the fragile weirdo who stressed about things that no one else stressed about. Was that me? I'd been playing the role of happy career woman long enough that it had started to feel real. It was disorienting to be reminded of that other side of myself, like seeing a ghost.

31

"I don't know. I haven't put much thought into my goals. I guess I'm still trying to figure out the meaning of life." I tried to force a casual laugh, but it sounded more like a sneeze-cough.

"Interesting", Joe said. I was surprised that he seemed genuine, since my answer was kind of lame. "So what do you think the meaning of life is?"

I took a long sip of my mystery drink. It was creamy with a vaguely burnt taste, and I decided I liked it. "Honestly, I have no idea. What about you?"

"Oh, to me it's clear", he said, as if I had asked him to add one plus one. "I grew up poor. My mom was a single mother. She grew up even poorer than I did—like, they used corncobs for toilet paper and didn't have running water when she graduated from high school."

"Seriously?" I interrupted. There were rumors at work that he'd come from a well-connected blue-blooded family, so I hadn't imagined this side of him.

"Yeah. We struggled constantly. A lot of times my mom didn't know how she was going to put dinner on the table. It sucked. So that's my meaning of life—to get out of all of that."

"Well, you're there, right? I mean, this is a pretty good job, isn't it?" I knew he had to be making six figures, and there was little question that he'd be promoted to VP soon.

He looked at me like we'd had some kind of misunderstanding and he was waiting for me to acknowledge it. Finally, he said, "No. I mean real financial stability."

I obviously still wasn't getting it.

"I have student loan debt that's more than a lot of people's debt on their houses", he explained. "I'm not talking about having a decent job and some extra cash to take a vacation once in a while. I'm talking about having enough assets to where you don't need to worry anymore. To me, that's freedom. And that's pretty much all I'm focused on right now."

"Wow. Well, good luck with that. Those are some big goals."

He shrugged. "They say that your first million is always your hardest. After that, it's not as much work."

I chuckled at his funny joke. He smiled politely, but he wasn't laughing with me. That wasn't a joke.

He held my gaze during the awkward silence that ensued, and I quickly looked down at my hands. That pattern had been repeating itself since we'd first scooted up to the table. When Joe spoke to people, he maintained eye contact for the duration of the conversation. His posture was relaxed but unyielding. When he talked about what he planned to do with his life, there was not a trace of hesitation, no twinge of uncertainty about whether his goals would actually come to fruition. He seemed to be supremely comfortable in the world, and I found that quality deeply appealing.

We spent almost two more hours talking in the coffee shop, and I delighted in every minute of it. It wasn't anything in particular that he said; rather, it was that ease with which he moved, and the force with which he conveyed his ideas. Whether it was announcing why the last version of the product sucked or detailing how he was learning the Java programming language to be more conversant with the tech team, every sentence he spoke burst forth like a proclamation. He kept asking questions about me, but each time I deflected the conversation back to him, just because I enjoyed watching him. Joe Fulwiler moved through the world as if he owned it. He knew what he wanted out of life, and anyone who had even a moment's interaction with him knew that nothing would stop him from getting it.

6

Everyone else saw it before I did. Day after day, Joe and I left the office within five minutes of one another and returned at the same time over an hour later, laughing, loudly talking over one another, and carrying matching coffee cups. But when the office manager pulled me aside and asked if Joe and I were dating, I was genuinely surprised.

Sure, I often came back to my desk flushed and giddy after our coffee meetings, feeling more alive than I ever had in my life. Joe seemed to enjoy hanging out with me as well, as I had concluded after the approximately ten thousand hours I'd spent wondering about it. I decided that he probably was not just being nice when he said I was "an insightful person" that time that we were at the coffee shop by the 360 bridge when I put too much sugar in my coffee and was wearing the yellow-and-black striped shirt (not that I had etched every last detail into my mind or anything), if nothing else because he was not the type of person who would waste time hanging out with people he didn't like.

Despite all of that, my belief that we could never be anything other than coworkers—friends, at best—was unshakable. In fact, the longer we spent time together, the less likely it seemed that anything would come of this acquaintanceship. Any time I was in Joe's presence, I felt like I had to make the most of these moments before they were gone. Joe carried with him an aura of someone who was perpetually about to move on to something else—something bigger, something better than what was here. Each Monday I was a little surprised that he was still in the office; I always expected to hear that he'd been lured away by another tech startup and didn't work here anymore. He gave me his full attention at our coffee meetings, but the moment he returned to his desk, his focus was back on his plans for world domination.

It seemed clear that Joe would only date someone who could keep up with him. I imagined him with a woman who went to business school at

Harvard and had used the millions she made from her work as an investment banker to invent a new line of microprocessors. One time we were talking about our college accomplishments, and it came out that Joe had graduated from Yale in three years, with honors. Unfortunately this revelation came to light after I'd revealed that one of my biggest accomplishments from college was that some buddies and I almost got on the *Jerry Springer Show* after a friend's boyfriend traded her car for a quarter bag of weed. I was sure that he looked at me as someone who would hold him back.

When he took me out to dinner at an elegant steakhouse, just the two of us, I didn't think there was anything between us. When he came with me to a Roots concert I assumed he was just a fan of hip hop neo soul music, even though he didn't seem familiar with any of the songs. We began going to parties together on the weekends, and finally, at a Hyde Park bungalow at four o'clock in the morning on a cold winter night, we kissed. And the next day, I wrote it off as a fluke.

It wasn't until we'd been dating for a month that I actually believed we were dating. We'd arranged our work schedules so that we could both attend a product strategy meeting at our company's San Francisco office, and we attended a Stanford GSB event while we were there. When Joe introduced me to his business school friends as his girlfriend, it finally sunk in that this was real.

I started taking time off work to join him when he visited clients in other cities, and soon I quit my job to work as a freelancer. When Joe traveled, he could easily get me a ticket with his frequent flier miles, usually with an upgrade to first class. All of our expenses except my food would be covered while we were there, and I could toss my laptop into my backpack and do client work in coffee shops. Our schedule became so packed with travel that I had to keep a calendar for the first time in my life. Sometimes we'd return from San Francisco in the morning and would have only a few hours to repack our bags before we rushed back to the airport for a flight to New York.

Spending so much time together only strengthened our relationship. We'd known we were compatible, but Joe and I were both surprised by just how well we got along. Loud arguments would erupt on rare occasions, but we eventually realized that they always happened when we were drunk and up too late, so we solved the problem by agreeing not to talk about anything controversial when we were drunk and up too late. Other than that, we almost never argued or even disagreed about much.

There was only one potential source of tension in our relationship, and it was a big one: Joe mentioned a couple of times that he believed in God. Inexplicably, he also said something about considering himself a Christian. I tried to tell myself that he meant it in a medieval way, like to indicate that he was a non-Muslim citizen of Christendom, but I'd seen a few clues that indicated otherwise. On the one hand, he hadn't gone to church once since I'd known him, he didn't talk about having any kind of faith, and I never saw him pray. On the other hand, he did own a Bible, and he mentioned that he'd been trying to remember to say *dammit* instead of the version of the word that included God's name.

In the six months that we'd been dating, the subject had never come up in any substantial way. Like Joe with whatever his beliefs were, I didn't hide the fact that I was an atheist, but I didn't volunteer it either. When we were at a Houston rodeo event that began with a prayer, I didn't bow my head or say "amen". Another time I wondered aloud what someone meant when she referred to another person as a "prodigal son", and Joe seemed to find it remarkable that I didn't know that the expression was from the Bible. Aside from these minor instances, we had an unspoken agreement not to put a damper on all the fun we were having with the dreary topic of spirituality.

* * *

Our first serious conversation about the subject of belief occurred thirty thousand feet above the New Mexico desert. Our flight out of Austin had been delayed, and I was drowsy from a gin and tonic I'd downed in the airport to pass the time. I pushed my back deep into the soft leather seat, ready to dream about the awesomeness that was in store for me on this trip. First we would spend a long weekend at a resort in Palm Springs where Joe's department was hosting a client retreat, then we'd head up to San Francisco for another week. I had recently finished a nightmare of a freelance project with a client who reminded me vaguely of Mussolini, and I was ready to do a whole lot of sleeping and sitting by sparkling hotel pools while Joe worked.

The lights flickered out in the cabin, and I closed my eyes, not sure whether I was trying to sleep or just simmer in bliss.

Joe nudged my arm. "Wow. Look at that." I opened my eyes and followed his gaze to the window. When I saw what awaited me outside the plane, I gasped.

A giant cumulonimbus cloud filled the sky to the right of us, its top towering probably forty thousand feet over the ground below. It was taller than Mount Everest and diffused the last rays of the sun so that it glowed like a child's nightlight. Between us and it was another plane, its lights blinking silently. Lightning illuminated the entire cloud every few seconds, turning the plane into a tiny black silhouette. It baffled me to think that there were other people on that plane, maybe even people I'd met before. How utterly unique in human history to pass by someone you knew, up among the clouds.

"I don't see how anyone could look at that and not believe in God", Joe said, his voice lowered as if out of reverence for this masterpiece of nature.

Maybe it was the influence of the gin and tonic, but I figured that now, when we were both happy and calm, was as good a time as any to have this discussion. "You know that I don't believe in God, right?" I said.

Joe kept his eyes on the cloud. "Yeah, I think you said something about that once."

I waited for him to elaborate on that statement; I'd expected more of a reaction. He remained silent, so I asked, "Does that bother you?"

"Nah", he said casually. "You're reasonable, so you'll get over the atheism thing eventually."

I turned to face him. "Excuse me? You're saying that being an atheist is *unreasonable*?"

"Yeah. Of course. I mean, what, you think the universe brought itself into existence?"

I didn't respond. I was debating whether to turn this into an argument about the fact that he had essentially just called me unreasonable in a backhanded way, which would be satisfying but would derail the conversation.

"Hey, did you hear that nobody built this plane?" Joe said. "It's the craziest thing—they just found it in a field."

"What?" Normally I would have seen where he was headed, but I was distracted by my righteous indignation.

"Yeah! They think that water washed over some aluminum ore and formed it into the hull, then a tornado came along and blew it all

37

together in the shape of a plane", he said, waving his hands dramatically at the "blew it all together" part.

"Oh, I see. I see where you're going with this."

He was on a roll. "Then a meteor landed right by the plane, and the debris hit the side of it so that it etched out the word *Delta*!"

"You can stop now."

"But wait! Don't you want to hear about the earthquake that turned the sand into glass, then ... I don't know ... bounced it onto the front of the plane?" He broke into laughter.

I exhaled a loud sigh to express my weariness.

"No, no, but that's the thing: You don't get to do the 'big sigh at the stupidity of my argument' routine", he said, still smiling, "because you believing that the first self-replicating cell was the product of random forces is the same as my saying that this plane is the product of random forces."

I didn't take the bait. One of the reasons was that, frankly, I thought the origin of life argument was one of the better ones that the theists had. It was pure craziness to suggest that a man in the sky brought life into existence with some sort of divine magic wand, of course, but I also didn't think that any of the current theories about abiogenesis were convincing enough to be worth arguing about.

"Honest question", I said, prefacing my next statement since it might sound like I was saying it just to be insulting. "If you're going to believe in supernatural beings that there's no evidence for, why stop with God? Why not throw in the Tooth Fairy and Santa Claus while you're at it?"

"I just gave you an example of evidence for God. Be sure to let me know when Santa creates an entire universe out of nothing—then I'll believe in him, too."

"Saying 'something exists and we don't know where it came from' isn't evidence. That's like saying that Santa must exist because there are bites out of the cookies on Christmas morning."

"That's not my argument."

"It *is* your argument: You have no evidence for your claim that God created life or the universe or whatever. Scientifically, we can't—"

"This isn't about science", Joe said. "What we're talking about here is the fundamental question, 'Why does something exist instead of nothing?' Why is there a universe at all? Science can't weigh in on that either way, because it's not able to investigate those kinds of questions."

The lady across the aisle looked from her book to us and cleared her throat conspicuously. I took a breath, then lowered my voice to respond: "But if you don't root yourself in scientific evidence, there's no end to the craziness you could believe. Why not believe that there are ten co-gods instead of just one, or that the universe was created by a master race of cats?"

"Are you aware that people have been writing about these kinds of questions for, oh, six thousand years? And that they've pooled their wisdom to come up with some pretty compelling conclusions? It's called philosophy."

"Yeah, philosophy's awesome. Take L. Ron Hubbard, for example ..."

"My point isn't that all philosophies are right. Obviously. It's that these aren't the kinds of questions you answer with material evidence alone."

I had a headache—in part from the drink at the airport, but mostly from this conversation. I wanted to circle back to the dangers of veering away from an evidence-based view of the world. It was tempting to hit the basics, like asking why God didn't just reveal himself to us if he cared about our knowing him, or why he'd sit back and let suffering rip through humanity. But, when I thought about it, I realized that I didn't care that much if Joe held some vaguely theistic beliefs. It wasn't worth starting my much-needed vacation with an argument.

There was one thing, though, that did concern me enough to be worth talking about. "Okay, fine. I disagree with the whole way you're thinking about this subject, but whatever", I began. "But you don't believe in ... you know ..."

"In what?"

"You know. All the other stuff. You're not into that, right?"

"What other stuff? I don't know what you're talking about."

He did know what I was talking about, but evidently wanted me to say it. "The Jesus stuff."

"Are you asking if I'm a Christian?"

I hadn't expected the question to sound as distasteful as it did, or to be as nervous about his potential response as I was. "Yeah. That's what I'm asking."

"Yes, I am."

I could feel my face flush red, which normally happened during only the most intense confrontations. "That's ... surprising."

"Well, it depends what you mean by 'Christian'. Obviously, I'm not religious. I haven't been to church in a year. I'm not going to hit you over the head with my Bible, I'm pro-choice, and I don't think the children in Africa who have never heard of Jesus are going to burn in hell. But do I believe in Jesus? Absolutely."

"Can you—" my voice was gravelly; my throat had suddenly gone dry. The stewardess was refilling the wine of the man in front of me, and I flagged her for some water. I coughed and tried again. "Can you explain that? I truly do not understand how someone like you could believe in something like that."

His tone was lighter now. "Look, I don't even know how many of the details I believe. Was Jesus totally divine? Did every single thing that's written about him actually happen? No idea. But do I believe in him? Yeah."

"Why?" I snapped. I hadn't meant to sound so exasperated. It was as if the pressure had been building and building inside of me, and when I opened my mouth it came rushing out.

The stewardess leaned in to hand me a cup of ice water, and Joe seemed to use the time to collect his thoughts. "I was baptized when I was thirteen", he began, speaking slowly, "in a full-dunk Baptist ceremony. When I came out of the water, I felt this— "

"But see, you're relying on experience there", I interrupted. "It's totally subjective. That's not good evidence. I was baptized when I was a baby—something my mom's parents wanted done—and it didn't impact me at all."

Joe didn't respond. The drone of the plane's engine filled the space where conversation should have been, and it occurred to me that I'd been rude to cut Joe off. It was unlike me to rebuff people when they were trying to share something personal, and it made me realize that I had more lingering irritation with Christianity than I'd thought.

"Sorry", I said. "What were you saying about your baptism?"

"Never mind. It doesn't matter." Before I could protest, he added, "Is any of this really worth arguing about?"

"No, it doesn't matter", I said, though I wasn't sure that that was true. I looked out the window, leaning forward to catch one last glimpse of the cloud before it drifted out of view. It was night now, and I could only see it when the storm filled it with light.

* * *

At the end of our trip to San Francisco, Joe proposed. We were meandering along the walkway of the Golden Gate Bridge, and when we got to the middle, he stopped and said he had a question for me. He held a diamond ring in his hand and asked me to marry him. Through tears, I said yes. With the skyscrapers of San Francisco at our backs, the wide-open Pacific Ocean in front of us, and the cold bay wind vigorously cheering us on, he slid the ring onto my finger.

It was the day after Valentine's Day, and that night we attended a Burt Bacharach tribute concert at the Bohemian Club. The Bohemian Club was an exclusive men's society that counted multiple world leaders among its members, and, according to the online research I'd done, was an endless source of fascination for conspiracy theorists throughout the world. Joe had attended one of their ultra-exclusive retreats at the Bohemian Grove the summer before, and he was now on the membership waiting list.

We settled into seats in the club theater, the cushions softened by decades of use. While a velvet-voiced gentleman belted out "What the World Needs Now Is Love," I twisted my ring back and forth, amazed by how it sparkled even in the dimmed lights. We were seated next to Joe's friend who was his connection to the Bohemian Club; his friend was not yet a member himself, but was sponsored by a bigwig CEO who had recommended Joe for membership as well. The CEO sat on the other side of Joe's friend, and the three of them frequently leaned in to make brief comments, occasionally chuckling quietly.

For the past week I had been plagued by a lingering stress about the religion discussion. Now, as I soaked in this scene, my worries evaporated. One day I would figure out how someone as sharp as Joe could believe in the supernatural, but in the meantime, it didn't matter. Regardless of what Joe believed about the creation of the universe, this—this moment, right here—was what he really cared about. The fact that he had the money to accept an opportunity to join the Club if it came up, and the connections potentially to get the offer in the first place, meant that his life was where he'd always hoped it would be.

And in that, we were perfectly united. Since Joe and I had begun this whirlwind lifestyle of endless travel and parties, I no longer felt like I was forever on the brink of an existential crisis. Though I never thought about it in detail, on some level I realized that our lifestyle was the lesson I'd learned in my grandfather's pickup truck so long ago writ large: My life was filled with wonderful amusements. Hardly a day went by that I wasn't engaged in some activity that entertained me. My life was one exhilarating rush of happiness after another, each one powerful enough to crowd out the despair-filled thoughts that once lurked at the edge of my consciousness. I hadn't found any great answers to those morbid questions I'd first uncovered at The Creek, but all these wonderful distractions had relegated them to functional irrelevance.

Joe turned to me and squeezed my hand. "This is great, isn't it?" He leaned over and kissed me on the cheek.

My throat felt tight with emotion, so I nodded in response. This *was* great. It was more than great. It was proof that, despite our differences of opinions on some things, Joe and I were in agreement about what we most wanted out of life.

7

I cleared the San Francisco airport out of bridal magazines, but dumped them all into a trash can when we stepped off the plane in Austin.

I was thrilled about planning our big day, but when I flipped through the pictures in the magazines during the flight, I realized that everything about the traditional American wedding was based on Judeo-Christian tradition. I'd never followed the customs of that belief system before, so why would I start with my own wedding? I wanted to do something different, something that reflected my own views, not the symbols of a dying religion.

I brought it up during a layover in Salt Lake City, and Joe was fine with the idea. In fact, he seemed enthusiastic about creating our own kind of wedding ceremony that had no religious elements to it (which confirmed for me that, whatever he meant when he said "I'm a Christian", it wasn't what other people meant when they said those words). While we waited for the flight to board, we examined each element of a wedding ceremony and asked ourselves whether that tradition made sense to us.

White dress? No way. With my pale skin that only broke into dark freckles any time I attempted to tan, white was the most unflattering color on me. In fact, I wanted something as close to black as possible—might as well go for a slimming shade if I was going to be in a ton of pictures.

Bridesmaids and groomsmen? No need for them. Bachelor/bachelorette parties? Pointless. People standing when the bride walks down the aisle? I didn't like the idea, but figured that people would do it anyway, and it might be weird to have someone shouting at them to sit down. Bouquet toss? That one definitely made no sense, considering that none of the women I knew cared about who would be the next to get married. I told Joe that maybe I should toss a copy of *Advanced Programming in C+* over my head and whisper to my friends that whoever caught it would be the first to be promoted to Director of Engineering.

By the time we took our seats for the Austin-bound flight, we'd decided that we didn't even want to be legally married by the state at our ceremony—we didn't need anyone else to tell us whether or not our union was valid, whether it was a church or the State of Texas. For legal reasons, we might get a certificate of marriage from the state at some point, but it wouldn't be at our wedding. We agreed to ask our friend Keith Ferrazzi to walk us through our vows, his role being more of a master of ceremonies than an official presider. We'd gone to his commitment ceremony to his boyfriend the year before, and we found that that event was far closer to what we were going for than the traditional American wedding.

The day after we got home I called One World Theater, an arts venue where we had recently attended a Hugh Masekela concert. It was a gorgeous, Tuscan-style building nestled in the tree-covered hills of west Austin, just a few miles down the road from the office where we met. It would be the ideal spot for our ceremony. I asked them if they rented out the building, then closed my eyes while I waited for the answer, telling myself not to be too disappointed if it didn't work out. They said yes, and I booked it on the spot. I opened up the calendar on my laptop and scrolled to Saturday, October 4, 2003. I looked at the square on the calendar for a moment before clicking on it and typing, *Wedding*.

* * *

We had big ideals about keeping the wedding simple, but when we couldn't get the invite list under three hundred people, we realized that this was going to take a lot of work to pull off. Unfortunately, our planning was interrupted by an unexpected turn of events in July.

I got a call from Joe one afternoon while I was doing some work at his place. His loft was in a building just blocks away from my biggest client's headquarters, so I had gotten in the habit of working there in case I had to run to the office for meetings. It was unusual to hear from Joe during business hours, so I figured he must have news.

"Meet me at Guero's", he said as soon as I picked up the phone.

"Guero's?" We'd become regulars at the trendy Tex-Mex restaurant on South Congress, but we didn't normally go there until it was time for after-work drinks, usually around nine o'clock. "When?"

"Now." He said he was already on his way.

When I arrived, Joe was seated at a table in the front waiting area. The waiter set down two narrow, cylindrical glasses filled with margaritas over ice. "No thanks", I said as I took my seat, motioning to the drink closest to me. "I still have more work to do today."

Joe pulled the margarita to his side of the table. "That wasn't for you."

Now I was really curious. "Okay, what's up?"

He took a long sip from the first glass, then said, "I quit."

"You quit what?"

"My job. I'm done."

"Okay", I said hesitantly. "Wow." He knew what I was thinking: We were in the process of buying a condo in the Westgate, a high-rise that was literally at the West Gate of the state Capitol building. It would be tight financially, but we decided to go for it since we loved the twenty-first-floor view, which stretched all the way from downtown and into the hills twenty miles to the west. Considering that I didn't have many freelance clients at the moment, Joe chose an interesting time to quit his job.

"I know. The timing isn't great", he said. He flagged the waiter and asked for a basket of chips, and I noticed that his movements were tense and jerky. "It actually wasn't entirely my decision. Tom and I agreed that things weren't working, and he offered me a nice severance package to step down." The company had faced one crisis after another in recent months, and Joe had been in the middle of a variety of political battles with the ever-changing group of executives. Tom, the interim CEO, had been hinting for a while that he wasn't going to be able to give Joe the resources he needed to run his department. In retrospect, I should have seen this coming.

Joe mindlessly tapped a tortilla chip on the table. "The good news is that it's a generous severance package. If we watch our spending, we might even be able to last a year while we figure out what's next."

"What do you mean 'what's next'? You're going to put out feelers for another job, right?"

"Not if I can help it", he said. He stared off behind me for a while. "It was never my plan to work for other people. I've always wanted to run my own company—just try it, see if I could do it."

"So you're saying you want to start that now?"

"I'm about to turn thirty-three. I have no job. I have severance to pay the bills for a while. If not now, when?"

45

I took a moment to process everything. My gut reaction was to freak out and ask him screechy questions about how we were going to make the new mortgage payment every month, but it only took a few seconds before my concern melted into confidence. First of all, nobody was more easily stressed about money than Joe. He didn't mind spending it, but if anything happened to threaten his income he immediately went into panic mode. One time there had been discussions of pay cuts at our company, and though his salary still would have been good by anyone else's standards, I could see him having flashbacks of his mother crying because she couldn't cover the monthly bills. He seemed to carry with him an omnipresent fear that he was a half step away from the poorhouse.

The other thing was that Joe had been thinking about starting a business for years. He knew dozens of entrepreneurs and had observed what worked and what didn't. He had plenty of connections at venture capitalist firms. In business school, they'd pored over countless case studies to discover what makes companies thrive. This wasn't a spontaneous idea; it was something Joe had been preparing for, for a very long time. The more I considered it, the more I thought it just might be a great idea.

I smiled—a big, genuine smile to let him know that he had my full support. "Great. So what business are we going to start?"

"Good question", he said. He reached into his pocket and produced a paper that had been folded into a square. He smoothed it out over the Tecate beer logo on the rickety Guero's table. The paper was filled from edge to edge with tightly packed columns of words and numbers, printed in what looked to be seven-point font. "Here is a spreadsheet I put together listing the pros and cons of various industries", he said, pointing to some inscrutable lines in the middle of the page. "I weighted each business based on growth potential. And notice here—"

I laughed and shook my head at the mess of text. "When on earth did you have time to put this together?"

"I started this file in business school. I add to it all the time."

"Okay, well, I can't make heads or tails of any of it. Just tell me what your top ideas are."

"That's the thing", he said. "Nothing is sounding right." Starting a tech company sounded promising since he knew the industry, he explained, but it was a ruthlessly competitive field, which significantly lowered the chances of success. He'd run the numbers on starting a wine bar, with an eye toward turning it into a chain, but the margins were too thin. His uncle was doing well as a wholesaler for medical supplies, but Joe had no interest in keeping tons of inventory in a warehouse.

He asked me what I thought about all his top ideas, but, not surprisingly, I had little to add. I couldn't come up with any new perspectives that he hadn't already considered in the thousands of hours he'd spent thinking about this.

It became clear that this was going to be a long discussion, so we ordered mushroom enchiladas for lunch. We were still talking long after the last bits of mole sauce had been scraped from the plates, and I gave in and ordered a margarita. By the time the sun was setting and the din of the dinner crowd filled the room, I could finally interpret most of Joe's spreadsheet. We'd been at this since before noon and still didn't seem any closer to finding a promising idea. Though neither of us said it, we were both starting to wonder if this dream of business ownership was unrealistic.

I held up the sheet, its top half drooping over at the center fold. As I scanned its contents, Joe thought out loud.

"What you want is an industry with barriers to entry, to find a business that not anyone could start", he said. "That's the thing with tech— even if you do have a good idea, some fifteen-year-old in his mom's basement may very well beat you to the punch."

He kept talking, but the words *barriers to entry* triggered an idea. "You're a lawyer, right?"

I'd interrupted him, but he didn't seem to mind. "Yeah, but not in Texas. I haven't practiced since I was in New York."

"Have you thought of starting a law firm?"

"I have. But I really hated law—that's why I got out of it. I got sick of pushing papers for corporations ninety hours a week."

"But there are other types of law, right?"

He tapped on the table for a moment, then answered absentmindedly, as if it were an afterthought to verbalize his thoughts. "Well, that's true."

"I mean, do you think you'd like any of the other kinds of legal work? Like, helping individuals?"

"Maybe helping startup businesses get going? Yeah, that doesn't sound too bad."

"And we wouldn't have to move—you could set up shop here in Austin."

"And I could do some management consulting in addition to the legal side."

A million unspoken thoughts filled the air between us. The moment this law firm idea came up, the tone of the conversation changed. We sat up straighter. Our voices got louder. We stopped lazily watching the parade of new customers walk by as we talked, and turned all our focus to this discussion.

"There's a lot to think about", Joe said. "I'm on 'retired from legal practice' status right now in New York and New Jersey, so I'd have to get reinstated with those bars before I could even apply for the Texas bar. We'd have to make sure there's a market for this kind of work."

"Right. Of course", I said, making a conscious effort to sound like I was being cautious, to disguise the fact that I was basically ready to pick out office space tonight. "Well, maybe we should just add it to the list."

"Yeah. Maybe we should", he said. He looked a little stunned, like someone who just found out he'd won the lottery.

* * *

Before we could devote any more attention to fleshing out the law firm idea, we had to get the wedding out of the way.

We wanted to host a late-night after-party at our new condo by the Capitol and also a welcome event on Friday. Between these two events, the ceremony itself, the dinner, and the official reception, that left us planning five events for the approximately two hundred and fifty people who had RSVP'd to attend. (Part of me wondered if the turnout would have been higher if I hadn't said in the invitation that children weren't allowed. I felt bad about it, realizing only in retrospect that it was probably offensive to people with kids. But I stood by it, since I didn't see what children had to do with weddings.)

By the time October 4 rolled around, Joe and I were overjoyed—not just to begin our future as husband and wife, but because getting married meant that we were finally done with wedding planning. At six o'clock in the evening, we stood backstage while guests took their seats in the theater. Our mothers gave me a final look-over to inspect my dress, a sequined strapless gown that was such a deep shade of purple that it appeared black in some light. My soon-to-be mother-in-law wished me luck, then ducked out the door to her seat in the front row. My mom took one last moment to brush a hair behind my ear. Before she left, she exchanged a long, tender glance with my dad.

Our parents had been nothing but supportive of Joe and me as we'd set out to create our unique brand of wedding. My parents would have undoubtedly applauded such outside-the-box thinking anyway, but I suspected that their views were influenced in part by the fact that they'd gotten divorced the year before. I'd never asked them detailed questions about what had happened; by then I knew enough about relationships to understand that they probably couldn't have captured all the reasons in words, even if they'd wanted to.

Ironically, they were a model divorced couple, just as they had been a model married couple. They continued to treat each other with warmth and respect, and never brought me in to any conflicts. And as they watched me plan my own wedding, they seemed especially pleased that Joe and I were doing it our own way, as if they had a special understanding that the traditional way of doing things offers no guarantees either.

The murmuring of the crowd faded out, and the sound of our entrance music took its place. It was time.

"Wait. Is this the song we decided on?" Joe whispered. It was an acoustic cover of Bryan Adams' "Heaven", which I'd forgotten to replace after Joe had denounced it as "goofy".

"Sorry!" I mouthed. He rolled his eyes in jest before turning to walk into the theater.

After Joe was out of sight, it was time for my dad and me to make our entrance. I could have given a long discourse about why the tradition of fathers walking their daughters down the aisle had lost its symbolism in the modern age, but I never considered removing it from the ceremony. It was something that my dad had been looking forward to from the moment he had heard about the wedding, so it stayed. I put my arm through his, and we walked into the theater.

We stood on the stage, and Keith did a marvelous job of walking us through our vows. We promised to respect one another, to make our home a welcoming place for friends. We swore we would "set big goals and pursue them vigorously". At Joe's request, we even said a line about making God a part of our lives, which, for my part, I took to mean that I wouldn't harass him too much if he wanted to hang a

49

decorative cross in the kitchen. I had gotten everything I wanted with the rest of the ceremony, so I was happy to concede one line about God.

We finished our vows. I couldn't recall what came next, but things seemed to be getting off to a good start. Just then, the theater filled with the sound of Iggy Pop's drum-slamming tune, "Lust for Life". That was our exit music. But why was it playing now? Keith announced, "I present to you Joe and Jennifer Fulwiler!" Joe turned toward the audience. Could the ceremony possibly be over?

Joe took my arm, and in a daze I followed his lead off the stage and down the aisle that divided the two main seating sections. Our guests stood and applauded, but people were exchanging confused looks as they clapped. Everyone was as puzzled as I was about whether we were already done.

Joe pushed open the door at the back of the theater, which triggered an explosion of light from the sun setting behind the hills in front of us. We stopped on the balcony at the top of the stairs outside, the double doors slamming shut behind us. One World was perched on a hilltop, and out ahead, waves of cedar and cypress trees covered the land. Palatial homes jutted up from the landscape here and there, all of it awash in golden light.

We looked at each other in wide-eyed disbelief, then burst into laughter.

"How long was that?" I asked.

Joe checked his watch. "I don't think it was even ten minutes. Seven at best."

I bent down to suppress another wave of laughter, worried that the people inside might hear me. "Well, lesson learned!"

"Yeah", Joe said. "Next time we reinvent the wheel on a tradition that's thousands of years old, we really need to *rehearse* it first."

A rumble from behind the double doors indicated that the guests were gathering their things and would soon be flooding through the exit. These were the last few seconds we'd have to ourselves for the rest of the evening. We embraced, and I closed my eyes to soak in the moment.

"I'm happy to be married to you!" Joe whispered.

"I'm so happy to be married to you, too", I said, though the words didn't even come close to capturing how I felt.

It felt like a momentous occasion, and not just for obvious reasons. I shivered in response to something I felt. It was like the vibration in the ground before a space shuttle launches, that rumble that precedes the unleashing of a great power. I was filled with a sense that something was about to happen for Joe and me—and that whatever it was, it would be big.

8

Four months after the wedding, we found out I was pregnant.

Joe's reaction was happiness mixed with panic: He worried enough about falling back into poverty himself, so the idea of not giving his own children a financially comfortable life sent him into overdrive. The day we got the positive pregnancy test, he stayed up until four o'clock in the morning getting his papers in order for the bar exam.

My reaction was profound, dizzying shock. In fact, it took me a few days and two more tests before I believed that it was true. I'd been diagnosed with polycystic ovary syndrome around the time Joe and I started dating, and an endocrinologist had assured me that I would never be able to have children without medical intervention. In recent months I had begun researching the concept of holistic health, looking into how everything from diet to lifestyle to psychological factors can impact your well-being. At first I wrote it off as hippie nonsense, but I came to think that the hippies just might have a point that combining constant travel, high stress, plenty of alcohol, and a diet in which Doritos had become a main food group could have a negative impact on my system. Now that I had been taking better care of myself, I probably shouldn't have been surprised that all my symptoms related to PCOS had gone away and I'd gotten a positive pregnancy test.

The real source of my shock, though, was due to the fact that I effectively lived in a world in which babies didn't exist. When I was a child, I never had a friend who had a baby sibling in the house. I'd never held a baby other than two of my younger cousins (which was more than Joe, who had never held a baby at all). None of my close friends had kids. We lived downtown, where few people had children. Our building's location next to the Capitol meant that it was populated almost entirely by politicians and lobbyists, most of whom were over fifty. In the back of my mind I'd almost started to believe that new human life was created in a cloning room at the back of a Starbucks, people coming into the world well into their twenties, complete with lattes and wire-rimmed glasses.

The idea of babies was freaky enough; the idea of *me* having *my own* baby was surreal to the point of being difficult to believe. I was happy—I did want to have a kid or two at some point. I just hadn't thought it would happen so soon.

I began to research the subject obsessively. The timing was perfect in terms of the law firm: Joe's severance pay took pressure off me to bring in freelance income, and there was nothing I could do to help the business get up and running until Joe passed the bar exam. So as Joe lost himself in studying the law, I lost myself in studying pregnancy. Sometimes we would sit in the living room for hours at a time, the city bustling beneath us as we read our books in silence.

When I was seven months pregnant, I went to the grocery store one morning to pick up some coffee for Joe. When I leaned down to grab his favorite brand, I pushed up against another grocery cart that was in the way. As I stood back up, I was startled to see a face at the edge of the cart: I was inches away from a baby. It was the closest I'd come to a kid that age in a very long time, and I stopped to stare.

The grocery store fell away, and all I saw was the child. It was a girl, nestled into the pink-and-yellow checked padding of her car seat. Her eyes were closed, and she occasionally wrinkled her eyelids, as if having a bad dream. It had never occurred to me how different a baby's proportions are from an adult's: If she raised her arms, the tips of her fingers would barely extend past the top of her head. The features on her little face were so compact and soft in contrast to the elongated, narrow features of an adult. And that skin! Her cheeks were like those of a doll, yet with a glow as if lit from the inside.

"Can you believe you're going to have one of those soon?" the mother said, motioning to my huge stomach.

Her voice startled me so much that I dropped the coffee container. I blurted out some polite acknowledgment of her statement as I bumbled around to pick it up and then stumbled off like the crazy person she undoubtedly thought I was.

After I checked out, I stood in front of the grocery store parking lot, staring past people pushing carts and lifting grocery bags into trunks. In a few weeks, I was going to have my own baby—like, a real human being. An actual person: part me, part Joe. It occurred to me that this was possibly *the* defining event of the human experience, and I had never even come close to it before.

* * *

Labor began at exactly midnight on the fall equinox. The night before, I had watched a documentary about a hiker who had to cut off his own arm after a boulder fell on it. As I watched the man reenact the angle into which he positioned himself to break his own bones, I admonished myself not to fear labor. I was nervous about my choice to have the baby at a birthing center that didn't offer epidurals, but this man's experience showed me that there was nothing to be worried about—after all, there are plenty of more painful occurrences in the world than childbirth. Fourteen hours into labor, I remembered the documentary and scoffed bitterly at the hiker's whining, wishing I could be so lucky as to only have to sever my own ulnar nerve with a dull knife.

The baby was born at seven o'clock in the evening, and we named him Donald, after my dad and grandfather. Per the custom of the midwife-staffed birthing center, we took him home hours later. We arrived home around eleven o'clock that night, but I didn't even try to sleep. I sat up in bed and placed the baby on my lap, pulling my knees in to prop him up, as if we were about to have a conversation.

I wondered if I would ever get tired of looking at him. I'd expected to have a child who resembled my baby pictures, with fair skin and a few wisps of reddish blonde hair. Instead, my son had the slightly darker complexion of Joe's ancestors from southern Germany, including a full head of black hair. Perhaps because he arrived five days after his due date, he was so much more awake than the sleepy newborn I'd imagined. He'd been born with his dark blue eyes wide open, and he hadn't shut them yet.

My main reaction to this moment was stress. The more I looked at this little baby, the more a feeling of dread spread within me. When we left the birthing center, the midwife told me to enjoy my "baby-moon", as she called it. She seemed to imagine that the next few weeks would be one moment after another of my joyfully gazing at my son. Did other women do this? I couldn't imagine. Who could waste time soaking in the cuteness of those little eyelash flutters when there was so much worrying to be done? I had only come up with twenty-eight ways the baby could die from household accidents—I hadn't even had time to research the most horrific childhood diseases. Only after I finished agonizing about that could I even begin to think about all the ways that other people might hurt him in his life.

At some point in the middle of the night, I needed to use the bathroom. I scooped Donald into my arms and crept out to the living room, where Joe was sleeping on the couch. Our plan had been that he would get a solid night's sleep so that he could help me tomorrow. I grabbed his shoulder and shook him.

"I need you to hold the baby", I whispered, though there was no need to lower my voice since the baby was still wide awake.

"Huh? What?" Joe grumbled as he shifted positions. "Okay, put him here", he said, and patted a spot next to him.

"No. You need to sit up." He was already back asleep. I shook him again. "Joe. You need to sit all the way up to hold him. It's the only safe way."

After a lot of groaning, which may have been from confusion, irritation, or both, Joe sat up and held out his arms for the baby. I passed Donald to him and rushed to the bathroom. I returned in a matter of seconds to snatch the baby back, hoping Joe noticed my look of disapproval that he'd slouched down on the arm of the couch.

Little did we know, this was only the beginning of my craziness. Soon I became fixated on the fact that our floors were made of stone. I'd found it to be a key selling point when the realtor told us that the previous owner had the tiles custom-made from the same pink granite used to construct the Texas Capitol building across the street, but now I wanted to have it all ripped out and placed with shag carpeting with a one-inch pad underneath. I was terrified of someone dropping the baby on this hideously hard surface (a 7 on the Mohs Scale of mineral hardness—I looked it up). I snapped at my mom when she cradled the baby in only one arm, and when my mother-in-law tried to burp Donald while she was standing in the kitchen, I rushed over with my hands outstretched as if she'd started to juggle him.

As the days oozed into weeks, I only got worse. When Joe suggested that I start letting Donald sleep in his crib, I reacted as if he'd suggested that I start letting the baby sleep in the crocodile cage at the zoo. Obviously, co-sleeping was full of dangers, too, so I usually slept sitting up, the baby nestled in my arms on top of a nursing pillow.

I also wouldn't set him down to do laundry, and developed a one-handed routine for folding clothes that probably qualified me for my own circus act.

When Donald was around two months old, Joe started going to the office every day. He had taken the bar exam, and now it was a matter of waiting for the results. He used the time to get the business going. He could practice federal law with his New York license, so he'd rented office space and was taking on a few bankruptcy cases. When he wasn't doing client work, he busied himself writing copy for the website and setting up the accounting system. I hadn't realized how much he had helped me when he was studying for the bar exam; now that he was gone, there was nobody else to make lunch or help me change the trash bag while I held the baby.

Finally, even I had to admit that I had a problem. Shortly after Joe signed the lease on his office, my mom took a day off work to help me. When she arrived, she took one look at my appearance and said she'd take care of the baby while I slept. I refused. I pushed my un-brushed hair out of my face, clutched the baby against the clothes that I'd been wearing for three days, and assured her through bloodshot eyes that I was fine, just fine.

Joe called to check in, and when he heard what had happened, he demanded that I give her the baby and get some sleep. I tried to argue, but when I found that I was having trouble making my words come together in a way that formed anything that could even loosely be considered a sentence, I gave up in disgust and went into the bedroom, slamming the door behind me.

I flopped onto the bed and mumbled to myself about how terrible Joe would feel if something happened to the baby while I was off duty. But then I thought through what, exactly, I was afraid would occur: When I had refused my mom's offer, it was because I was convinced that the baby would fall over our balcony as soon as I left the room. My mom was the most attentive, careful grandmother imaginable, not to mention the fact that I had firmly established the rule that nobody could hold the baby within five feet of the balcony door (I showed everyone the edge of the living room rug that they couldn't pass). Also, it would require defying the laws of physics for any kind of accident to move the baby from a position in my mom's arms to the edge of the balcony—even then, the heavy glass doors would have to be open, and the baby would somehow have to bounce over the railing. Yet, to my mind, it seemed like a real concern.

I sighed and pulled a pillow over my head. Okay, there was something wrong. I had to admit it. This wasn't like me. The obvious explanation was that it must be a hormonal imbalance—maybe I had postpartum depression, or postpartum obsessive-compulsive disorder, if such a thing existed. But I knew that there was something more. Post-baby hormones may have been a factor, but I was aware that what was really driving this madness was something much deeper than that.

* * *

The blocky red digits on the clock next to the bed announced that it was 3:02 A.M. The power nap I'd taken while my mom was here had given me a burst of energy, and now sleep was even less likely than it normally was. An infomercial for the Mix Magic blender played silently on the muted television, and the room got brighter or darker depending on the colors on the screen. I knew this one by heart: The female host was shaking her head in skepticism that this product could really be so amazing; next it would flash to the black-and-white vignette of the man trying in vain to use a traditional blender to make a milkshake. He'd end up exasperated and covered in ice cream, as if the complexity of the task was akin to disarming a bomb.

I flipped off the television and tossed the remote onto the bed. I'd spent the whole night trying to distract myself, but now I was out of options. There was nothing on TV, and I was too strung out to read. I was tempted to go out to the living room and wake Joe to see if he wanted to split a glass of wine, but he needed rest for all the work he had to do tomorrow, which is why he was sleeping in the living room in the first place.

I slid Donald down to the bed next to me. I watched him to make sure he stayed asleep, then forced myself to get up and leave him lying there. I walked to the sliding door at the end of the room, slid it open, and stepped onto the balcony. Briefly, I felt the strange exhilaration of being out in the city at night, safely tucked away hundreds of feet in the air.

Even though I hadn't thought much about it, I knew what fueled all my crazy behavior. I could always tell when this idea was creeping

57

nearer, like recognizing the smell of your archenemy's cologne. I closed the balcony door, leaned back against it, and slid to the cold concrete floor. I let my head drop back until it smacked into the glass. I took a breath, and let it all in.

It was that awareness of human mortality that had first occurred to me at The Creek, of course. That's what had been gnawing at me since the baby's birth. If I thought it was bad to internalize the reality of my own meaninglessness in the grand scheme of things, doing so for my child was enough to drive me over the edge—in fact, it almost had.

In the decade and a half since the first time it all sunk in, I'd encountered wise atheists who didn't seem to think it was all so bleak. They agreed that all of our experiences are products of the chemical reactions in our brains. They believed, as I did, that our very selves are nothing more than the result of a bunch of neurons firing. They understood as well as anyone that nothing of a person lasts beyond his death, that all of his dreams and hopes and joys and sorrows simply cease to exist when he breathes his last. And they didn't think any of that was depressing.

I admired them. I wished that I could be more like them. But I could not, for the life of me, make sense of their views.

On the rare occasions that I let myself think about this kind of thing, a passage from Bertrand Russell's essay "A Free Man's Worship" always came to mind. He wrote:

That man is the product of causes which had no prevision of the end they were achieving; that his origin, his growth, his hopes and fears, his loves and beliefs are but the outcome of accidental collections of atoms; that no fire, no heroism, no intensity of thought and feeling, can preserve an individual life beyond the grave. That all the labors of the ages, all the devotion, all the inspiration, all the noonday brightness of human genius are destined to extinction ... that the whole temple of man's achievement must inevitably be buried. All these things, if not quite beyond dispute, are yet so nearly certain, that no philosophy which rejects them can hope to stand.

Russell went on to recommend that people go ahead and build their lives on a "firm foundation of unyielding despair". That was my kind of atheism. Granted, I had chosen to build my life on a series of vain distractions that helped me forget about the truth, but I agreed that the unyielding despair route was the most intellectually honest one.

I closed my eyes and waited for it all to sink in. No more denial. No more running away. My head had been three feet into the sand for over half my life, and now that I had a child, it was making me crazy. Whatever might come of it, I had to stop shoving these thoughts away. It was time to accept them, whatever that meant.

I waited, but nothing happened. My hands didn't shake like they did that day at The Creek; I didn't even feel depressed. Why not? I thought through it all again: the fact that I was nothing more than chemical reactions, and that everything that I thought of as "me" would disappear like a mirage in the desert. The fact that Donald too was destined for a fate like those fossils frozen in the rock wall—I thought about it all. Yet it elicited in me no reaction.

What was going on? Had I become like the atheists who were somehow cool with all that? Was I still in denial despite my best efforts to accept the truth?

I sat like that for what felt like hours (though was probably just a few minutes), lost in thought, breathing in the icy wind that wound through the skyscrapers. Finally, I stumbled across the answer, and the words rang through my mind like a bell:

I don't think it's true.

My eyelids burst open and I sat up straight. As impossible as it sounded, that was it. It had been years since I'd put serious thought into this topic, and in the meantime, something had changed. I'd met Joe. I'd given birth to a son. And through my new family, I had been plunged into an experience of love that I'd never had before. My parents and I loved each other, of course, but becoming a wife and a mother exposed me to a different type of love, one that had the power to alter everything within me.

Atheism could not account for the bond that Joe and I shared. It offered no lexicon for capturing what I saw in my child. An atheistic worldview could offer an accurate explanation of the way my brain chemistry had been altered to experience more of the sensation we label "love", but I was certain now that that explanation would stop short of the full truth. It would be like confusing a picture of the Grand Canyon with the actual place; there's nothing false about the picture, but it would be foolish to confuse the piece of paper with the real thing. There was more to human life than the atoms that made up our bodies—I was sure of it.

In fact, I wondered if this was part of the reason for my postpartum insanity: Maybe humans really did have souls that really did have a connection to some other dimension. Maybe people are more than the sum of their molecules, and I'd been driving myself crazy by denying this most fundamental of truths. Perhaps the inner agony that had erupted since Donald's birth had been caused by the friction of trying to jam the square peg of atheism into the round hole of reality.

Before I could talk myself out of it, I lowered my head, and I did something. It was an internal opening, a willingness to get in touch with any nonmaterial entity that might be out there. It was a silent hello, an unobservable communication, in which I told whatever or whoever might be out there that I was open to knowing it, if it did exist. It was simultaneously the most awkward thing I'd ever done and one of the most natural things I'd ever done. I supposed I had to admit that I had just said a prayer.

As soon as I did it, I felt ridiculous. It was one thing to re-evaluate my views, but reaching out to the supernatural like a kid chatting with her imaginary friend was another thing altogether—definitely an indicator that it was time to go inside and get some sleep. I tiptoed back into the warm bedroom and sat down next to Donald. My movements caused him to inhale a startled gasp, then let out a squeaky sigh.

I was in dangerous intellectual territory. Becoming a mother had undoubtedly triggered an evolved instinct to value my offspring, so my biology would tempt me to be open to any idea that told me that Donald was valuable on a cosmic level. On top of that, the love I felt for him, regardless of where it came from, left me feeling exposed and vulnerable. Maybe fear had weakened me to the point that I'd be willing to believe in souls or fairies or angels or whatever would make me feel safe. Maybe I was confusing what was actually true with what I needed to be true.

I ran my finger along Donald's cheek, then rested my hand against his face. I would think about this more later, when my head was clear enough that I could make sure that this wasn't simply the delusional mental wanderings of a woman who really needed to get some rest. But as I watched my tiny son sleep, the curves of his body illuminated by the city lights that filtered in through the window, I couldn't escape the feeling that I was no longer an atheist.

9

It was daytime—late into the morning, judging by the level of light in the room. I sat up and brushed matted layers of hair out of my face. Donald was asleep next to me. The clock said it was almost ten, which meant that he slept an unprecedented four hours in a row. Normally, I would have stood in awe at the profundity of that event, but something had woken me up. A noise outside the bedroom door.

I unwrapped myself from a tangle of covers and headed for the living room. When I opened our bedroom door, I jumped to see Joe in front of me.

He stopped and smiled. "Oh, hey, you're awake!"

I checked the clock over my shoulder. "Why aren't you at the office?"

"I was. I tried to call. I guess you didn't hear the phone ring?"

I shuffled past him into the living room, squinting in the daylight. "I was tired", I said, not mentioning the part about staying up until four o'clock in the morning to fundamentally re-evaluate everything I believed about human existence. At some point I'd tell him about that, but preferably not when I was exhausted to the point of feeling like I had the mental capacity of a bowl of oatmeal. "Why are you home?" I asked.

"I got some news", he said, pausing to grin. In a more coherent state I might have been able to guess what it was, but I was surprised when he announced, "I passed the Texas Bar Exam!"

The news jolted me out of my haze. I actually bounced on my heels as I told him congratulations and gave him a hug. Tears stung my eyes, and only partially because I was still frazzled from the night before. Hearing that Joe passed was one of those moments of not realizing how stressed you are until the stress has been removed. If Joe had failed the exam, it would have been six months until he could retake it, and we didn't have the funds to last that long. It may have set us back seriously enough to stop the entire law firm dream in its tracks.

Joe radiated happiness. "Want to come down and check out the office? I've got it almost all set up—I think we can start hiring next week."

I looked down and noticed a crusty stain from where I'd dropped a meatball on my shirt four days ago. "Let me, umm ..." I motioned to my outfit.

I didn't need to finish my sentence. "Yeah. Go ahead and get yourself ready—take your time."

After I showered and changed clothes, we put Donald in his car seat and made the short drive to Joe's office, which was so close that we could've walked. He had rented out a bank of rooms in a two-story building off Enfield Road, which housed other small law and accounting practices. It was nestled in the downtown neighborhood that used to be a residential area, but whose historic early-twentieth-century houses had now been taken over by businesses.

With the baby nestled in a wrap sling, I followed Joe past the receptionist and into the hallway that led to his office space. When people walked by he greeted them by name, and we stopped so that he could introduce me to another attorney whose office was on the first floor. It occurred to me that while I had been shuttered in my bedroom at the Westgate, stuck in my twenty-first-floor, self-imposed prison like a frumpy Rapunzel, Joe had been living a real life, making new friends, and getting a lot of work done. I was suddenly conscious of the feel of pants that were not pajama bottoms—even if they were ill-fitting maternity jeans—and the structure that these strange "shoe" apparati imposed on my normally bare feet. I wondered if I should maybe start to make an effort to get back into the real world again.

At the end of the hall, on the right side was an open office area. Currently, it functioned as a graveyard for cardboard boxes and broken desk chairs, but Joe was planning to transform it into a workspace for two or three paralegals to share. On the left were two office doors, one of which would eventually house another attorney. Joe opened the door to the other, his own office.

The last time I had seen it, it was an empty room with a few stacks of books resting in the corner. Now it was a real workspace: An oak desk filled the center of the room, and behind it were two floor-to-ceiling windows that looked down upon the grounds of a historic mansion across the street. A panel of bookshelves lined the left side of the room, the wood stained a few shades darker than the desk, two of its shelves already filled with legal tomes leftover from Joe's days practicing law in New York. On the wall across from the desk were Joe's framed degrees.

Joe sat down behind his desk, as if to make sure I got the full picture of the office in action. "What do you think?"

"I love it!" I slid into a leather chair on the other side of the desk, imagining being a client of the Fulwiler Law firm.

"I have something for you", Joe said. He produced a brown cardboard box from a drawer and reached across the desk to hand it to me. He flipped the lid open like it was a jewelry box and revealed a rectangular row of neatly stacked business cards. I pulled one out to see the "FULWILER LAW, P.C." logo against the rustic tan and burgundy background colors, made more vivid by the card's glossy sheen. In the center of the card were the words:

JENNIFER FULWILER
Business Manager

I was conscious of the fact that we would one day look back on this moment as the beginning of our success. A decade from now, we'd gather our many employees at the Fulwiler Law Christmas party and tell them about the time that Joe handed me the first company business card. Everyone would shake their heads wistfully and note that they could hardly imagine this firm having only two employees.

"There's something we need to talk about", Joe said. His tone had changed. He didn't sound upset; rather, he seemed more concerned that I would be upset by what he had to say.

Trying not to wake a sleeping Donald, I leaned down and slid the business card into the pocket of my purse. "Sure. What?"

"I've been looking at our finances over the past few weeks. I've run the numbers a bunch of times, and I don't see how we can make everything work." He had an expectant look in his eyes, as if he had more to say, but he was waiting to let that sink in first.

"What do you mean 'make everything work'?"

"It's going to take the firm longer to make money than I thought. We're also burning through savings. I don't know if you've taken a look at our budget lately, but our spending is insane. We can't start a business with those kinds of expenses—not unless we got investors, and you can't have investors with a law firm."

I didn't understand what he was saying.

"If we're serious about starting this firm, then we have to slash expenses", he explained.

"Okay. I think I could shave some money off the groceries—"

"I said *slash*."

I patted Donald through the taut canvas of the sling while I thought about it. "You mean, like we'd try to get by with one car?"

Joe stood and came to sit in the other client's chair, next to me. I turned to face him. He leaned forward and said with gentle urgency, "I mean get rid of it all. Sell the condo. Get rid of the Jag. No more trips to that salon you go to. No more travel."

A whirl of concerns hit me at once. I wasn't sure where to start. "Wait. You said get rid of the condo. Where would we live?"

"Well. That's the main thing I wanted to talk to you about."

Uh-oh. I forgot about everything else and stared at him, waiting for whatever he was going to suggest.

"Your mom has her house all to herself. She once said that we could always move in with her, and I don't think she was kidding."

"My mom? You want us to move in with my mom?"

He paused, searching my face for something, probably any sign of agreement. "Yes. I do. I think it's the only chance we have of making this thing work."

Donald stirred slightly, and I stood to walk him around. Everything I loved about living downtown flashed before my eyes: the walks to Whole Foods and bookstores and my favorite sushi restaurant on Congress Avenue. The Texas Book Festival took place literally at the front door of our building each year. And then there was the Westgate itself: The building had a full gym, a doorman, and 24/7 staff. The lieutenant governor lived a couple of floors down from us, and I sometimes chatted with him when we were on the treadmills at the same time. And of course there was the rooftop pool and patio, where we had had more than a few memorable parties. Joe was suggesting that we leave all of this? For the remote suburbs where my mom lived?

"Are you open to it?"

I turned around to face Joe, who was still sitting in the chair. I found within me a surprising willingness to make this sacrifice. Joe still exuded

64

excitement despite the tension in this conversation, and it made me understand for the first time just what this meant to him. When he was a kid, sometimes his mom couldn't afford to run the heat in the winter. She'd wrap him up in a blanket and cuddle him in a rocking chair, turning her head so that he wouldn't see her tears. When he was older he'd have to hurry through homework each night so that he could help her clean office buildings until midnight, and then he'd wake up at four-thirty in the morning for swim team practice, in hopes that it would help him get a scholarship to a good school. What kept him going through each of those moments was the vision of this moment, right now: sitting in his own office, the founder of what was sure to be a successful business. It was no exaggeration to say that this was everything he'd ever wanted.

"It won't be easy", I said under my breath. As soon as I spoke, I regretted it. Of course he knew it would be hard; Joe was the one who had been working sixty hours a week trying to get a law firm going. "But we can do it", I added. "I know my mom would be fine with it. We can make it work."

Joe let out a long breath, then rose to his feet. "I really think this is the right decision."

"So do I." Joe may have been dreaming about owning a business longer than I had, but I wanted it as much as he did. And I was willing to make it work, even if that meant letting go of our lifestyle for a few months.

10

I took my time as I strolled along the sidewalk in front of Central Market. I stopped Donald's stroller just outside the grocery exit, next to the birds who pecked at crumbs by the store's outdoor restaurant. Soon I would need to wrap this up. I'd treated myself to a leisurely lunch in the gourmet grocery store's café, offering Donald bites of the mashed potatoes that came with my grilled tilapia. Alas, now it was time to make one last trip to the bathroom, change Donald's diaper, and head back to my mom's house to get back to work unpacking. I turned toward the parking lot and imagined what awaited me as soon as I returned to my new suburban home. The boxes. The furniture assembly. The grocery shopping. And the boxes.

It had taken us the rest of the fall, as well as winter and most of spring, to get to the point that we were ready to move in with my mom. I told myself that the holdup was because there was so much to do: We had to get our condo ready to sell, meet with potential realtors, and strategize with my mom about the setup in her house. In reality, though, it was a long exercise in procrastination. The thought of trading in my view of all of west Austin for the view of a backyard fence pained me more and more as the reality of it got closer, and I always managed to find one more reason to put it off. As the late spring temperatures rose and our bank account balance fell, it was time. Now, in the last days of May, we were finally moving.

Donald had begun to doze off in his stroller, and not even a group of birds fighting over a discarded hunk of bread was enough to keep him awake. Now would be the perfect time to leave. But surely there was something else I had to do. The sign of a bookstore at the far corner of the strip center caught my attention. That was it: I needed a book. I couldn't face the Sisyphean toil that awaited me back home without a new read. I'd grab one quickly, and *then* I'd get on the road.

When I pulled open the glass door to the bookstore, the stroller wheels caught on a metal plate on the floor. I bent over to jimmy them free, and when I straightened up, an object caught my attention. At the far end of the store, against the back wall, was a book. I didn't even see the thousands of other books in the store; it was as if only this one existed. It had a light cover, and it almost seemed to glow the way it stood out in my perception amidst the clutter.

I moved intently toward it. I'd never been to this bookstore before, and I didn't know what section I was headed for. I stopped short when I saw the sign, above and just to the right of the book: CHRISTIANITY.

I'd never been in the Christianity section of any bookstore or library before; the closest I'd come was when I'd taken all the Bibles in my elementary school library and moved them to the Fiction section, in what I was certain was the most erudite prank the whole fourth grade had seen all year. When I got close enough to see the title, I laughed. *The Case for Christ*. I leaned the stroller on its back wheels to turn around, but the book's subtitle caught my attention: *A Journalist's Personal Investigation of the Evidence for Jesus*. Mainly, it was the word "journalist". That was annoying.

I was a journalism major for a few semesters in college, and it gave me enough of a glimpse into that line of work to know that you have to be a quick, clear thinker with an eye for detail and an ability to sift through large amounts of data in order to be successful in the field. It was irritating to see Christians co-opting that title to try to sell books, when by "journalist" this author undoubtedly meant "I wrote a couple of blurbs for my church's Sunday bulletin." I picked up the book, looking forward to simmering in the indignation that would come with my discovery of the loose use of the term.

It turned out that the author, a guy named Lee Strobel, was a Yale Law grad and the former legal editor for the *Chicago Tribune*. Okay, so he was a journalist. I was about to put the book down when another note caught my attention. It said that he was a former atheist, and that he'd "investigated" his way into believing in Jesus. I fished my mobile phone out of my purse to check the time. I did need to get back home. But first, I had to deal with this book.

Atheist journalists do not become Christians based on investigating evidence. If he wanted to claim that he had had some sort of vision, I could believe that: Even otherwise normal people could be misguided by powerful emotional experiences sometimes. But to say that he'd *investigated* his way from atheism to Christianity was absurd. It would be like saying that you investigated your way into believing that there really is a cauldron full of shiny gold coins at the bottom of every rainbow.

I put the book under my arm and pushed the stroller over to the store's café. Amidst the smell of burnt coffee and the sounds of hissing espresso machines, I settled into a chair in front of a small table and opened the book.

Strobel started with a story about a Chicago police shooting case he'd covered for the *Tribune*, where he thought he knew what had happened, because the evidence all pointed in one direction. After a call from a tipster, he took a second look at the facts and found, to his great surprise, that an entirely different story took shape. He asked readers to do the same with this Jesus stuff: Take another look at the case, consider new evidence, look at old evidence from a different angle.

Strobel seemed like a nice guy, and I believed he'd really been an atheist. He didn't seem to be exactly the same type of atheist I was, at one point mentioning that he was initially resistant to learning about Jesus because he didn't want to give up his immoral lifestyle. That would never have occurred to me, since I knew right from wrong without receiving instructions from a holy book, but he wasn't using the term "atheist" as loosely as I'd expected he would.

My phone buzzed, and my mom's number appeared on caller ID. She was undoubtedly calling to ask where I was, since I said I was only going out for a quick lunch. I put the phone back in my pocket; I'd call her back once I was on the road.

I stood and hoisted my purse on my shoulder. It was time to head out. Yup. Time to walk away from that book. Just leave it there, or maybe put it back on the shelf.

But the thing kept drawing me back to the table, each time I tried to step away.

If the past few months in the grinder of new parenthood and new business ownership had taught me anything, it was that I didn't have it all figured out. My late-night epiphany on the balcony at the West-gate had made me consider that I might have been missing fundamental truths about the human experience. Could it be possible that there was something here that was worth looking into further?

My phone buzzed. My mom again. Time to go. I took the book over to the checkout counter, telling myself that I could return it later since I'd probably never pick it up again.

On the drive back to the house, my purchase sat on the passenger seat, wrapped tightly in the bookstore bag. I assured myself that any eagerness I felt to read it must be due to an extreme desire to procrastinate, and that the excitement that fluttered within me must be late-arriving emotions about the move to my mom's place.

* * *

"What's in the bag?" my mom asked when I got home.

"What bag?" I looked down. "Oh, the bag in my hands? I don't know. It's a book."

My mom sat at the command center of her massive network of desks, which covered two entire walls in her home office. Her job managing the finances of an eye care company had her especially busy that day, and she kept turning her attention back to the computer screen as we talked. "Any book in particular?"

"I can't remember the title. Or what it's about."

Donald came to the rescue and crawled up next to my feet as we spoke, a concerned look on his chubby face as if he were on an important mission. My mom swung her chair around so that her back was fully to her computer and leaned forward to beckon Donald. "And how did my little man do today? Was he a good boy?"

I started to answer, but then saw that she'd been speaking to the nine-month-old baby. It became clear that this would be a meeting with an extensive agenda: My mom and Donald would need to go over what he had for lunch, whether he was da cutest widdle man in the entire world, and possibly review what the kitty–cat says. "Would it be okay if I went into our room for a while?" I asked. "I should probably get back to unpacking."

My mom picked up Donald and propped him on her lap so that he was facing her. He giggled and tried to take her glasses, and she responded by initiating a game where she would lean in so that her glasses were just within reach of his outstretched hand, then she'd pull back and Donald would explode in guttural giggles. I tried again to ask if it would be okay for the baby to hang out with my mom, but it was clear that even my questions were an interruption to this convocation of their mutual admiration society.

The bedroom door hit up against a box after opening only halfway, and I pressed my back against the wall to squeeze through the opening.

The room consisted of my mom's double guest bed, her dresser, her two bedside tables, and a tall, narrow bookshelf—the bookshelf being the only piece of furniture we owned in the room. It was a small room, with only a few feet between the sides of the bed and the walls, and I had to move past the boxes like someone on a boulder-climbing expedition. I sat down on the bed and pulled the book out of its cellophane bag. In just a minute I would get back to work unpacking. First, I just wanted to read a few more pages—only to get to a stopping point from where I'd been at the bookstore.

For someone who didn't care about reading *The Case for Christ*, I did an amazing impression of finding it riveting. I stretched out on the bed and smoothed the book flat at my side. Whether or not Strobel perfectly nailed every single one of the dozens of points he and his experts raised, he made a good case that Jesus as a historical figure did exist and that his life did have an eerie similarity to ancient Jewish prophecies.

Two pages into a new section, I heard my mom's voice out in the hall. "Do you need more time?" she asked through the crack in the door, which still couldn't be opened because of the boxes. "I need to run errands and was going to take Donald with me."

I jolted up and fumbled to straighten a lampshade, as if that would make it look like I was being incredibly productive. "Yeah. I could use a while longer."

She and Donald chattered down the hall, and a few seconds later I heard the *beep-beep-beep* of the alarm system announcing that they'd exited the house. I returned to my book, where Strobel was interviewing a man who detailed the shockwave of changes that radiated across the globe shortly after Jesus' death.

"When Jesus was crucified, his followers were discouraged and depressed. They no longer had confidence that Jesus had been sent by God, because they believed that anyone crucified was accursed by God", said Strobel's interviewee, a Ph.D. philosopher with a background in chemistry named J. P. Moreland. "So they dispersed. The Jesus movement was all but stopped in its tracks."

Moreland then pointed out that, soon afterward, these people dramatically regathered, abandoned their former ways of living, and dedicated their entire lives to spreading the specific message that they had seen Jesus risen from the dead. And, finally, many of them died heinous deaths rather than recant their claims that they personally had witnessed

Jesus alive after death. As Strobel pointed out, some people are willing to die for beliefs that they mistakenly think are true, but nobody will die for beliefs that they know are false.

Moreland also pointed out that something huge happened in Jewish culture during that time. He began by describing five ancient social structures, such as keeping the Sabbath and the practice of animal sacrifice, which were the very center of Jewish life at that time.

"Now a rabbi named Jesus appears from a lower-class region", he continued. "He teaches for three years, gathers a following of lower- and middle-class people, gets in trouble with the authorities, and gets crucified along with thirty thousand other Jewish men who are executed during this time period.

"But five weeks after he's crucified, over ten thousand Jews are following him … And get this: They're willing to give up or alter all five of the social institutions that they have been taught since childhood have such importance both sociologically and theologically."

Regardless of your religious beliefs, Moreland said, you had to admit that something explosive happened to Jewish culture in first-century Palestine. His own explanation was simple: "They'd seen Jesus risen from the dead."

I paused. Was it so crazy to believe that this could have happened? Was I crazy for thinking it might not be crazy? I kept bouncing back and forth. *It's crazy*: Reasonable people cannot believe that anyone ever rose from the dead. *It's not crazy*: If some kind of God does exist, then presumably he could hook up that sort of thing. If you're willing to believe in the divine at all, it's not that much of a stretch to believe in Jesus' Resurrection.

What made Christianity's story so challenging was its specificity. If the idea had been that Jesus was a special guy who had a special gift for coming up with insights about spirituality, I wouldn't have hesitated to consider it. There was comfort in vagueness, which was one of the reasons I found Buddhism appealing. All the teachings of Buddhism resided in the ether of thoughts and experiences. In contrast, here was Christianity, talking about corpses rising from the dead and guys transforming water into wine at a party that happened at this one house on this one day. Buddhism allowed some bet-hedging: You're never going to look like a fool for believing that *dukkha* exists. It's just a concept. But to say, "I believe that on a certain day, two thousand years ago, a man came

71

along and healed another man who was blind"—that was a different deal. Specificity makes an easy target.

I set the book down and sat motionless on the bed. The house was still; the neighborhood outside was still. The only sound was the soft click of the air conditioner as it turned off. A thought approached. I tried to fight it, to reject it, to do everything not to let such an insane idea into my mind, but it overwhelmed me like a tidal wave. And I asked myself with a frightening level of openness:

What if it were true?

The words sunk in slowly, one by one.

All of reality suddenly shifted, so forcefully that I shivered with vertigo. What if there were a God? What if he did enter into a human body at one point? What if he were here, now, aware of this moment, wanting me to know that he exists?

My skin tingled with the possibility that I was not alone in the room— that I'd never been alone in my life.

11

The next morning I settled into my chair in the guest room that I was using as an office. I set my cup of coffee next to a jumble of wires that went with my printer and called Joe to catch up. We'd been sleeping in different places most nights. Each day he'd work fourteen hours at the office, then go to the Westgate to pack, make a run to the storage shed we'd rented in north Austin, then return to pack some more. He'd been sleeping on a mat on the floor in the condo to avoid the long commute back and forth to my mom's house.

I could tell he was busy when he answered the phone; his voice sounded distant, like he was cradling the handset on his shoulder. A drawer opened and shut in the background. I'd debated whether to tell him about my latest read, but decided to go ahead and get the embarrassment over with.

"I bought a book the other day", I said after we exchanged hellos. "It was actually a book about Christianity. I read it, too."

"That's great, sweetie! It did seem like you'd been more interested in religion lately. Glad to hear it." I was surprised that he'd noticed anything about my changing views. I hadn't said anything about it, simply because I had mostly forgotten about the subject in the months that passed between my middle-of-the-night revelation and when I found the Strobel book. The only thing he might have noticed was that I left a website about Buddhism up on the computer at one point, and another time I asked him if he thought humans had souls (and didn't argue with his answer). Actually, now that I thought about it, that was a lot more than I used to do.

"The book wasn't perfect", I continued. "Some of their points were pretty weak. But, you know, overall, I didn't hate it." I waited for a reaction, but heard only the rustling of papers. "Actually, it's got me wondering about Jesus. I think I might read some more about it."

There was a pause, then the sound of a keyboard clicking. "Great", Joe said, his voice trailing off while he finished typing. The background sounds stopped, and he turned his attention back to the call. "That is very cool. Really. I can't wait to hear all about it. Now, if I send you the updated text for the estate planning page on the website, do you think you could get it up by noon? I have this online ad that's about to drop, and I just realized we never finished that section of the site. Oh, and don't forget to set up the email account for the new paralegal. He starts Monday."

"Yeah—" I stammered, trying to catch up to this new course the conversation had taken. "Yeah, sure, I think I can get to that."

"Thanks! Gotta run. I have to do another trip to the storage facility tonight, but I'm headed up there after that. Should be home before midnight."

True to his word, Joe got home at 11:47. I met him in the kitchen and got to work heating up the leftovers from a crock-pot stew. Joe poured a glass of milk for himself, and as he moved, I thought I noticed a slight limp. The moving process was wearing him out.

He started on his bowl of microwaved stew, and I pulled up a chair next to him. We didn't even bother to turn on the light above the table.

I let him have a chance to eat, then asked, "Could we go out to dinner tomorrow night? Maybe Guero's? My mom said she could watch Donald."

Joe finished another bite, leaned back, and wiped his hand on the bottom of his undershirt, which was so filthy with dust and grease that the new smidgen of stew sauce was not even noticeable. "I don't really have time for that right now."

"The condo is closing next week, and you should have more time to work after that. Could you take just this one night?"

"Okay. Sure. Is there something wrong?"

"I'm not sure", I said. "I think I just need to get out."

* * *

"It's the Fulwilers!" a voice shouted as soon as Joe and I pushed through the double doors and into the high-ceilinged waiting area at Guero's. A waitress came over to ask how the baby was doing, and the hostess came from behind the counter to give us hugs. I inhaled a long breath to savor the heavy aroma of spiced, slow-cooked meat.

Our usual table was taken, so we sat at the one next to the hatch door in the floor, unused since this building had been a feed warehouse. I sipped from the slender glass of margarita on the rocks, letting the rough salt crystals from its rim dissolve slowly on my lips. As I did, it was as if I was melting back into my real self.

So much had changed so quickly, I sometimes felt as if I'd been thrust into someone else's life. Not that long ago I was a childless atheist who lived downtown; now I was a suburban mother who was reading about Jesus. It was a lot to process. Tonight was a chance to step back into my old shoes for a while, to go to a place I knew well, to think about the things I was comfortable thinking about. Immersing myself in the familiar smells and sights of this place was like easing into a warm bath.

"So what's the occasion?" Joe asked.

I took another sip of my drink like I was in a commercial for Guero's margaritas. "Nothing, really." I remembered his concern about losing work time for this dinner, so I quickly added: "Well, I mean, I needed a break. Badly."

"You don't like living with your mom?" he asked.

"The house itself is great, and my mom has been nothing but awesome. But it's insanely hard to keep Donald quiet when she's on business calls. He wants to run into her office every two seconds."

He winced at the thought of it. "Yeah. Raising a toddler in a house where someone works from home is not going to be the easiest thing we've ever done."

"Also, I don't know anyone up there. It's a forty-minute drive each way to meet my friends for lunch, which means that I basically never see anyone. And I can't even imagine what we're spending on gas for your commute."

"It's not ideal, but you have to keep your eyes on the vision", Joe said. "Picture the grand opening of the Dallas office. Picture living in one of those houses that overlooks Town Lake. Picture doing all of this with a firm that actually helps people make their lives better."

I nodded. I was going to mention being a little bummed that the vast majority of our worldly possessions had either been sold or locked in a storage shed, but I already sounded like enough of a whiner.

Joe sensed my lack of enthusiasm. "Maybe we should get back to hosting parties. We're too maxed out right now, but we could aim to do it in a few months."

"At my mom's house?" Her house was nice, but it didn't quite have the ambiance of a twenty-fifth-floor rooftop downtown.

"I doubt people would drive that far, but maybe we could do it at the office. I think it would be good for you—it would be a fun project, and help you feel a little less isolated."

He was right. Joe and I had thrown parties regularly since the beginning of our relationship. Sometimes they were more along the lines of our hip-hop karaoke event where attendees were required to dress like their favorite rappers, other times they were low-key wine tastings, but they were always a great time. As an introvert, I was surprised by how much I enjoyed getting people together and helping them connect with one another. By the time Joe and I left the Westgate, we were getting weekly emails from people we didn't know, asking if they could get on the invite list. Our last few parties had grown to the point that we'd had to hire staff to handle them, and our reputation as people who knew how to throw a good bash had become an integral part of our identity as a couple.

"You know, I would really love to get back to that", I said. I'd already begun considering themes for the next shindig.

Joe was about to say something when a man approached our table.

"May I use this seat?" he asked.

I looked up to see blues legend Clifford Antone towering above us. He'd been a Guero's regular for months, and Joe and I ran into him almost every time we went there. We had spoken with him a few times before, but I was still star-struck every time I saw him.

He took a second look and said, "Joe and ... is it Jennifer?"

"Yes, hi!" I'd been so anxious to respond that a wad of chewed-up food almost fell out of my mouth.

Joe motioned to the chair in Clifford's hand. "You can have it, but do you want to sit with us?"

It was a quintessential Joe move. I would never have thought to ask a living legend if he wanted to hang out with us. This man had been friends with Stevie Ray Vaughn and John Lee Hooker. He'd hung out with B.B. King and Fats Domino. By starting the Antone's record label and store, he single-handedly changed the face of blues recording and was instrumental in launching the Austin live music scene. The godfather of blues did not share tables with random Guero's customers. But Joe didn't see boundaries like that. One time we were at a function where we ran into a widely acclaimed author, and I wrung my hands while trying to figure out if it would be okay to say hello. Joe walked up to her and said, "My girlfriend loved your book and wants to take you out to lunch on Monday." She accepted.

So, of course Joe asked Clifford Antone to sit down with us. And he accepted.

Joe took over the conversation by asking for Clifford's opinion about a current controversy regarding city ordinances about downtown clubs' decibel levels, and then the subject turned to business. Clifford asked what we did for work, and we told him about the law firm. I was surprised at the energy that filled me when I explained that, to us, this was more than just a job—it was our first big step toward our dreams for a fulfilling life.

Clifford nodded with a restrained enthusiasm. He had a baby face that was incongruent with his fifty-odd years, which gave him an aura of being both childlike and wise. "In a way, I'm right there with you", he said. "My life has been one way up to this point, and now it's like I'm starting over, trying to do it right this time." We understood that he was referencing the fact that he'd recently gotten out of prison. Pretty much everyone in Austin knew that he'd served time for drug charges, since his arrest had dominated the local news five years before. "It's not always easy, is it?" he asked, his smirk indicating that he assumed we knew exactly what he was talking about.

"No. No, it's not." It may have been the effect of the margarita, but I had to resist the urge to get teary-eyed as I answered. The stress from all the changes had been wearing me down, and the fact that Clifford Antone could relate to it touched me to a surprising degree.

Clifford glanced over his shoulder to make sure no one else was within earshot, then lowered his voice. He told us that he had recently been in a limo with a friend who was a well-known musician, and the musician and his crew started smoking pot. Clifford asked them to stop, pointing out that he could end up back in jail for this, since being around people doing drugs was a serious violation of his probation. His friend laughed off his request and continued smoking. Clifford had to ask the driver to pull over so he could get out, and he walked home alone.

"So, yeah", he said at the end of the story. "You try to make changes, and everything gets tough. Sometimes you lose things, like friends." He'd recounted his story casually, but there was visible hurt in his eyes when he spoke of what happened in the limo.

When it was time for us to go, Joe brought up one last thing. "My wife and I love throwing parties. We were just sitting here talking about how we could get back into that once the law firm is off the ground", he explained. "Would you be interested in co-hosting events with us? Maybe we could start with a benefit for musicians, or a charity thing?"

I turned to Clifford, morbidly curious to see how he'd get out of this awkward request. Instead, he replied, "I'd love to. When?"

I was ready to ask what he was doing this Saturday, but ever-prudent Joe said that we needed to wait a few months until things stabilized with us. While he and Clifford batted around ideas for themes and charities, I thought of how the invitation would read: "Clifford Antone and Jennifer and Joe Fulwiler invite you to ..." Or maybe it would be better to keep it more simple, to begin with "Clifford Antone and the Fulwilers ..." I could hardly wait for the moment that some friend called to see what was new, and I could casually remark that I was changing the baby's diaper, thinking about dinner—oh, and working on that thing we're doing with Clifford Antone.

As the two guys brought the conversation to a graceful close, Clifford said, "Let me give you my phone number so we can talk about this some more." Joe produced a blue ball point pen from his pocket, and Clifford scrawled a number on a napkin. When he finished, he handed the pen to Joe and the napkin to me. "This is going to be great. I look forward to it."

We stood, and I said "thank you" about three times as I shook his hand. I wanted him to understand how much he'd brightened my spirits. The vision of getting back to hosting great events—and doing it with Clifford Antone—was exciting enough to make me willing to sacrifice just about anything to achieve it.

Joe walked me to my car, and we kissed and parted ways. He would go to the Westgate for one last night of moving work, and I would embark on the voyage back up to my mom's house. Before I started the car, I pulled my purse onto my lap and slid the napkin with the number on it into the special compartment where I kept my house key. I looked at it one more time before I closed the zipper over it.

12

I leaned awkwardly into the booth at the restaurant of the Inn of the Mountain Gods in Ruidoso, New Mexico. I positioned myself to face the main room, so that everyone could see that I was reading a collection of essays by Augustine of Hippo. Occasionally, I would glance over the top of the book to see if anyone had noticed the title and was now running toward me to ask me if I'd gotten to the part where he falls into the Manichean heresy. Every time I saw only disinterested hotel guests milling around the buffet line, I was disappointed.

If the visit to Guero's had brought out Normal Jen, this vacation to the mountains of southern New Mexico brought out Reading about Christianity Jen, and she had evidently been dying to make an appearance. Joe was the only person who knew about this side of me, and he didn't seem to have the time or the interest to talk about it. None of my friends in Austin were religious—only one or two even considered themselves spiritual—and most were at least vaguely aware that I was an atheist. I didn't want to deal with the ribbing I'd get if it came out that I was interested in Jesus, so I kept this part of my life carefully separate from everything else. The result was that I was bursting with a million thoughts on the subject, but had no one to share them with.

Now, being so far away from home made me salivate at the opportunity to have a real conversation about faith without word getting out to anyone I knew. A busboy took my empty plate, then leaned across the table for my drained cup of water.

"Don't mind my book", I said loudly, moving it slightly so that it would be directly in his line of vision. "I was just reading it here." No response. "Yup, got completely sucked in."

He hesitated as if struggling to communicate something, and I remembered that some of the employees here spoke only Spanish. I pointed to the book again: "*Mi libro. Es muy interesante.*"

"I speak English", he said. "I was going to ask if you were planning to go through the buffet line again." He looked back over his shoulder at the crowd of guests by the hostess stand. "You've been here since after breakfast."

Mortified, I told him I was just about to leave. I fumbled for my purse and paid the bill, leaving a 60 percent tip. I relocated to the hotel's lobby, where I hoped I would be able to restrain myself from foisting my latest Jesus book on unsuspecting resort employees.

Coming here had been Joe's idea. Part of it was to celebrate: The Westgate sale was final, we'd gotten rid of Joe's car shortly after that, and now, in early August, the business finances were finally moving in the right direction. Plus, living with my mom was going as well as could be expected. I still felt like I was going to lose my mind trying to keep Donald quiet while she worked, but we were all getting along well.

The main reason for the trip, though, was to make connections. Joe was here with a group of attorneys from Austin to participate in an annual golf tournament. We'd hesitated about spending the money, but he pointed out that these guys were deeply connected in the local legal world and could be an important source of referrals for him. When my dad offered to pay for our airfare as an early gift for our second anniversary, we decided to do it.

The back of the lobby was enclosed by two stories of window paneling, tilted away from the inside as if to point to the lake and mountains that lay ahead. A single row of upholstered chairs lined the walkway in front of it, with no televisions or stacks of magazines nearby, almost demanding that you sit down and think about something deep.

Joe wasn't even halfway done with the thirty-six holes of golf they would play that day, and Donald had stayed home with my mom. As I eased into a chair and pulled a new book from my orange travel bag, I felt like I had nothing but time. The sounds of ancient pan flute flowed from the Apache-owned hotel's sound system, adding to the sense that I'd slipped into a time and place that were totally disconnected from my normal life. I stretched my legs and cracked open *Mere Christianity* by C. S. Lewis.

Lewis was an Oxford don best known for his beloved children's book series the Chronicles of Narnia. He was an atheist before he converted to Christianity; *Mere Christianity* was his summary of why he believed, based on a series of radio talks he gave to wartime Britain. As I pored over the pages under the watch of the Sarasota Mountains, I was delighted by what a good read this was. What shocked me most was the brilliant simplicity of it. This author was the kind of guy who, along with his friend J. R. R. Tolkien, belonged to an Old Norse reading club at Oxford. If his treatise on Christianity had been an unreadable mess of obtuse references to philosophers I'd never heard of, it wouldn't have surprised me. Instead, Lewis' prose was powerful and unadorned, as if he knew these concepts were powerful enough that they didn't need embellishment.

He began his book by noting that all humans have an innate sense of right and wrong—one that each of us refers to all the time, whether we realize it or not. He pointed out that when people argue about one another's behavior, they almost always appeal to a universal moral code. If one man steals another man's seat on a bus and an argument breaks out, the first man wouldn't make the case that stealing seats isn't wrong; he'd make the case that he was justified in using the seat, that he hadn't "stolen" it at all.

Lewis suggested that this is because we are all born with the same core sense of right and wrong. Cultures may disagree as to the details of their moral codes, but, underneath it all, we know goodness when we see it. He called this the Law of Nature.

"If no set of moral ideas were truer or better than any other, there would be no sense in preferring . . . Christian morality to Nazi morality", he wrote. "The moment you say that one set of moral ideas can be better than another, you are, in fact, measuring them both by a standard, saying that one of them conforms to that standard more nearly than the other."

I'd been waiting for him to bring God into the picture, and that's when he did it. He suggested that we humans are aware of these unseen laws because of our souls' connection to their origin. God isn't some man in the sky who tells us to be nice and loving, Lewis explained. God is the very *source* of all goodness. Our yearnings for a perfectly peaceful world are yearnings to be in union with God—and that union is the entire purpose of human existence.

I stopped. This depiction of God was more interesting than the caricature I'd always imagined—and I would have loved to have thought about it more but, oh, the pan flute. At some point in the past hour it had changed from lovely ambiance to musical torture. It seemed to be the same short clip played on an infinite loop—either that or my appreciation of the subtleties of pan flute song composition was totally lacking. It was invading my brain like a parasite, my thoughts overridden every few seconds with the sounds of the same few whistle-like notes.

I escaped outside to the paths in front of Mescalero Lake, where the only sounds were waves lapping against the lakeshore and the occasional hum of a golf cart motor. The mountains rose up just behind the lake, looming over it as if on guard. The hills themselves had a mysterious hazy quality, despite the fact that I saw no fog or smoke or other sources of haze. I understood why the Native Americans believed that this was sacred land.

I wondered about the Apache who lived here hundreds of years ago. What would they think of Lewis and his Law of Nature?

I knew what the first European settlers who encountered them would say. The Mescalero Apache were one of the most feared tribes of the Old West. They were skilled guerilla fighters who raided settlements and earned a reputation for violence and ruthlessness. The Westerners who encountered the Apache would probably point to them as a prime example in the case against Lewis' Law of Nature: To these natives, brutality and killing were a way of life, the settlers would say. They had an entirely different moral code that seemed to have no overlap with that of civilized people.

I looked from the mountains down to the golf course, where the descendants of those same settlers now laughed and drank beer. Though the Apaches technically owned this place, it had only been given to them after everything else was taken away. And so the Apaches would probably point to white people to make the same case: These newcomers trampled across the natives' ancestral homeland without a second thought toward how it might impact the people who had been living there for generations. They claimed ownership over that which could not be owned, and, to the Apache, appeared to have an entirely different and irreconcilable notion of right and wrong.

Yet when I considered this tragic clash of civilizations, walking on the very land where it took place, I did see a common thread of morality.

When the Apache attacked the settlers, they said they were defending their homeland. The settlers may have disagreed about who owned the land, but they never said that people don't have a right to defend their homes. The settlers justified their own actions by saying that the land didn't belong to the natives—or, on the rare occasions that they did admit that the land may have been theirs, they rationalized their choices in the name of progress.

"Think of a country where people were admired for running away in battle, or where a man felt proud of double-crossing all the people who had been kindest to him", Lewis said in defense of the Law of Nature. "Men have differed as regards to what people you ought to be unselfish to—whether it was only your own family, or your fellow countrymen, or everyone. But they have always agreed that you ought not to put yourself first."

I traced the side of the lake by walking the golf cart path. When I reached the side furthest from the hotel, I paused. I took in my surroundings through a new lens, much like I'd done when I looked around the room at my mom's house after considering that Jesus might exist. Only a few moments before, I'd seen the tourists and the resort's Apache owners as fundamentally different people. The Apache spirituality that was woven all through the grounds struck me as mainly being an attempt to enhance the visitor experience.

But now I remembered the statues of dancing warriors at the front of the hotel, the beads and fringe of their deerskin garments shooting out like flame, frozen in an eternal moment from a sacred ritual, and I saw a people reaching out to something real and extant. I thought of all the evils that had been committed by both sides in the wars that once scorched this land, and I saw the tragedy of people who, in their hearts, knew better.

The sun drew close to the tops of the mountains, and the sky's color was darkening to match the lake's ancient blue. I slid my book back into my travel bag and walked the gravel path back toward the resort.

Back in the room, I shuffled through the resort's literature while I waited for Joe to return. I picked up a brochure from the top of a stack on the table by the door and flopped onto the bed to peruse it. For some reason I flipped it over to the back first, where there was a quote from the Apache warrior Geronimo: "There is one God looking down on us all. We are all the children of one God."

13

We were still unpacking our bags from New Mexico when news reports began to filter in about a hurricane called Katrina. It had already hit Florida and was moving westward. Residents of the Gulf Coast were told to prepare as it crept toward them. As the days went on, the reports grew more dire, the warnings more urgent. The storm was gaining strength, and it threatened to level anything in its path.

On the night of Sunday, August 28, Joe and I stayed up late watching a Bourbon Street webcam on my laptop. Like most people in Austin, we considered New Orleans to be part of a close-knit family of weird Southern cities, our crazy Cajun cousin to the east. We'd walked among the Bourbon Street revelers many times, and so it was creepy to see the grainy image of the desolate street on the computer. As the wind picked up, empty cups blew by faster and faster. Then the rain began. When we woke up the next morning, there was a black box where the webcam screen had been.

The next weeks were filled with images of bloated bodies rotting in the sun, children clinging to tattered toys at overcrowded shelters, and muddy streams of water interrupted by triangular rooftops. Then the stories broke through the screen and into real life: Houston was overloaded with refugees, and busloads of recently homeless New Orleans residents were sent west to San Antonio, then north to Austin. People we knew began talking about friends and family who had been impacted by the hurricane. The driveway at the end of the street was clogged with cars bearing Louisiana license plates.

The country was still sorting through the chaos when I started ramping up my work at the law firm. Joe pointed out that we could save thousands on bookkeeping expenses if I could run the billing system, so we worked out a temporary arrangement with my mom where she would watch Donald in the mornings so that I could go into the office.

On my first official day of work, I wandered the halls until I found my new workspace, a desk in an administrative office that I would share with employees of a few other lawyers in the building. I dropped my purse on the floor, clicked the power button on the computer, and hoisted a stack of time sheets from my desk drawer. The old computer groaned to a start, and I flipped through the papers while it booted up. One-point-one hours for this client. Two-point-three hours for that client. The program to input the data was cumbersome and confusing, yet it was critical that I get everything in correctly, since clients didn't tend to have a sense of humor about being charged for work done on someone else's account.

The computer, which would have been better placed in a museum of 1990s technology, sputtered and froze every time I entered a new time record. Approximately five trillion hours later, I had only gotten through a quarter of the time sheets. My back ached and my hands hurt, not so much from the amount of time I'd been sitting at my desk—I'd been known to work twenty-four hours at a stretch in my programming days and loved every minute of it—but out of anger at this stupid computer and the overwhelming nature of the task.

Two women who worked for another lawyer burst through the door, chirping and gasping and gripping one another's arms. "It's disgusting", one of them said.

"People like that just make me want to scream", said the other.

I was never sure what the protocols were for shared office interactions. I glanced over my shoulder with a pleasant expression in case they expected me to talk. Luckily, they didn't seem to see me, so I hunkered over the keyboard and tried to seem intensely focused on my work.

"I swear, Sue, that man is as useless as tits on a boar hog." I felt a warm hand on my shoulder. "Honey, I'm sorry, I hope we're not offending you."

I swung the chair around. "No, you're fine!" I was wondering if I should introduce myself or just go back to the time sheets when she continued, as if I had been part of the conversation all along, "I'm just so mad about what that man said. I'm so mad I could spit!"

"Which man?" I asked.

"Pat Robertson. You didn't hear? He said that God sent Hurricane Katrina to New Orleans as punishment!"

The woman next to her shook her head. "Those Bible-beating idi-ots." She quickly looked at me and added: "I'm sorry if you're religious, I just—"

"Oh, no. I'm an atheist", I said. I needed to stop saying that since it technically wasn't true anymore, but I just couldn't bring myself to say *agnostic*. It was like saying you're bisexual. I always thought that agnostics and bisexuals needed to make a decision one way or the other.

"Well, I'm religious. I mean, I'm a Christian", said the first woman. "But this man is just plain wrong. This is not Christian doctrine."

"My pastor used to say it was", said the second woman. "That's why I stopped going to church. Anything bad would happen, he'd say it was because God's mad at us again."

"You should go to Hill Country Bible Church. The pastor there never says anything like that."

"*Now* he doesn't. But who knows what he'll say tomorrow? I'm done with church."

"Anyway, sorry to disturb you, honey", the first woman said to me. They rifled through a drawer, pulled out a file folder, and chattered their way out the door.

I turned back to the computer. My eyes were set in the direction of the screen, but I saw nothing. I thought of the children cuddling ragged toys, their only possessions left on earth. Images of bodies floating face-down in filthy water glowed in my mind. All other thoughts fell away, and I became instantly obsessed with a single question:

Who is Jesus?

If I was spending all this time reading about a passive-aggressive deity whose preferred method of hinting was Category 5 hurricanes, I needed to know right now so that I could stop wasting time on this religion. I pulled the keyboard close and started typing. My first search led me to the page of a pastor who said that no, it was not Christian teaching that Katrina was God's punishment. He condemned any other Christian leaders who would accuse God of such a terrible thing, and listed Bible verses that bolstered his case. I looked them up on a website and found:

For God sent the Son into the world, not to condemn the world, but that the world might be saved through him. (Jn 3:17)

We know that in everything God works for good with those who love him, who are called according to his purpose. (Rom 8:28)

86

For the Son of man is not come to destroy men's lives, but to save them. (Lk 9:56, KJV)

Okay. This was good. I liked this portrait of God. Much like C. S. Lewis, he described the Almighty as the source of all goodness and love. God never actively wills for bad things to happen to people, the pastor explained.

I was about to close the page when a reader's comment caught my eye. A man wrote in accusing this pastor of heresy and pointed him to the writings of another pastor who shared the Pat Robertson view that this hurricane was an act of God in direct response to man's sinfulness. I went to that page and found:

> For behold, the day comes, burning like an oven, when all the arrogant and all evildoers will be stubble; the day that comes shall burn them up, says the LORD of hosts, so that it will leave them neither root nor branch. (Mal 4:1)
>
> But the wicked perish; the enemies of the LORD are like the glory of the pastures, they vanish—away. (Ps 37:20)
>
> For the wages of sin is death. (Rom 6:23)
>
> He who has the Son has life; he who has not the Son of God has not life. (1 Jn 5:12)
>
> By turning the cities of Sodom and Gomor'rah to ashes he condemned them to extinction and made them an example to those who were to be ungodly. (2 Pet 2:6)

In the comment boxes on both pages, an angry debate raged about who was interpreting the Bible correctly. It was Team God's Wrath vs. Team God's Love, and the fight was vicious. God's Wrath accused God's Love of willfully overlooking verses that they found inconvenient. God's Love hit God's Wrath hard with lines from John and Galatians. But God's Wrath came back strong, throwing around some Revelation and a little Romans 2. They agreed that God loves us and doesn't want us to die, but said that that only refers to eternal life, and thus the occasional city-demolishing hurricane is needed as a wakeup call. In the end there were excommunications by combox for all involved, and each side walked away content that it had the Bible on its side.

I picked up my purse and dug through it. I pulled out a pocket-sized book with a nondescript black cover, the edges of its thin pages gleaming silver. It was my Bible.

It still felt weird to use the words *my* and *Bible* in the same sentence. We never had one in the house when I was growing up, other than a dusty heirloom copy that spent years in the attic. My dad would bring it down to show me the handwritten notes on the first pages that recorded dates of family births and deaths. He enjoyed the Old Testament as mythical literature, and would occasionally read it to me as a cultural heritage lesson before putting it back in the box where we kept all the faded, sepia-toned pictures. When I stopped by the bookstore to buy my current copy, I ended up with something called an English Standard Version, but that meant nothing to me; I'd simply picked the one that looked least like a Bible.

Since each side of the God's Wrath/God's Love debate accused the other of taking verses out of context, I flipped my book open and looked up verses for myself. I thumbed through page after page, passing books with names like Lamentations and Zephaniah. I found one of the key verses from Team God's Love at the beginning of chapter 3 in the book of John. I eased back into the chair and started reading.

A loud knock startled me so badly that I almost dropped the book. I turned to see our new paralegal. "You seen Joe?" he asked.

It was then that I noticed that I still had the God's Wrath page up on my screen. So there was Joe's wife, studying her Bible, reading a website titled HURRICANE KATRINA: GOD'S PUNISHMENT FOR A SINFUL WORLD. I tossed the Bible on the floor in the general direction of my purse and scooted between the paralegal's line of sight and my computer screen. "Nope. Haven't seen him. No idea where he is", I said.

As soon he disappeared from the doorway I clicked off the computer monitor, picked up the Bible, and ran through the lobby and into the main hallway. I searched my mental map of the building for a private place. The conference rooms were shared by other businesses, so that was out. Obviously my office was a hub of endless activity. There was only one place where I could get some time to myself to read this thing.

I pushed through the door into the women's bathroom, mumbled a hello to a lady washing her hands, and locked myself in a stall. I looked down at the toilet seat and hesitated. It would be nice to have somewhere to sit, but ... what the heck. I wiped it off with toilet paper and sat down in my slacks.

Listen, God, I said silently. Then I realized I was addressing the Almighty from a toilet. Surely there were rules about that. I stood and continued: *We seem to be missing each other here. I don't know whether I'm doing something wrong or what. Or maybe you don't exist, and I'm sitting here talking to myself, in a bathroom—damn, this is weird—but if you do exist and want me to find you, you're going to have to help me out. Amen.*

I sat back down on the toilet and opened my Bible.

I read and read and read. For at least an hour, maybe two, I flipped back and forth between pages. High-pitched voices exchanged greetings over the creaking of the soap dispenser and the rushing of sink water. I kept reading. Two or three times my door rattled, and one woman would ask another, "Is someone in there?" I'd forcefully spin the toilet paper roll as an answer, and then I'd go back to reading.

By the time my legs and back started aching from sitting there so long, I was no closer to clarity than when I'd first come across the debate. Team God's Love made a powerful Scriptural case to back up their convictions—but so did God's Wrath. I closed the book, and put my head on my knees.

It was time to admit that Christianity wasn't checking out. In theory, I had been open to that possibility all along. This was a search for truth, after all, and therefore must be conducted without the slightest whiff of emotional bias. But I had sensed something. In that dizzying moment in the room at my mom's house when I had first opened my mind about Jesus, something within me screamed, *Yes! This is it, this is right! You are going to find out that it's all true!* When I read C. S. Lewis, the feeling only grew stronger.

But evidently all those feelings were baseless, because Christianity was not holding up to scrutiny. What I had found, not only in the Love/Wrath debate but in all the years I'd lived among believers, was that there was not agreement among Christians about who God is. One Christian had faith in a Jesus who was a sensitive guy who just wanted everyone to be happy. The Christian next to him had faith in a Jesus who was disgusted by what he saw in this wicked world, the flesh-and-blood presence of a God who did not hesitate to punish disobedience severely. These two Jesuses were not the same person.

Christians wanted us nonbelievers to have faith in Jesus, but in order for that to be possible, we would first have to know *who Jesus is*. And, evidently, there was no way to get a clear answer about that.

What I had seen was that the Bible had enough content that you could pretty much make God and Jesus whomever you wanted them to be—and the upshot was that each Christian had a different image of whom they were following. This was not a religion where people came together to focus on the same deity; it was a religion where each person projected a hologram of the divine based on their subconscious issues and desires, and worshipped that.

The toilet next to me flushed loudly. It was late, and my legs were getting sore. I took one last look at my Bible, then closed it and went back to work.

14

I was now working for the law firm so much that we decided to get someone to help me with Donald. When I went to call the family friend who we heard was looking for babysitting work, the phone seemed heavier than usual. When she answered, I strained to sound upbeat about this turn of events.

The truth was that I was delighting in Donald's childhood, more than I could have imagined I would. I never had yearnings to be a mother when I was younger, and until I met Joe I figured that I might not have kids at all. Even when I was pregnant with Donald, I worried that I wouldn't be able to connect with him because I was missing whatever gene makes women maternal. Now that he was here, though, I found myself surprised anew every day at how much I enjoyed being a mother. It was a wonder to watch his little face come alive as he discovered new things about the world. I was fascinated by how he used his limited vocabulary to express his ideas, like the time he pointed to the crescent moon and turned to me with great concern to ask, "Moon? Broken?"

As I talked to our friend, a fifty-year-old lady named Irma, I thought of what Joe would say about my hesitation. He'd remind me to keep my eyes on the goal. He'd tell me that these are the kind of sacrifices you have to make to have a successful business. He was right. I shooed away that sense of sadness, and booked Irma for four days a week.

On her first day of work, Donald warmed to her immediately. He ran over to show her his "twactor" toy, and she scooped him up in her arms. She spoke to him in Spanish, and he listened as if he understood every word. It was as if he could sense the decades of history that her family shared with ours. Irma's sisters had arrived in this part of Texas thirty years earlier, and my dad's parents were among the first people they'd met. My grandparents spoke fluent Spanish from the years they'd spent living in Mexico, and they helped her sisters get on their feet in their new country. Our families had been close ever since.

My mom came in from her office, and she and Irma hugged. They exchanged pleasantries despite my mom's limited Spanish and Irma's limited English, and I excused myself while they talked.

I sat down at my desk in my bedroom office. I was planning to take time for some mindless web surfing, but an email marked urgent caught my attention. It was from Joe, and its subject said *Call me as soon as you get this*. Our search engine rankings had plummeted, Joe wrote, and he and the employees were in a panic. "We've had no new leads in the past ten days", he reported in another email. "Before our rankings dropped, we used to get over a dozen people contacting us every week. I need you to fix this now."

I'd configured the Fulwiler Law website so that it was one of the first results when people searched for terms like *lawyer in Austin*. The results were better than we could have dreamed: The day we reached the number-two spot on page one of the rankings, the electronic sound of the office phone ringing was like background music that played all day. Queries from potential clients popped up in Joe's paralegal's email inbox one after another. Doing well in search engine results generated tenfold more qualified leads than even the most expensive traditional advertising campaigns. Best of all, it was free.

The downside to all of this was that we'd come to live and die by our search engine rankings. We'd cut the thousands of dollars per month that lawyers traditionally spend on advertising from the budget, and had hired another employee with the money saved. Now we'd lost our page-one position and all the revenue that came with it, and I didn't know why.

The phone rang. "How long do you think it'll take to fix this?" Joe said, the sound of his keyboard clicking in the background.

"Once I make the changes, we could see results in as early as a few days", I said. "But the problem is that I don't know what changes to make. I looked at—"

"Okay, just do what you can, as fast as you can. I gotta go." Before hanging up he said *loveyoubye* as if it were one word. Our end-of-call terms of endearment had been getting shorter and shorter lately, down from "I love you, sweetie! I hope you had a good rest of the day", to this *loveyoubye* thing.

The sounds of Donald and Irma's intermingled laughter floated in from the living room, but I blocked it out to focus on this task. I typed frantically, opening multiple pages at once, making changes to the web-site code then checking it against ranking tools. The tweaks seemed to help slightly, but I suspected that they wouldn't take us back to where we needed to be. Something big must have happened for us to fall so far.

When four o'clock rolled around, I picked up the phone to tell Joe that I'd had no luck. Just before I dialed I stumbled across a news story, released only hours before, that announced a fundamental change to the algorithm of one of the big search engines. I set the phone down. This must be it. It had to be. I leaned forward and read the article, taking time to absorb every word. This was the answer. I needed to do more research in order to know exactly what changes to make, but once I made them, we could probably get the phones ringing again by the end of the week.

I dashed out a search to get the details of the new algorithm. Instead of the list of search results I expected to see, my browser hung on the page with the news story. I clicked around, trying to resubmit the search, but nothing happened. I tried again, and this time an error page thudded onto the screen. My internet connection was down.

A line from one of Joe's emails came to mind: "Every day that our rank is down, we have to reach into our personal expenses to cover the loss of business." I clicked again. Same error page.

I called out to my mom, and she confirmed that she couldn't get online either. I tried one more time, then slammed my fist on my key-board at the sight of the error notice. What I wished for most—even more than I wished for the problem to be solved—was that my internet cable could feel pain. It would be worth the whole thing having hap-pened if I could give it a good stomping to punish it for doing this to me.

There was nothing to do. I called Joe and left a voicemail letting him know what was happening. Now all I could do was wait.

I tried to busy myself with other things. I reviewed the code I'd saved on my computer, paced the room, tried to check email, became exasperated when I remembered that no internet connection meant no email either, then went back to pacing. Every few minutes I'd return to the same screen and type my query again, slam the Enter key to submit the search—as if maybe it would be afraid to mess with me after wit-nessing such a display of power—and then shout expletives when I saw the inevitable error page. When I began addressing the computer with direct personal threats, I knew it was time to step away.

I stalked into the hall, giving my computer one last warning glance before I left. Now what? If Donald saw me he'd probably cry for me, and if I picked him up he'd cry harder when I had to go back to work. Then Irma would behold the scene and think about what a terrible mother I was, and twenty years from now Donald would write about it on his tell-all confessional blog called "Memories of an Awful Childhood". So, clearly, I needed to avoid the living room. The only other options were to go to my room, Donald's room, my mom's room, or maybe just keep standing in the hallway. I chose our room.

As soon as I entered, my Bible caught my eye.

I hadn't been able to walk away from Christianity yet. Despite its issues, there were still too many unresolved questions. How did C. S. Lewis have that uncanny ability to describe the universal moral laws of humanity with such accuracy? How did Augustine of Hippo have such an intimate understanding of the human experience? How did Newton, Copernicus, Galileo, Mendel, Kepler, and Boyle—some of the great minds of science, unquestionably rational men—make sense of the logical flaws with Christianity?

And there was the mysterious figure of Jesus himself. Even if I didn't have clarity on exactly who he was, there was no question that he single-handedly started a religious revolution that was still going on thousands of years later, despite the fact that he was a poor man who was executed. As Joe pointed out when he first saw me reading these Christian books, "No founder of any other major world religion claimed to be God." Cult leaders throughout the ages had tried to pull it off, and their religions always petered out once they made the very un-godlike move of dying and staying dead. So what did Jesus have going on that allowed his religion to spread like a shockwave through the ancient world despite his grandiose claim, and despite the fact that being a Christian often meant persecution or death?

I continued staring at the Bible. I could not escape the feeling that there was something real that I had yet to find, some treasure buried beneath these words. As if the book had its own gravity field, I felt drawn to it, to pick it up, to read it. But I'd done that dozens of times by this point, and each time I walked away only more confused. I turned to walk out the door, but I couldn't. I had nowhere else to go.

Okay, God, let's try this again, I whispered. I took the book in my hands. My heart was full of so many worries and questions that I didn't even know where to start. Should I pray for a resolution to the search engine issue? Or just ask for help figuring out if God exists? I packed it all up into a ball of hope and yearning, and did that thing where I sent it out in the form of an unspoken prayer that I hoped someone could hear.

I closed my eyes and ran my hand along the faux leather cover. Augustine of Hippo once opened a book of Paul's letters to a random page and received a profound message from God. Maybe that's where I'd find the answers I was looking for, too. My fingertips moved blindly over the edges of the pages and worked their way into an opening. I slid my finger down the delicate paper and stopped when it felt right. I opened my eyes to see what message awaited me:

"In the twelfth year of Joram son of Ahab king of Israel, Ahaziah son of Jehoram king of Judah began to reign."

"Oh, come on!" I snapped the book shut and stood up. Okay, this was it. This religion was obviously making me crazy, Exhibit A being that I was now turning to random pages in the Bible for answers to search engine optimization problems.

I stacked the books on my bedstand: *Mere Christianity*, *Augustine's Major Writings*, *The Case for Christ*, and the Bible. I wasn't ready to shove them under the bed or into a box yet, but I was close.

From out in her office, my mom called that the internet connection was back up. I finished the last of the code changes just in time to take Irma home. I strained to make conversation on the drive, my mind awhirl with stresses and questions about everything from the existence of God to how to get the law firm website back on page one of law-related search results. I briefly attempted to tell Irma about the work I'd been doing, but when I said in Spanish that "our word is low on the computer and now I am anger", I changed the subject to the weather.

15

As soon as Joe got home, I collapsed into bed for a nap. I awoke after dinner time and found him out in the living room, Donald asleep on his chest. My mom was playing tennis, so the two of them were alone in that part of the house. Before Joe saw me, I stopped and watched him for a moment. He was frowning at a stack of legal papers piled on the couch next to him; in contrast, Donald looked so peaceful with his eyes shut, his head cradled between his daddy's shoulder and neck. Donald wasn't a baby anymore; he'd just turned one. I wished Joe had more time to enjoy his childhood.

Joe saw me and put down the paper in his hand. "Hey, it's the super-woman who can fix all search engine problems!" he announced in a joyous whisper.

I said thanks, and he immediately turned back to his papers, moving his lips silently as he reviewed the pages packed with small type.

I cleared my throat. "Can I talk to you about something?"

Joe turned toward me, his body language screaming that he was desperate to get back to work. "Sure. Of course."

"I used my Bible today", I said.

"That's great. How did that go?" It was comical to watch him try to ignore his documents and wriggle himself into the role of Husband Who Is Delighted to Have Bible Chat with His Wife.

To save time, I just spit it out: "Okay, look, I did that thing where you open to a random Scripture passage to look for an answer. I got nothing—this line about someone being the son of Captain Ahab."

"I think you mean just Ahab. Captain Ahab is in *Moby Dick*, not the Bible."

"Whatever. The point is that it was this stupid moment of despera-tion, and I only did it because it really seemed like there was something to this religion, but if God even exists then he's totally ignoring me, and I can't get any answers from Christians about what their doctrines are, and it all makes me feel like I'm going insane."

Joe began to say something, but I was just getting started. I unloaded on him about how confusing the Bible was, how I was baffled by all this stuff about Passover and a Feast of Tabernacles and burnt offerings and unclean food and gentiles, Jewish terms that I had zero familiarity with. It was like I was eavesdropping on someone else's conversation: I was reading about first-century Jerusalem, stories of men and women whose lives were separated from mine by a yawning gulf of seven thousand miles and two thousand years. I could pick up the gist of what they were saying, but never for a moment did I think I understood the full meaning of their message.

Then I started on the issue of Christians not being able to agree on how to interpret any of it, but Joe stopped me. "If I remember correctly from Sunday School, John 3:16 basically lays out Christian theology", he said. He took a moment to search his memory before reciting the quote: "God so loved the world that he gave his only begotten Son, and whoever believes in him will have eternal life."

"So ..."

"So you're getting way too bogged down here", he said. "Don't worry about the minutia of Jewish culture. Don't worry about the details of the phrasing. It's really simple."

"But it's not! A lot of people say that God wanted Hurricane Katrina to happen to New Orleans as punishment. I read online yesterday that some pastor said that people who haven't heard the name of Jesus will go to hell forever. If that's really who Jesus is, then no, I can't believe in him."

Joe didn't respond. I leaned over to fling a teddy bear back into the toy bucket at the corner of the room, and I noticed that he was sneaking glances at his paperwork when it seemed like I wasn't looking. He didn't want to talk about this right now. The poor guy—he was just about working himself to death trying to make our dreams a reality, and I was distracting him with my theological flailing.

"You know what, it's cool", I said. Since it wouldn't be out of character for me to say that in a passive-aggressive way and then go stew about it, I made sure to sound sincere when I added, "We can talk about this another time. You can get back to work."

I gave Joe a kiss on the forehead, patted Donald on the back, and went into my office. I had an idea. It was something I'd been thinking of doing for a while, a way to find an outlet for talking about my spiritual wanderings without distracting Joe. I took a seat in the desk chair and wiggled the mouse to bring my laptop to life.

I pulled up the webpage of a free blogging platform and clicked the button that said START YOUR OWN BLOG.

Using only the name Jennifer F., I told the unknown reader that I had been an atheist all my life, but had started to think that God might exist. I explained that my search for him had been kind of a mess so far, and that if I were ever going to find him, I was obviously going to need some help.

* * *

The next morning, after Irma arrived I blew off work to play around with my new blog. My first task was to recruit some readers. I came across an atheist site where a handful of Christians debated the author and his readers in the comment boxes at the bottom of his posts. I picked through the discussions to identify Christians who did the best jobs of defending their faith. Anyone who appealed to subjective personal experience was out, as was anyone who quoted Bible verses with the unquestioned assumption that they spoke truth. Those who remained were the ones who made linear arguments, explained their beliefs using reason, and seemed familiar with the common atheistic objections to faith.

Many of these people had email addresses as part of their commenting profiles, and I sent notes to each of them to ask if they would comment on my blog. That morning I sent more than a dozen emails. Half of them bounced. Of those that didn't, three people replied.

That group of Christians told their friends about my blog, and within a few weeks I had a small but active following. Interacting with these people was like what I had experienced with C. S. Lewis and Augustine: I saw people who were made more, not less, reasonable by their faith.

In one of my first email exchanges with a reader, a man named Steve G. caught my attention when he made the case that humans don't really have free will if the atheistic worldview is true. He wrote:

Under atheistic materialism, the universe is by necessity strictly deterministic because every "decision" you make is completely the result of previous brain states combined with current sensory and somatic input.

98

In a classical physics based model, all inputs are processed in the brain in a deterministic manner. Every step of the processing is completely determined by the sensory input and the previous brain states, which in turn have been determined by sensory/somatic input, genetics, and environmental factors.

In order to deviate from a strictly deterministic outcome at any of these decision points, some source of information other than the strictly physical is required. By this very definition, the source of the required additional information must be supernatural. So, we have free will if there is a supernatural information source that can inform our decision outside of the dictates of natural law.

He went on to address new research in the field of quantum mechanics that supposedly made free will possible within the atheistic worldview, pointing out that "quantum mechanics predicts events only in terms of probabilities, which casts some doubt on whether the universe is strictly deterministic. However, if an action is taken due to quantum randomness, this in itself means that free will is still absent, as such action cannot be controllable by someone claimed to possess such free will."

These were the kind of people I'd been looking for. Whether they were right or wrong, they were knowledgeable and willing to take a clear-eyed look at the world. In fact, I enjoyed my conversations with them so much that I started to stay up late just to reply to emails and blog comments. I felt like I was at an intellectual all-you-can-eat buffet: These people were presenting me with a rich spread of topics to devour, each one more fascinating than the next, and it never seemed to end. One night I might be up until one o'clock, reading and re-reading a long comment about how the ancient Greek philosophers conceived of God. I would reply to the comment's author by email, and the next night I'd scoot up to my computer screen with a cup of chamomile tea (or, if it were a weekend night, maybe a glass of cabernet sauvignon), and linger over his reply.

Yet underneath my excitement lingered an awareness that there were still major flaws with this belief system. As much as I was enjoying talking with these Christians on my blog, I could not continue to explore a religion that fundamentally didn't make sense. At some point, if I didn't find answers that resolved the problems I'd encountered, I'd have to wrap up this investigation and move on to . . . I had no idea what.

* * *

I made the decision one night when the blog was four months old. I was sitting with Donald in my lap, both of us nestled into the avocado green chair in his room, and I'd been thinking about whether or not it made sense to spend any more time exploring Christianity—I'd had plenty of time to think, given that it usually took me over an hour to get my sleep-hating child to finally drift off.

My pile of religious books had migrated from my bedside table to the side of the green chair as I'd come to spend more and more time next to Donald's crib in a (mostly futile) effort to get him to sleep on a regular schedule. I picked up the Bible from the top of the stack. I opened it, the feathery pages lit by the dim glow of Donald's Winnie the Pooh nightlight. I wondered if this would be the last time I opened a Bible.

C. S. Lewis and Augustine—and even my blog readers—had an amazing grasp of both the natural world and the human experience. I did still have lingering questions about how Christianity spread and how Jesus pulled off a lasting religion while claiming to be God. But still, it was probably time to call it quits with this religion.

For months, I'd been trying to piece together the Christian moral code. With every major question, I encountered the same theological imbroglio as the God's Wrath vs. God's Love fight after Hurricane Katrina. *Is abortion okay?* Some Christians said yes, some said no, each had Scriptures to back up his claims. *Is euthanasia okay?* Some Christians said yes, some said no, each had Scriptures to back up his claims. *Is gay marriage okay?* Some Christians said yes, some said no, each had Scriptures to back up his claims.

Over and over again, I encountered the idea that none of this really matters: *All Christians agree that you have to have faith in Jesus to come to know God, so what's the big deal if there's some disagreement about the Christian moral code?* Aside from the fact that I had not encountered "some" disagreement, but rather had seen more disagreement than agreement, that theory simply did not work.

At the foundation of this religion was the belief that God is good—he's the very source of everything we sense and know to be "good". To define a moral code, then, is to sketch a portrait of the Almighty himself: To separate good from not good is to separate what is God from what is not God. By the tenets of their own belief system, Christians didn't have the option of disagreeing on their moral code.

With Donald draped across my left arm, I used my right hand to flip the Bible closed. The moral code concerns were enough to make me ready to move on from this religion, but the death knell had come, ironically, in the form of the book itself.

Every time I read my Bible, I was distracted by the knowledge that, before the printing press, each Bible had to be hand-copied using a feather quill pen. It was an arduous process that took thousands of hours. One medieval scribe complained that "it dims your eyes, makes your back ache, and knits your chest and belly together. It is a terrible ordeal for the whole body." Bibles, along with all other books, were necessarily expensive and rare. Before the printing press, the idea of the average person being able to pore over his personal Bible—let alone own a concordance or other supplementary books—was out of the question.

And then there was the issue of literacy. I could not believe that an all-knowing God would create a system in which a person had to be literate in order to know him. Most people throughout history could not read. Even now, the world literacy rate was only 80 percent; there were dozens of countries where fewer than half the citizens could understand the written word. Yet here was Christianity, saying that not only did you have to be able to read in order to know God, but you had to have strong reading comprehension skills—not to mention the leisure time to be able to gain an encyclopedic knowledge of the Scriptures so that you could interpret them in context with one another.

I didn't see the fingerprints of the divine anywhere in this system. Instead, I saw a structure created by well-meaning people—people who had found comfort and peace in the Bible, who wanted to share it with others, who did their best to spread the words from which they'd derived inspiration. But, like any other human creation, it was flawed with imperfections that would ultimately doom it to collapse.

I set the Bible on the floor next to the chair and strained to get to a standing position while still holding Donald. I lowered him into his crib a millimeter at a time, lest any sudden movements wake him and leave me to begin the hour-long process all over again. When he was safely on his mattress, I crept out of the room and eased the door shut behind me.

I'd expected to tiptoe into my own darkened room since it was past midnight, but I opened the door to find that the overhead light was on. Joe sat on top of the bed, covered in a mound of papers as if he'd been caught in a file folder avalanche.

"What are you doing up?" I asked.

"I have a hearing tomorrow. That Jaworski case."

I tensed upon hearing the name. I'd been filling in for paralegal work when Mr. Jaworski first came in for a consultation. I was moved by his story of being swindled out of his life savings at eighty years old, and I'd encouraged Joe to represent him. What we didn't see coming was that the swindler hired a guy who had a reputation for being one of the most vicious and conniving lawyers in the state. Now that I saw Joe working feverishly late into the night, I wondered whether taking the case had been the right decision.

"What about you?" he asked. "Are you going to bed now?"

"Actually, I was going to blog."

Joe glanced at the clock radio on his bed stand. "Don't you think you should try to get some sleep? Isn't Donald due to wake up again in a couple hours?"

"Yeah, but I have something I need to get off my chest." I pushed aside a fat manila envelope and took a seat at the end of the bed. "Are you really a Christian?" I asked.

"Of course", he said.

I took the time to find the right words. "Okay. But you do see the problems with this religion, like the ones we talked about a while back. You have to."

Without looking up from his work, he said, "Sure. And I might not fit everyone's definition of a Christian. But do I believe in Jesus? Absolutely."

"Okay—" I stopped to calm myself so I wouldn't start ranting again. "But you can see how strange this looks from my point of view. You don't do this in any other area of your life. You would never say 'a geocentric model of the solar system doesn't stand up to scrutiny, but I believe it anyway'!"

"Jesus stands up to scrutiny. Maybe the religion that's been built up around him doesn't, but he does."

"In what way?"

Joe set down the papers. He closed his eyes, keeping them shut for so long that I thought he wasn't going to answer. "I was baptized when I was thirteen", he began.

102

"That's right, I remember your telling me that", I said. He hadn't brought it up in years, not since that flight to San Francisco before we got engaged. Last time, I cut him off before he could tell me what it was that he experienced. This time, I listened.

"Something happened. I'm not sure if it's anything I can explain, but when I came up from the water, and for a long time afterward, I felt a presence. There was something there, something powerful and pure. Like light, but light that I could feel inside. It threw my sense of self into contrast. Like, I saw myself differently."

I started to speak, but he wasn't finished. "Look, I agree that your questions are good, and I don't have answers for you. But I do know that what I experienced that day was real."

"Uh, wow. Wow, that's definitely great." I was trying so hard to show my sincerity to make up for last time that I sounded like a bad actor. "Do you still feel that presence?"

"No. I still believe, but ... no. I haven't felt that for a long time." His face flickered with sadness, as if he were speaking of a lost friend he couldn't find.

"So what would you say about someone like me?" I asked. "I haven't had any experiences like you have. On top of that, I see major flaws in this belief system."

"Jesus is not a belief system."

"Okay. But whatever or whoever he is, he sure doesn't seem to be reaching out to me. It's looking to me like he doesn't exist at all."

"You'll eventually believe", he said.

A staccato laugh burst from my lips before I could stifle it. "And what makes you think that?"

"You'll find him because you're honestly looking for him, and he exists." Joe added a little shrug, and if he'd just made the most obvious statement in the world.

"Well, great. I look forward to my profound conversion to Christianity", I said, not sure if I was joking or not. "In the meantime, I'm going to go tell my blog readers that I don't think I'll ever become a Christian because their religion doesn't make sense."

"Have fun with that", Joe said. He was smiling as if he knew something I didn't. He really seemed to think that I would be a Christian one day.

I took a seat in my darkened office, where only the monitor lit the room. I was too afraid to turn on the overhead light—if even one photon made it into Donald's room across the hall, it wouldn't be worth it.

I looked at the finished draft. Title: *Thanks for everything*. It was a farewell that announced the end of my short-lived blog and expressed gratitude for the kindness my readers had shown me. Without going into detail, I explained that this religion had not checked out for me and wished my readers well.

My cursor hovered over the PUBLISH button.

I'd miss the blog. In the short time that I'd been having conversations with this group of readers, they'd shown themselves to be some of the friendliest and most interesting people I'd ever encountered. I'd also miss the Bible itself. Even though I couldn't figure out what to make of the book as a whole, the writers themselves had charmed me. Some of my favorite parts in the whole text were the passages that nobody ever quotes. I smiled as I read Paul's warm greetings from prison to his friends Philemon and Apphia. I thought it was cute that he interjected a note written in his own handwriting in the letter to the Corinthians—I never expected to see "Hey from Paul!" in the Holy Bible. I loved all the shout-outs throughout his letters, to men and women like Aquila and Prisca, Stephanas, Fortunatus, and Achaicus, with the occasional interjection about how nice it was to have the church meet in their homes or how fondly he regarded their friendships. Within the books of the New Testament I'd sensed an earnestness among the writers, an utter lack of self-consciousness about whether or not the reader would accept what they wrote. I spotted no sly attempts at coercion; I believed that they believed it was all true.

I moved the cursor from PUBLISH to DISCARD. Though I was fairly certain that this would be the end of my investigation into Christianity, it didn't feel right to make an official announcement just yet. I clicked the DISCARD button and started over.

Feeling for the right letters in the darkness, I typed out an honest account of my problems with Christianity. I laid out everything I'd been struggling with and thinking about. When I was finished, my eyes ached from the glare of the screen. And this time, I hit PUBLISH.

16

On a warm October morning, I found myself standing in the bathroom, staring at a positive pregnancy test. Donald was over a year old, and we'd been hoping to have another kid sometime soon. Since neither Joe nor I had siblings, it seemed like it would be nice for Donald to have a brother or sister who would be close enough in age to be a buddy. Now that I was actually pregnant, though, my worries overshadowed my daydreams about Donald frolicking hand-in-hand with another Fulwiler child. For one thing, what would we do about our living situation? Things were already cramped here at my mom's house; I couldn't imagine how we'd squeeze a new baby into the mix.

I called Joe to tell him the news. He was excited, but I'd caught him five minutes before a big meeting, so we didn't get to chat much. It was Irma's day off, so I couldn't distract myself with work. I tried flipping channels in the living room while Donald colored, but there were no good shows on, and Donald seemed more interested in shredding the pages of the coloring book than creating art with them.

Finally, I couldn't take it anymore. I turned off the television, strapped Donald into his car seat, and headed into Austin. It was time to take action.

* * *

"Will your husband be meeting us?" the realtor asked.

"No, it's just me", I said, resting Donald on my hip as I peered through a window into the empty house.

She unlocked the door, and I stepped into a long living room. It had the musty smell of a house built in the 1970s and none of the charm of its restored bungalow neighbors, but there was plenty of space. The hallway at the end of the room led to four bedrooms, and the porch outside the sliding glass door would only need a few touch-ups to be perfect for parties.

"It just went on the market yesterday morning", the realtor said, raising her voice to get my attention as I admired the brand new stove, and the dishwasher that had more buttons than a space shuttle.

My heart beat faster as I inspected the bedrooms. Just how I liked them: not too large, saving most of the square footage for the common rooms. There were no fancy touches like a garden bath or a sitting area in the master bedroom—but that was even better, because it made the house within a price range that two people starting a business could afford.

As if reading my mind, the realtor added, "You're not going to find a better deal for miles."

Really, this house was all about the location. It was a mere two blocks from Lake Austin, a short walk to the popular restaurants that lined the lake, and only two miles from downtown. It was in the coveted Tarrytown neighborhood, the lush, tree-lined part of town where hipsters went to live when they got promoted and had kids. Though most of the houses were expensive, none were ostentatious; Tarrytown denizens invested tens of thousands of dollars renovating their bungalows to make them more charming. The architecture was simple, the houses tucked away in the embrace of cedar elm and oak trees.

I stepped onto the back porch, where the air was heavy with the scent of lake water. Boats whined in the background, on their way to dock at the funky Hula Hut restaurant down the street. All along the block, native plants grew wild in carefully planned environmentally friendly yards, buffalo grass and leathery agave plants lining driveways paved with artisan-carved stones.

Our new life appeared before me, each detail vivid: I wake up in the morning and jog down to Mozart's Café for a cup of coffee. Feet propped on a chair, I blow on my drink to cool it as I plan my day. As I stroll home, I wave hello to my neighbors, well-networked executive types who have introduced us to industry paragons who have been critical to the firm's success. When I get back to the house, Joe has already started breakfast for Donald and his sibling, their ages now seven and five. After a leisurely meal, Joe rides his bike to work, I drop the kids off at their blue-ribbon school, and then I return to the house to plan our upcoming party, to be hosted in our recently refinished back yard. *Only two blocks from Lake Austin*, the invitations would note.

The vision was so clear, it seemed destined to become a reality.

"Great space, isn't it?" the realtor said, stepping through the sliding door behind me.

It was more than a great space. This was my new life. Right here, in this house. It would make everything come together. For one thing, we would have our own space. My mother had shown saint-like patience with our living with her, but the strain of trying to raise my child in someone else's house was starting to wear me down. Also, we'd be back in a central location. I could meet working friends for lunch, we could go to our favorite restaurants on date nights, I'd have someplace to walk with Donald other than a desolate suburban playground. And the parties. We could finally start planning events, get back into the social scene, and get our lives back. We'd be the same Joe and Jen that everyone knew, just with a couple of kids, and living by the lake instead of downtown.

I turned to the realtor. "How do I put in an offer?"

"You'll just need to follow me to my office. It's a few blocks away, by the organic market", she said. She pulled out her phone and began pushing buttons. "I'll call ahead to have the paperwork ready."

Okay. I did need to call Joe. Definitely. I could not go around putting in offers on houses without my husband's knowledge, even if it was a fantastic deal. I briefly went through the scenario of doing it anyway, starting our next phone call with, "Promise me you won't be mad when you hear what I'm going to tell you ...", but I quickly shut it down.

"Wait", I told the realtor. "I need to talk to my husband. I'll just call him real quick to get his okay."

I pressed the button to call the number. In the moment of silence between when I dialed and the first ring, I thought a dozen times, *Please don't say no, please don't say no, please don't say no* ... A coarse ring rattled through the speaker. *Please don't say no, please don't say no, please don't say no* ... The receptionist answered. I asked for Joe and was put on hold. *Please don't say no, please don't say no, please don't say no* ...

He answered, and I jumped immediately to the purpose of my call. Obviously, we needed more room now, I explained. I recounted my tales of woe of trying to keep Donald from interrupting my mom's work in her home office, emphasizing that it would be impossible—totally impossible!—to deal with that once I had morning sickness. And, plus, it's not like a family of four could live in someone else's house for too long anyway. And then there were the parties, the lifestyle, the location we'd have if we moved here. And had I mentioned the price? Wasn't it hard to believe that such a good deal could possibly exist? Really, this house would be an investment—we should think of it as *making* money more than spending money.

After a long silence, and what sounded like a stifled sigh, Joe responded. "Are you serious?"

Donald crawled into the kitchen, and I followed him as an excuse to step away from the realtor. "Are *you* serious? What, you want to keep living with my mom for the rest of our lives?"

"It doesn't matter what I want. The firm isn't there yet financially."

"You have been working fourteen hours a day, six days a week. How is that not translating into money in our bank account?"

"For one thing, we're still paying off startup costs. But the Jaworski case has been taking up all my time for weeks, and it's not like I'm getting paid anything for that—"

"He's not paying us?" The question came out like a yelp of pain. The realtor looked up, and I moved further into the kitchen.

"I told you that, remember?"

I hadn't worked on the case since I'd gotten busy with the firm's website, but I had a vague memory of Joe leaning over my shoulder and telling me to input this client's hours differently back when I was doing time sheets. "I didn't realize this was going to take up so much of your time", I said.

"Obviously, I didn't either. But I'm knee-deep in it now. Do you want me to tell him to find another lawyer?"

Here's where I was supposed to say no. This was my cue to tell Joe emphatically to do whatever he needed to do to help that man salvage what was left from the wreckage of his life. And it's not like I didn't want to. My heart ached to think of an old man without anyone to defend him, and a part of me wanted to insist that Joe help anyone like this who walked through his door.

But most of our possessions had been stuffed into a discount storage facility for six months. I was trying to raise my child in someone else's home. And now I had a real chance to get my life back. Over there, just past the kitchen entry, was the place I had picked out for our ebony buffet table. We'd dust off the cream-colored couch and put it just across from the fireplace. There was Joe, unrolling the beige area rug, with Donald giggling and jumping on top of it. Outside was the patio bar we'd added, where the caterers and waitstaff were setting up for our first party. I did care about Mr. Jaworski. Truly. I wished him all the best. But what about my happiness?

"I take your silence as a yes?" Joe said.

My tone was cold when I responded. "I know you don't want to get off the case."

"You're right. I don't know what would happen to this guy if I didn't see this thing through."

I cupped my hand over the phone and lowered my voice. "Okay. So we can't put in an offer right now. But if you get this case done as fast as possible we could put in a bid later if the house is still available, right?"

"Let's talk about it. That would still be a huge mortgage to have hanging over our heads."

With every terse word Joe spoke, my new house disappeared a little more. "But it's an investment!"

"I haven't even seen it!"

This conversation wasn't getting me any closer to my goal, so I wrapped up the call and Joe and I exchanged clipped goodbyes. "Looks like my husband can't make it over here today", I called to the realtor as I picked up Donald. "We're very interested, but may need a few days to get things in order."

She walked with me to the front door. "Okay, well, I don't expect this one to stay on the market very long—not at this price."

Fear shot through my stomach like a cannonball. I had to get started.

After I strapped Donald in and got behind the wheel, I unzipped the back pocket on the inside of my purse. I pulled out an old napkin, smoothed from months of being pressed into the small space. There was Clifford Antone's number.

I wondered if I should call. If I could get something on the calendar with Clifford, maybe Joe would be excited about it. It would remind him of everything we wanted from our lives, and surely the house wouldn't be a hard sell after that. I fished my phone from the pocket of my jeans and typed the number into the keypad.

The realtor lingered in the driveway in front of me. We met eyes, and she waved for the third time. Since she seemed to be waiting for me to leave, I tossed the phone onto the passenger seat and put the napkin back in the compartment in my purse. I pulled the car into the driveway to turn around, and when I did I paused to focus on the front door. I wanted that to be the door that I walked through each day. I wanted to enter it with Donald and his younger sibling after picking them up from school, and push it open with my foot when I brought in bags of groceries. I wanted to stand behind it while welcoming guests to our parties, and crowd through it with the whole family when we went down to the lake on summer nights.

I put the car in gear and started down the street, back to the highway that would take me up to my mom's house. But before I lost sight of the door, it occurred to me that there was nothing that I wanted more than this.

17

With a stack of new time sheets piled on my lap, I logged in to my blog. I wasn't eager to do battle with the old computer again, so a little procrastination was in order.

The Christians had responded to my post where I pointed out that their religion had logical flaws. Part of me thought I might get a series of short comments saying, "You're right. Anyone know where the nearest Buddhist temple is?" But they weren't going down that easily.

"America is fundamentally a Protestant nation", the commenter Steve G. said. "The idea of just picking up the Bible and being able to discover God and Christ is deeply ingrained in this culture to the point that the average American with no foreknowledge of Christian history (yourself, for example) would think this is the norm."

He explained that there's another theory: Before Jesus left the earth, he founded a Church and instilled it with his own authority. The Church is still around today, the theory went, recognizable by the fact that its leadership can be traced back in an unbroken line, all the way to Christ himself. God still guides its doctrines to articulate the truth for all times and places. It was this God-guided Church that chose the books of the Bible. It is through this Church that illiterate people and those with poor reading comprehension skills can come to know what is true about God. The thousands of Christians who lived in the three hundred years before the New Testament coalesced were part of this Church, and through it they practiced their faith before the Bible as we know it existed. To this day, the majority of Christians throughout the world belong to this Church.

I set the stack of time sheets next to the desk and leaned forward. Was he saying what I thought he was saying? Footsteps shushed past the office door, and I almost broke the keyboard trying to get another page on the screen. Our employees had already seen me staring at crazy Jesus websites; the last thing I needed was for them to see me staring at *my own* crazy Jesus website. Nobody came in, so I pulled the blog back up and kept reading.

Steve went on to say that the question of who has the final authority on matters of doctrine is *the* fundamental issue in Christianity. He went so far as to suggest that I would not have clarity on anything in this religion if I didn't first tackle this issue. "As a Catholic, I am obviously going to be biased towards one view, but ..."

He's Catholic! I thought back through all the discussions in blog comments and emails, remembered terminology from passing remarks, and realized with a start: *They're all Catholic.* These readers whom I had handpicked to comment on my blog based on their ability to defend their beliefs against atheistic arguments ... every one of them was Catholic.

Joe poked his head in to ask a question, and at the sound of his voice I banged on the keyboard to close browser windows again. "It's just me", he assured me. "You surfing Jesus sites again?"

"No. I was looking at porn. I swear!" We both laughed, which was a relief. Things had been tense ever since this house situation had come up, and it was good to have something to talk about that was only minimally controversial. I motioned him over. "Come look at this."

Joe put his hand on my shoulder and leaned toward the screen. He whispered words intermittently as he read. *The Bible nowhere claims for itself that it is authoritative ... also the issue of canon, which books to include ... if the Bible doesn't provide an infallible index, we can't know what's inspired ...*

Joe stood up. "He's a Catholic, isn't he?"

"Yes! Isn't that nuts? They all are!"

"You need to stop messing around with these people. Catholics believe weird stuff."

"Well, yeah. If I'd known they were Catholic, I wouldn't have invited them to read."

Here is where I would have expected Joe to change the subject back to whatever business matter he'd come to talk about, but he didn't. "Have these people never studied history? Do they not know about the pagan influences, the abuses? The Reformation happened for a reason, guys."

"Right, right", I nodded vigorously, basking in the unity that this subject created.

Joe kept staring at the screen. "This stuff about the Church's authority would be like saying that the Supreme Court is a higher authority than the Constitution. They want to elevate humans over written rules? C'mon."

"Right!"

As he glared at the words on the screen, he whispered, *Jesus chose twelve disciples, gave them authority . . . promised the Holy Spirit would protect them . . . they had successors, more successors . . . same line of successors today.* "That's crazy. If even one evil person had gotten into the mix—which undoubtedly happened—then that screws up the whole thing. That's why you have to have written rules to come back to."

"Right!"

"How do you write a new blog post?"

"Ri—what?"

He yanked a chair away from the desk behind us and sat down. He slid the keyboard in front of himself and stretched his hands as if getting ready to type for a very long time. "Don't worry, I'll say it's you writing the post", he assured me.

Joe? Writing words that would be attributed to me? I almost threw myself across the keyboard. "Oh, you know, I was going to shut this thing down. I mean, why waste our time with these people?"

"Cool, you're already logged in. Is it just this New Post button here?"

"Oh, gosh. Don't say anything crazy."

"What are you talking about?"

I didn't even need to respond. If Joe thought someone's idea was stupid and wrong, he would express his opinion by saying, "That idea is stupid and wrong." His German heritage instilled him with a love of efficiency, and he would view any embellishments to the statement as a waste of time. If I, on the other hand, thought someone's idea was stupid and wrong, I'd start with some hand-wringing preamble about their positive qualities, drop a couple of hints that I might have a slight problem with one aspect of what they said—just a small thing, really—and end up blaming myself and telling them to have a nice day.

"I'm writing as you", Joe said. "I'm not going to go all 'Joe' on them. I'll be easygoing. See?" He pointed to an opening sentence he'd already written: *Catholicism is a corrupt belief system that is not true Christianity.*

I grabbed the keyboard. "Why don't you tell me what you're trying to say, and I'll translate it."

"Okay. I'm wondering why otherwise intelligent people would blindly follow popes and bishops, when they know that plenty of them have been shameful sinners."

I typed: *If you don't mind, my husband just had a quick question about some of the issues we discussed about authority. There's just one thing about the issue*

of Church leaders having authority, given that maybe they're not totally perfect
100% of the time . . .

We went on like that until we had a post that Joe approved of as truthful enough and I approved of as polite enough, and I published it. Joe told me to let him know if anyone responded. When he left the room to go back to his office, I noticed that he'd forgotten to bring up whatever business matter he'd originally come in to talk about.

* * *

"Joe, the internet's talking to you", I called when I saw him walk by on his way to the break room.

He turned instantly and came into the office. "Has that Steve guy responded?"

"Yeah. Right here."

With his eyes fixed on the screen, Joe nudged me to let him sit in the chair. I stood and read over his shoulder.

"The fundamental question is: Can God convey truth through imperfect people?" Steve said. "Rejecting the Church doesn't get you out of that quandary. Christianity has always been composed of imperfect people, all the way back to the authors of the Bible."

Steve went on to say that the Constitution analogy actually supports the theory of there being a Church acting as a sort of divinely guided Supreme Court. "Imagine if, instead of setting up the Supreme Court, America's founding fathers had distributed the Constitution to individual citizens and said, 'Make of this what you will.'" He drew out the obvious answer: There would be chaos. There'd be bickering over meaning, different groups banding together to advocate for their particular interpretations, and endlessly splintering factions. "It would seem strange indeed that the founding fathers would be wise enough to set up a system for handling the interpretation of the Constitution, but that God Almighty wouldn't be equally wise and do the same basic thing."

"I'd rather have chaos than be bossed around by a bunch of guys in the Vatican." I nudged Joe on the shoulder, waiting for his gesticulations of fervent agreement, but he was still.

"Well, they would say the Church's teachings are from God, not the leaders of the Church themselves."

"People believe that? What century are we in?"

Joe scrolled up and down the page, occasionally highlighting passages and re-reading them. "Yeah, it's kind of crazy ... although it's the same theory about the writers of the Bible. What he's saying is, 'Can you believe that God can convey perfect truth through imperfect people, or not?'"

It was only then that it dawned on me. "Are you agreeing with him?"

"No. Well, maybe this point has some validity, but there are plenty of other issues."

"Wait. How do you suddenly know so much about Catholicism?"

"I had Catholic friends when I was growing up. That and I just spent like four hours researching it."

"That's all you've been doing since we wrote the post?"

Joe didn't answer. He was reading. I tried not to calculate how much money that just cost us in lost billable hours.

"American Christianity is a mess", Joe continued. "I just saw that there are over thirty thousand different Protestant denominations now, and they disagree about the most basic stuff. Like, some say infant baptism is critical, and others say it's unnecessary and invalid. Those are mutually exclusive claims, yet everyone thinks they're right. I have to say, there are some glaring problems with authority there."

"Wow. I didn't see that coming."

"You don't think this is compelling at all?"

It wasn't that, exactly. If Steve had been talking about a Christian sect I'd never heard of, I would have been intrigued. But the Catholic Church? I didn't dislike the Church's members—my maternal grandparents were Catholic, and though I didn't know them well before they died, they left me with a positive impression of Catholics as people—but the Catholic Church as an establishment was a different story. When I heard the words *Catholic Church*, images of an archaic, corrupt institution came to mind. It struck me as organized religion at its worst, a church run by power-hungry men who concocted absurd doctrines to secure their own power and fill their coffers. So while Steve's theory might make sense in a vacuum, I didn't know how to reconcile that with the fact that he was talking about Catholicism.

Before I could explain any of that to Joe, a paralegal came in to say that he was needed in a conference room. Joe stood and offered the chair back to me. After he left, he ducked his head back in the door and said, "Would you send me that guy's email address? I have some questions for him."

18

My mom and I sat at the table, picking at a breakfast of hash browns and scrambled eggs while we coaxed Donald into saying some of his new words.

"You look awfully nice for a Sunday morning", my mom said to Joe.

He walked into the kitchen in khaki slacks and a pressed white dress shirt. He was ready earlier than I'd expected, but I was excited to see how seriously he was taking this. "I don't think the realtor would mind if you wore jeans", I said. "But that's great if you want to dress up to see the house!"

"I hear it's gorgeous", my mom said. "Jenny told me about the entertaining area in the back yard, how close it is to the lake. I'm so excited for you!"

Joe didn't respond. He scraped hash brown scraps from the pan on the stove, downed half a glass of milk, then walked back toward our room. "Jen, can I talk to you?" he called from the hallway.

I knew what it was about before I even got out of the chair. He wasn't dressed up to look at the house. He'd forgotten all about it. "We are going to see the Tarrytown house, right?" I whispered.

"What about church?"

The word was like a stress bomb, and its explosion made me want to go back to bed. "That wasn't this weekend, was it?"

"Yes! You've been telling me for two weeks that we'd go today."

"But you said we'd visit the house today!"

"I forgot what day it was. But this was planned first. Besides, I thought you wanted to do this, too."

I did, sort of. I'd been reading up on Catholicism ever since our back-and-forth with Steve, and was pleasantly surprised by what I'd found. I even wanted to check out one of their services at some point. But none of that mattered compared to the house.

Before I could respond, Joe made a proposal. "The plans for church predate the plans to go to Tarrytown. And the house thing is moot anyway because we can't afford it. But if you want to flip for it, I'll go with that."

"Tails."

I followed Joe into the room, where he dug in the metal change container on top of the desk and pulled out a nickel. He flicked it up, grabbed the shimmering coin in the air, and slapped it onto the top of his left hand.

Heads. We were going to church.

* * *

I had been to church only a handful of times in my life. Sometimes I would tag along with friends' families after Saturday spend-the-nights when we lived in Dallas, and I usually managed to be a bad influence. Before she met me, my friend Sandy used to study her children's Bible during Sunday services. Then I suggested that it would be way cooler to conceal our Walkmen in our jean jackets so that we could listen to Bangles tapes during the service. The process of hiding a three-pound plastic device the size of a small unabridged dictionary proved to be more arduous than I'd imagined, but I walked away satisfied that we were the raddest kids in the entire First Methodist church that day.

Here at Saint Francis de Sales Catholic Church, we managed to make it through the front doors without any Atheist Detector sirens going off. But then there were bowls of water on pedestals near the front door. I stopped so suddenly that the man behind me almost ran into me. Was there an action item for me here?

Joe was already halfway down the main aisle and motioned for me to hurry up. He was carrying Donald, who was excitedly pointing to all the sights in this strange new building. I ran to catch up with them.

We were a few minutes early, and the room was more than half-full, with about three hundred people in attendance so far. Joe stopped in front of a pew on the left side of the sanctuary and motioned for me to go ahead. Just as I walked forward, I saw a family sit down across the aisle—but they did something first. They each knelt down and made a cross gesture while looking at the stage area at the front of the room.

Oh, no. Were we all supposed to do this? Would I seem rude if I didn't? For a half second, I paused with the intent to do the kneel motion. But then my imagination flashed forward: I was lowering myself down, and just as my right knee touched the floor, someone shouted from the back pew: "SHE'S NOT CATHOLIC!" It turned out that this was a sacred ritual that becomes the most vile blasphemy when done by the uninitiated. Children gasped and pointed. An old lady fainted, dropping to the floor like a sandbag.

Joe seemed to find it amusing that I was frozen in the aisle, my eyes wide with panic. "It's a pew", he whispered. "You sit in it." I dashed forward and sat down quickly, hoping nobody saw that I skipped the kneeling thing.

Shortly after we settled in, the service began. Music erupted from the choir area at the front of the room, a peppy song accompanied by tambourines and what sounded like a harmonica. Everyone around me stood in unison, and I scrambled to my feet. Then they all sat again, listened to something from the Bible, sang some really repetitive song, listened to the Bible again, then everyone stood for yet more Bible.

After we all returned to our seats, I became engrossed in a program I'd taken from a stack by the front door. It was as if I'd discovered the clandestine communications of a secret society. There was talk of "Eucharistic Adoration", and they threw around acronyms like RE and RCIA and NFP. I tried to imagine what would go on at a Rosary group, or what a Liturgist would do.

Joe nudged me. "Get ready", he whispered, picking up a folded collection of papers he'd brought with him. "Here comes the good part." He'd been researching the early Church and had discovered that much of the writing of the first Christians had been preserved. Even better, it was all available for free online, a discovery which used up the last of my printer paper and half of an ink cartridge. This particular set of printouts contained excerpts from the letters of Justin Martyr, who was born around the year 100, and Hippolytus of Rome, born in 170, both of whom described the Christian church services of their time.

Joe flipped to a wrinkled page and pointed to an underlined passage from Justin Martyr: *And on the day called Sunday, all who live in cities or in the country gather together to one place, and the memoirs of the apostles or the writings of the prophets are read.*

"The 'memoirs' of the apostles—this is from before the Bible existed!" Joe said. "They're talking about the writing that later became the New Testament! Isn't that amazing?"

Justin was a pagan philosopher who converted to Christianity, and in A.D. 150 he wrote to Emperor Antoninus Pius and to his son Verissimus the Philosopher (who would become Emperor Marcus Aurelius), explaining Christian practices and beliefs in hope of ending the rampant persecution of Christians.

Joe nudged me again and ran his finger under Justin's words: *There is then brought to the president of the brethren bread and a cup of wine mixed with water.* A man and woman walked to the front of the sanctuary and handed a pitcher of wine and a basket of round bread wafers to the priest.

Everyone stood, and Joe took that as a cue to flip to another page, this one titled *Hippolytus of Rome.* He pointed to something Hippolytus had written around A.D. 215 describing Christian worship. I tried to imagine the appearance of this Hippolytus, deciding that I envisioned him to have a long beard and thinning hair on his head. Did he write during the day, with sunlight streaming over his paper, the sounds of people walking by the window, or in the silence of the night, using a quill by candlelight? I scanned over the part where he recorded that the leader of the ceremony would say "The Lord be with you", and the people would answer, "And with your spirit."

"The Lord be with you", the priest called from the front of the room. I snapped my head up, disoriented.

"And also with you", said the people around me in one voice.

"*Lift up your hearts*", wrote Hippolytus.

"*We have them with the Lord*", replied the Christians of two thousand years ago.

"Lift up your hearts", I heard the priest say.

"We lift them up to the Lord", everyone here in the church replied.

"*Let us give thanks to the Lord.*"

"*It is proper and just.*"

"Let us give thanks to the Lord", the priest said.

"It is right to give him thanks and praise" came the response from all around me.

"Okay, that's cool", I whispered. I wasn't thrilled to be here at church, but it was amazing to experience something so old. Some woman stood in a church on a Sunday in the year 200, and she heard the same words I was hearing now. Century after century lurched past, generations came and went, wars were fought, countries were created and dissolved, and here was I, almost two thousand years later, sharing an experience with that ancient woman. If we were to meet each other, somewhere outside of time, we would have something in common.

Everyone knelt, and Joe and I were forced to do the same because the people behind us needed to lean on the back of our seats. Joe now flipped to a page titled *Ignatius of Antioch*. It had a bunch of details about Communion that he seemed to find riveting, but I couldn't get into it.

I turned back to the program. At the top of one of the pages was a guest column from a local nun—or, rather, a former nun. Mincing no words, she railed against the injustice of the all-male priesthood and spoke of the pain it caused her to know that she would never be able to administer the sacraments. Therefore, she was renouncing her status as a Catholic nun. She planned to join a Celtic Christian church, where she would begin the formation process for the priesthood.

Now Joe and I were both staring at papers. He was entranced by the writing of a first-century Christian, and I was equally taken with the writing of this nun. As I read her words, I readied myself for the inevitable reaction. I was prepared for the surge of enraged sympathy that would surely rush in any second now . . . but it never came.

I set the program down, straightened my back to kneel erect, and bowed my head to listen. The priest's deep voice boomed from the speakers and filled the sanctuary: "This is my body, which will be given up for you." I recognized those words from my Bible reading. Jesus said them only a few hours before his friend handed him over for execution. The discomfort that I had been so acutely aware of earlier in the ceremony faded away, and I became still, losing myself in the rhythm of this ancient ritual.

* * *

It was a mild November day, and after the service we stopped to let Donald toddle around the church grounds.

"What did you think?" Joe asked.

"It was good", I said.

"You don't seem very excited." He motioned to the program. "Was it the nun's thing in the bulletin?"

"Actually, no", I said. I'd been thinking about it, and I realized why her argument didn't resonate with me. She claimed that she was still a Christian, yet she was talking about the religion that said that God became a guy and hand-picked only other guys to spread his message. God could have come down as a woman, or as a hermaphrodite, or maybe manifested himself as a brother/sister team. But he didn't. It seemed undeniably clear that, if Christianity spoke truth, God didn't see the roles of men and women as being interchangeable.

There was a time when I would have looked at this setup as a blatantly unfair, but motherhood had slapped me upside the head with some perspective about gender and equality. There's nothing like nine months of pregnancy and eighteen hours of childbirth to make you see that men and women are really, really different. Men can't gestate and birth new human life. Women can. There's a huge area of activity that the sexes do not share. Whether the author of life is God or simply Nature, it seemed to declare that people can have vastly different roles, unavailable to certain other people, and yet all be valued equally.

So the nun's rallying cry fell flat for me, but there were other things that bothered me about Catholicism. "Look, the service was fine. Kind of neat, actually", I said. "But I'm not sure that it was a better use of time than going to see the Tarrytown house. It's not like we'd ever become Catholic."

"Right. It does seem unlikely."

"If nothing else, the anti-abortion stuff."

"Yeah, speaking of which, I got this flier from the lobby just now. Check it out." Joe produced a pamphlet from the bottom of his stack of papers. In big blue letters, the title said *PRAY TO END ABORTION*.

I stepped back. He couldn't have shocked me more if he'd whipped out a baggie of crack cocaine. "What are you doing with that?"

"Just read it and see what you think." He held it out for me.

I didn't take it. "Are you kidding? Why?"

"Let's face it: We're both interested in Catholicism. I don't know if it'll all check out, but we've found some pretty interesting stuff. So we might as well hear them out about abortion."

"I don't plan to change my stance on that issue", I snapped.

"Then you might as well stop looking into all of it right now. The beliefs that life is sacred and life begins in the womb go all the way to the core of Catholic doctrine."

121

Though I didn't show it, I winced at the idea of turning my back on Catholicism. I'd had mostly good experiences with this religion since I'd been looking into it. I loved chatting with my blog readers, and the more I considered what Steve G. pointed out about the issue of authority, the more the theory of a God-guided Church clicked in a way that really felt right. In fact, I'd been checking the mail every day for a new book I'd ordered on the subject. Yet, now that I thought about it, why *was* I wasting my time on a belief system I would never consider adopting?

"So you're not even open to hearing the Catholic point of view?" Joe asked. He seemed to be genuinely perplexed.

"About abortion? No, I'm not. I'm not interested in the viewpoints of slavery advocates or Holocaust deniers either, in case you were wondering."

Any positive feelings I might have had during the service were now forgotten. The nun got it wrong: If she wanted to reveal the Catholic Church's true anti-woman side, she should have skipped the priestess stuff and talked about its stance against abortion.

"Can you throw that thing away?" I glared at the pamphlet.

Joe slipped it back in his stack of papers. "So you think abortion is always okay, all the time? Like the day before a woman's due date? What if she's in labor, but the baby isn't out of the birth canal yet? Is it still her choice?"

I thought I detected a hint of dismissiveness when he said the word *choice*. I couldn't believe this was happening. We had always agreed on this issue. A group of women in flowing skirts passed by, their cross necklaces gleaming in the sun as they bubbled about the service. I wanted to point at them and shout, "You did this!"

Joe frowned. "Let me get this straight. You're telling me that even though every other thing about this Church has checked out so far, you will not consider looking further because of one single issue?"

I started sputtering out an answer, but stopped myself. I wanted to get this right. I took in a breath, closed my eyes, and weighed each word before I spoke. "It's not one random issue. This is about freedom. A person who does not have control over her body is not free."

Joe was about to respond, but I held up my hand. "This Church says it gets its teachings from God, right? They also say that God is the source of goodness."

Joe nodded cautiously. He was with me so far.

"If that's all true," I continued, "then the anti-abortion stance is not only offensive, but it's *illogical*. An all-good God wouldn't oppose freedom."

After processing what I said, Joe seemed to agree. "That's a fair point. There doesn't seem to be internal consistency there."

I was ready to wrap things up and pretend the discussion never happened, but Joe wasn't done. "I think it's worth just listening to the Catholic side of the story. I know we don't agree. But they've had two thousand years to think about this, and they keep saying the same thing. Why not hear them out?"

I didn't answer the question. This discussion was over, and we both knew it. Joe hoisted Donald up in his arms, and we walked back to the car in silence.

19

A week later I sulked in the back seat, my head resting against the window. Another Sunday, another car ride in the wrong direction.

My mom made conversation with my grandfather in the front seat, telling him funny stories from a recent vacation she took with some friends. Even though he was my dad's father and my parents were divorced, my mom and grandfather remained close. He lived in the town just north of us, and she saw him at least once a week. She'd stop by and sip Gatorade after she played tennis on the courts near his house; on evenings when she didn't have plans she'd join him for a cognac, even though she normally didn't drink.

I leaned over Donald's car seat and tapped Joe, who was dozing off after working late the day before. "Do you think we can see the house today?"

With his eyes still closed, he mumbled, "It depends on how long this trip takes."

So, no, we would not be going to Tarrytown today. A wave of nausea trickled through me, and I couldn't tell if it was from morning sickness or from thinking about the house. It was still on the market. If we acted quickly, in a matter of weeks I could be supervising movers hauling our possessions from the storage shed into our new home. I could walk Donald down to the lake, let him run around on the dock by the Hula Hut, tell him that this was where we lived now ... Another surge of nausea came up. I needed to stop thinking about this.

My mom spotted the unmarked entrance at the side of the rural highway and navigated the car down the gravel road that wound through a loose jumble of trees. The familiar sounds of rocks crunching under the tires, punctuated with the occasional screech of thorny branches down the side of the car, let me know we were almost there. Joe woke up from his catnap, and my grandfather picked up the bouquet of flowers that had been lying on the console. We approached the old chain-link fence and let ourselves in to the family cemetery.

Immediately I was greeted by familiar names. Of the hundreds of tombstones, dozens bore surnames from branches of my family tree. Bishop, my maiden name. Hurt, my grandfather's mother's maiden name. Hampton, Donnell, and Sybert, all names I'd heard mentioned as belonging to blood relatives. Some were proclaimed in large, clean text, modern gravestones that had been carved by machine. Others were eroded chunks of limestone with rough-hewn, uneven letters, chiseled out by poor farmers of bygone eras.

Just inside the gate stood a large pavilion, which held enough picnic tables to seat two hundred people. Behind that were the barbecue pits and a dilapidated outhouse. The setup was for the cemetery association's annual potluck, called the Cemetery Homecoming. (Which always prompted my mom to remark, "Who comes home?!" She was raised in the Northeast, where evidently people didn't hang out at cemeteries for fun.)

At the homecoming, a brief blessing was always offered under the pavilion's tin roof, led by a Methodist or Baptist minister, as the smells of slow-cooked meat wafted over from the barbecue pits on the hot summer breeze. Folding tables were covered with corn casseroles and green beans glistening in bacon and butter sauce; bowls heaped with fruit salad stood next to rows of pies, cakes, cookies, and homemade peach cobblers with hand-rolled crusts. Everyone walked around and caught up with old friends and distant relatives, the sounds of chatter and laughter mixed with the smells of food.

But today the benches stood empty, the pavilion silent. The barbecue pits were cold and dark, even the ashes stripped clean by the fall winds. The dry grass crunched underfoot as Joe, my mom, and my grandfather made their way toward my grandmother's grave. My grandfather would pull weeds and tidy the area around her headstone, then lay fresh flowers in front of it, as he had done almost every week for the past fifteen years.

I would join them in a minute, but first I wanted to take Donald on a stroll through the grounds. Per the longstanding family tradition, we stopped by the graves of great-grandmothers and great-great-grandmothers and people whose names I recognized from handwritten notes on the backs of old pictures. I carried Donald with me, telling him what I knew of each person, even though at just over a year old he was more interested in the birds than anything I was saying.

Toward the back of the grounds were the older graves, the ones from the settlers who first arrived by covered wagon in the mid-1800s. I'd wandered around these graves all my life, noting the unique first names like Miria, Alvia, and Eskalana. I passed the stone of J. T. Bentley, one I'd seen many times in my life. When I was a kid, I always pictured Mr. Bentley to be a proper old man, with a big belly, a top hat and a gleaming monocle (which showed that I wasn't very familiar with the standard dress of nineteenth-century Texas farmers). I waved hello to Mr. Bentley and encouraged Donald to join me. As he giggled his own greeting to the old man, the engraving at the bottom of the stone caught my eye. I'd never seen it when the sun was at this angle, and for the first time dark shadows revealed its words:

Sweet remembrance of our darling babe

At the top, the name was proceeded by *Miss*. And the dates: August 1898–July 1900. J. T. Bentley was a little girl. And she was lowered into this grave a month before her second birthday.

I moved away from the grave as if repelled by a magnetic field, not even sure where I was headed. The sounds of Joe and my mom and grandfather talking faded away as I drifted toward the back of the cemetery, stopping just next to the fence that separated the trimmed grounds from wild land covered in cacti and mesquite. Next to a sprawling pecan tree, I saw another stone I recognized: Lona Harper. I had also assumed her to be an old woman, her white hair pulled back just over her neck in a neat bun. For the first time, I looked at the dates: 1882–1900. She was eighteen. And for the first time, I noticed that her tombstone was in a row of four. Next to her lay Quille Harper, 1898–1900. Then Charlie Harper, 1900–1900. My throat burned, and I wasn't sure I even wanted to look at the last one. Dorcey Harper, 1884–1900. One family, probably distant relatives of mine, lost four children in the span of ten months.

My stomach churned to think of it. I turned to go somewhere else— anywhere where I wouldn't have to look at those four tombstones— and encountered two identical tombstones, both with the same simple inscription: *Murray baby*. I stumbled over to a pecan tree and pressed my back against its cold, wide trunk. I held Donald close, his warm body moving against mine. In all the years that I'd strolled through these grounds, I never understood that I was walking through a cemetery full of children.

The knowledge hit me with the same freight-train force as my realization at The Creek when I was a child. What troubled me this time wasn't the awareness of human mortality itself, but the awareness that it's possible to lose it all. I suddenly understood with burning clarity that my entire sense of well-being was as fragile as an empty eggshell. My whole approach to life only worked because I happened to be a twenty-first-century American. If I were to be tossed into a time machine and thrown out into 1850, I'd find myself utterly unable to cope with the suffering and toil that my ancestors experienced. My current strategy of seeking happiness in comforts and amusements would be impotent against the knowledge that any year could be the year I'd lose a child.

I could see how a moment like this might lead a person to run off to a cave to spend the rest of his life meditating on divine truths. To realize that nothing—absolutely nothing—in this world will last is to realize that seeking the transcendent is the most important thing you could do with your life. But that was the problem. I *had* been seeking the transcendent. I'd read lots of books about God. I'd even prayed once or twice. And despite all that, I had gotten only silence from the cosmos in return. I may have made an academic decision that there was probably some kind of spiritual realm, but that offered little comfort now that I found myself surrounded by tombstones with kids' names on them.

I wasn't even positive that I believed in God, but I was already angry with him. *So this is how it is?* I railed in a prayer, once again half-suspecting that I was talking to myself. *You sit there and do nothing, and we're supposed to just take your word for it that you exist? You let all these terrible things happen to people, and then don't even offer us any comfort in the face of it?*

Maybe my plan of rooting my happiness in the material world was a great idea after all. Sure, it depended entirely on a steady flow of money and perfect health for Joe and me and everyone we loved. It meant blocking out entire categories of the human experience, living under a willful delusion that everything I enjoyed in this life would last. But at least it worked. It did bring me some peace, even if it was fleeting.

Donald began to squirm, so I set him down so that he could toddle over to my mom and Joe. I followed behind him, staring at the hard winter ground so that I'd avoid reading any more tombstones. When I met up with everyone else at my grandmother's grave, Joe could tell something troubled me. He stood back where my mom and grandfather couldn't see him and mouthed, "What's wrong?"

I rolled my eyes and shook my head dismissively to indicate that I didn't want to talk about it.

* * *

I forced a few smiles and threw out a few positive statements when we got home, but it wasn't enough to convince Joe that nothing was wrong. He asked me if I needed anything to eat to help with morning sickness and offered to let me take a nap while he watched Donald. When none of that helped, he tenderly suggested that we look up the Tarrytown house on the realtor's website.

We went into my office, where the page was already up on my screen from when I'd checked the status that morning. "That kitchen is surprisingly big", he said from behind me. He was saying something else, but his voice sunk into the abyss of my dark mood.

He tapped me on the shoulder. "Did you hear me?"

"What? Sorry. No."

"How many blocks away from the lake did you say it was?"

"Oh. I'm not sure. Maybe two."

He made a few more upbeat remarks and then said something involving the words *financing* and *investment*. He was talking about getting the house. I instantly perked up at the news, only to have the happiness fall flat instantly, like a wave collapsing on itself. The trip to the cemetery seemed to have temporarily neutralized the house's power over me. I'd probably get back to feeling excited about it. But right now, it seemed like just another thing that would one day be gone.

Joe was pointing at a picture of the patio when I pushed the chair back from my desk. "I need a sec", I said. I didn't wait for his reply before I left the room.

Like that day at Joe's office, I found myself with few options for private spaces. Once again, I locked myself in a bathroom to pray. I slid down the wall and sat cross-legged on the floor next to the bathtub. I bowed my head, as much from exhaustion as from reverence, and said silently, *Let's try this again.*

I apologized to God for speaking disrespectfully at the cemetery. I told him that I was lost in a no-man's land, caught somewhere between seeing the hollowness of the things of this world, yet coming up with nothing every time I sought answers in the spiritual realm. It was good that I wasn't speaking aloud, since trying to capture all my thoughts in words would have been like trying to capture a waterfall in teacups. My eyes filled with tears as I told God that he really, really needed to help me if I was ever going to find him. This time, instead of the usual jokes and caveats about how I was probably talking to myself, I just said, "Amen."

* * *

I sat in the darkness with Donald, waiting for him to sleep. When his eyes fluttered closed for the last time, I lowered him into his crib. I flopped back into the green chair, not sure what I would do next. Among the shadows I noticed a fallen stack of Christian books by my feet. One had slid under the chair, and only a triangular edge poked out. I picked it up to see the familiar cover of *Mere Christianity*.

I was always loath to leave the room right after I put Donald down since it might wake him up, so I leaned closer to the nightlight and opened the book. I thumbed through the pages and re-read passages I'd bracketed, remembering the first time I encountered the starred sections. Then I came across a paragraph and sat up with a start:

When you come to know God, the initiative lies on His side. If He does not show Himself, nothing you can do will enable you to find Him.

I'd seen it before—I must have—but this time it caught my attention like a siren. I was shaken with a feeling that from the beginning of time, I had been destined to read this passage on this night at this moment. Lewis continued:

[God] shows much more of Himself to some people than to others—not because He has favourites, but because it is impossible for Him to show Himself to a man whose whole mind and character are in the wrong condition. Just as sunlight, though it has no favorites, cannot be reflected in a dusty mirror as clearly as in a clean one.

I whispered the last sentence, louder than I should have, not even worrying about whether it would wake Donald:

129

Yes. A feeling cascaded through me, my body physically relaxing as so many things that hadn't made sense now fell into place. *Yes.* This was the key that I'd been missing.

No spiritual teachers ever said you could access divine truths without transforming yourself first. All my life I'd brushed by this idea that some lifestyles lead to enlightenment more than others. One thing that had always piqued my interest about Buddhism was the idea that you must go through rigorous practices in order to gain deep understanding. Buddha didn't come up with the Four Noble Truths while rambling around the streets, throwing down some smack with his friends, eating and drinking whatever he wanted. It took days of fasting under the Bodhi Tree. Even when I was an atheist, everything I knew of the human experience confirmed that this was true. Maybe you could absorb data under any circumstances, but to attain *wisdom* you would have to be in the proper position, lifestyle-wise, and it probably wouldn't be comfortable.

I read the excerpt again. I'd been approaching it all wrong.

I closed the book and set it in my lap. Everything within me said that this was it, that there was something about my approach to the question of God that had been blocking my ability to sense him. Something about my "mind and character" was in the wrong condition. Something about my life and my existence had to change. Now, I just needed to find out what it was.

20

"Take off your wedding ring", Joe said. His eyes were fixed on the road in front of us, his hands cemented to the steering wheel. "It's better if these guys don't know you're my wife."

I slipped the unadorned gold band off my finger and tucked it into the back pocket of my purse, next to our house key. It was a chilly mid-winter day, everything around us hard and gray from the weeks of cold. Even with the car's heating vents all the way open, I couldn't seem to get warm.

"As far as they know, your role doesn't go beyond paralegal. Introduce yourself as Jennifer. If they ask for a last name, use your maiden name."

We arrived at the nondescript strip center where the Jaworski deposition was to take place, but Joe drove past it and turned the car into the parking lot of an abandoned building down the street. He put it in park and turned to me. There was something in his eyes, something so unfamiliar that I had trouble placing it. Stress, for sure. But I could have sworn I also saw fear.

"Do you have the camera?"

I fumbled with the canvas bag at my feet. "Yes."

"Videotape?"

"Yes."

"Backup tapes?"

"Yes."

I pulled out the main tape we would use, a mini-DV cassette. As part of my preparation, I'd pressed a fresh label across the front and written the date and client name with a black marker.

"That's the wrong date." Joe grabbed the tape out of my hand. "Do you have another label? We've got to be more careful about that."

I did a double-take before I reached into the bag for a new label. Small mistakes didn't usually upset him. "Are you okay?" I asked.

"I will be when this case is over", he said. He reached into the bag at my feet and handed me a sheet of paper that another paralegal had typed up, titled with the con artist's name, Eric Rayburne. Now that Mr. Jaworski was bringing a case, other victims had come forward and begun to tell their stories, many of them elderly or disabled. There was a widowed woman in Amarillo whom Rayburne had met in an online grief support group. He got to know her, convinced her to invest all her savings in a nonexistent business, and left her with an empty bank account. She had no children and had even lost the house she'd lived in for thirty years. Now she lived in a state-run nursing facility.

I scanned down the page, past stories of five thousand stolen here, a car "borrowed" and never returned there. At the bottom of the page I saw that a disabled woman had accused him of sexually harassing her daughter. She didn't have much evidence and didn't want to drag her child through court, but she was adamant that he'd done it.

I folded the paper and put it back in the bag. "What kind of lawyer would defend someone like that?"

"People tend to find lawyers with personalities like their own. His lawyer is Amos Adler, and they knew each other for years before this case." He fixed the mislabeled tape, his motions jerky as he ripped a new label off the sheet. While he worked, he recounted times that Adler had been caught in lies, and other occasions when Adler had exploded into the phone and seethed with threats and insults when they disagreed. It got so bad that Joe started telling Adler that he was taping their phone calls to moderate his bad behavior. When Joe's attorney friends found out whom he was up against, they all told him to try to get off the case. Nobody wanted to go into any detail, but everyone who had encountered this man grew grave when his name came up.

After recounting a particular call in which Adler laughed about a new accusation of fraud against his client, Joe grew quiet. "I hate him", he finally said. "I'm not using the word lightly, either." There was a darkness in his demeanor, and I had only ever seen it when he talked about this case.

* * *

At the deposition site, we stepped out of the car and into a swirl of dead leaves and dirt whipped around by the winter wind. Just inside the double doors at the entrance of the building, I saw two men talking.

132

"That's them", Joe said. He glanced down at my ring finger before he started forward.

I slung the heavy bag of video equipment and file folders onto my shoulder and stepped slowly toward the entrance. As the figures behind the glass took form, my heart thumped faster as I prepared to meet them. My jaw was rigid, the muscles in my shoulder as hard as steel.

Joe entered before I did, and one of the men said something to him. He was now interacting with both of them, and I stopped, wondering if I should get my mobile phone out in case someone started swinging. They seemed to be exchanging only words for now, so I pushed the glass doors open and entered the building. The man to Joe's left had thick, yellowed hair, recently smoothed back by a comb. He stopped his conversation and stared at me. Fear surged under my skin, and I instinctively took a step back.

His face relaxed into an eager smile, and he coasted toward me with his hand extended. "Hello there!" When we shook hands, he clasped his other hand around mine for a moment. "I'm Eric. So nice to meet you."

"Hi", I sputtered. "I'm Jennifer—" I stopped, remembering. "Bishop. Jennifer Bishop."

"You must be Joe's paralegal", he said, releasing my hand gently. "This is my lawyer, Amos Adler."

Adler acknowledged me with a nod before returning his attention to Joe. He wore a dark suit over black cowboy boots, and a crisp white shirt without a tie. His face was long and large, topped by wispy graying hair. There was something troubling about his demeanor, but I couldn't pinpoint it. Maybe Joe had biased me, but whatever I sensed about this man was so strong that I felt certain that he would have caught my attention, even if I'd had no idea who he was.

Rayburne was about to say something else to me, but his attention suddenly focused over my shoulder. I turned around to see Mr. Jaworski's hunched figure silhouetted in the doorframe, a nurse leading him by the hand. I instinctively flashed my attention to Rayburne to gauge what level of confrontation was about to transpire. I was shocked by what I saw on his face. It was just a flicker of an expression, so brief that I would have missed it if I hadn't turned around at that moment. It wasn't rage or vengefulness that I would have expected. Instead, it was hurt—genuine, spontaneous hurt.

We all moved in to the deposition site, and I got to work setting up the video camera. The conference room was a narrow, windowless space with a bank of fluorescent lights overhead. It was as if the glare of the lights sucked all the oxygen out of the room, leaving only an airless haze.

Adler and Rayburne took the chairs on the side of the table that faced the door. Mr. Jaworski and Joe sat directly across from them. Joe and Adler watched one another's every move so closely that when Adler dropped his pencil, Joe jumped. Before we began, Adler asked the nurse to leave the room.

Joe argued about it, knowing that Mr. Jaworski would be more comfortable with her there, but, ultimately he dropped it. He wanted to get the deposition over with and not give Adler any excuse to delay it further, since Jaworski was old and in poor health.

Adler leaned back in his chair. His eyes filled with a serpentine stillness as he looked across the table. "How old are you, Joe?"

Joe didn't answer. He continued ordering the stack of papers in front of him, setting them into piles by type.

"I asked you a question", Adler said, raising his voice.

Joe didn't look up. "That's none of your business."

"How many years have you been practicing law?"

Joe snapped his head to me. "Jennifer, start recording now. I want this on video."

My fingers shook as I fumbled for the red button. Adler sat up in his seat and addressed Mr. Jaworski. "I wish you luck, sir. You're going to need it."

The deposition began. A clear, tenor voice, as smooth as a song, came from the other side of the table. I looked up to see that it was Rayburne speaking. "I met Mr. Jaworski at the church where I was a volunteer prayer minister", he said in answer to something Joe asked. His face exuded a wistful ease, his eyes focused far in the distance, as if he were reliving treasured memories.

"When did you first approach my client about investing money in your business?" Joe asked.

Rayburne seemed gentle, almost vulnerable, in contrast to Joe's direct, businesslike tone. "It was really more his idea than mine. I asked him to pray with me about it, and when he found out that I needed investors, he volunteered."

Joe scratched a note. "Did you tell him that the business did not exist?"

"Objection!" Adler barked. "Watch it."

"Mr. Adler, it is a matter of record that your client was not operating a business at that point in time."

Rayburne jumped in. "You're right, Mr. Fulwiler. I wasn't." He lowered his head. "I'm not so good at this kind of thing. I didn't know about incorporation and all of that. I was running the business out of my kitchen."

"Do you have any paperwork that shows that you were doing business?"

"Nope. Afraid I don't. I never could get any deals going."

Joe pointed to a line on a spreadsheet. "What about the trip to Italy? You went there five weeks after a ten-thousand-dollar check from Mr. Jaworski was put into your bank account."

He nodded, making casual, confident eye contact with Joe. "Research. I was aiming to start a business supplying healthy meals to nursing homes, juvenile facilities, other residential places like that. I went to Italy for training."

"Do you have any receipts from cooking schools, classes, anything like that?"

"No. It was all private lessons. I paid cash."

Joe moved his pen one row down. "The Mediterranean cruise?"

"I had to relax!" he said, his voice slipping into a whiney tone, the first time I'd seen him show any signs of stress. "I was working my butt off over there in Italy. I put all my love into this business. All of it. Yes, I took a cruise. But it was after working away, taking lesson after lesson, all day every day for two weeks!"

He rubbed his temples. I shot my hand up to rub my own forehead. No matter how deeply I inhaled, I couldn't seem to get enough air. Things were going as well as could be expected, yet I wanted to get out of the room with the desperation of a person trapped in the hull of a sinking ship.

Joe slipped out another page from his stack of papers. "In June of 2002 my client gave you another twenty thousand. It was immediately transferred to an online poker website."

"Yeah, that was a mistake, okay? It was a mistake. But I was trying to raise money for the business. I guess I have a gambling problem—I ought to get treatment for it—but at the time I thought I could make some money and get this thing going." His face grew red, his motions more erratic.

Joe kept reading. "Another six thousand to something called 'Lacy's Erotica'?"

Rayburne smacked the table so hard it made me jump. "I said I had to relax! I'm not crazy about the name either, but it's a legal massage parlor. Lacy just uses the name because it gets her free word-of-mouth advertising. You know how people talk. But it's a legitimate massage therapy center." His eyes shimmered with indignation as he thrust his finger at the elderly man across from him. "I put everything into this business. Now he is dragging me through the mud, making me talk about every embarrassing mistake I ever made, all because he's pissed that he made a bad investment!"

I was standing behind Mr. Jaworski and could only see the back of his head, which shook almost imperceptibly, as if he had early Parkinson's.

Rayburne shoved his chair back from the table and cupped his hand over his mouth. A single tear slipped down his cheek. The room was silent except for his sniffling as he wiped his hand over his face and struggled to regain composure. "I love to cook. Back when I was a little boy, my dream was always to bless people through cooking. It was my whole life's dream. I thought that Ray Jaworski shared that with me."

Mr. Jaworski began to speak, but Joe held up his hand to stop him.

With an expression that glowed with conviction and sincerity, Rayburne addressed Jaworski directly again. "I am sorry, Ray, that it didn't work out. I thought we'd build something great together, too, that we'd help folks." A sob welled up, but he choked it down. "I wish the money wasn't gone, too. But I don't know why you're doing this to me." With the final words, the tears got the best of him, and he began to weep openly.

I caught myself. Witnessing the innocent honesty that he exuded, it would be so easy to tell myself that I was looking at a well-meaning guy who had simply made a few mistakes.

I pictured the old widow in Amarillo, sitting alone in a run-down nursing home room, looking around at her last few possessions as she remembered her beloved house. I thought of all his other victims, vulnerable people whose life circumstances left them unlikely to pursue a court case. I looked at Rayburne. He was drying his tears with the collar of his polo shirt.

Oh, no ... A realization rolled over me like thunder. *This man isn't lying. He believes it.*

My head throbbed to the point that I was dizzy. Ever since I'd been in the presence of Rayburne and Adler, I'd felt physically ill. My breathing quickened, and I closed my eyes to steady myself.

"Your paralegal is having a problem over there, Joe", Adler said. He smirked, as if he took perverse pleasure in my weakness.

Joe snapped around, his face tense with concern. He caught himself and straightened up to address me with intentional offhandedness. "Are you okay?"

"No." I darted toward the door, not caring whether I was still needed in the room. "I need to step outside for a second."

I ran down the empty hall and shoved open the double doors that led to the parking lot. It was cold, colder when the gusts of wind ripped by, and I'd left my jacket in the conference room. I didn't care, though. I drank in the fresh air, inhaling until my lungs hurt, but it wasn't the air that refreshed me—it was being away from Rayburne and his lawyer. I leaned against the locked car, trying to process what I'd just seen.

When I considered what I experienced in that room, there was only one word that came to mind: *evil.* And when I considered how it had operated, I knew that I'd never see the world the same way again.

When I used to come across tales of people committing atrocities, I would promptly decide that they were Bad People. This was a tidy conclusion that contained the problem of evil in a box and placed it on a distant shelf, safely away from my own life. Because I was a Good Person. And while Good People might occasionally make honest mistakes, we didn't get involved in anything seriously evil. After all, we weren't Bad People.

All my life I had imagined that, as a Good Person, under no circumstances would I have anything to do with evil. If I'd been a Hutu in 1990s Rwanda, I would have stood against the mass murders of the Tutsi. If I'd been a German in the 1940s and had friends who were getting involved with the Nazis, I would have decried their sickening ideals. If I'd lived here in Texas a couple hundred years earlier than I did, I would have been a tireless abolitionist. From the moment I could think about such things until the moment I walked into the deposition room, that idea was at the foundation of my identity.

And now, out in the parking lot, with dead leaves scuttling across the ground in front of me, I understood that it was supremely unlikely that

that was true. In each of those examples, large segments of civilization bought into the evil, so the odds were not in favor of my being one of the few crusaders for good. So how could it happen? How, then, could people like me, average folks who thought of themselves as Good People, get caught up in horrific crimes against humanity? Nobody ever wakes up in the morning and says, "What I am going to do today is evil, and I'm okay with that."

When I thought through each of the examples of society-wide atrocities, examining them through the new lens I had gained in that deposition room, immediately I saw it: In every single case where people cooperated with evil, they used eloquent lies to assure themselves that what they were doing was actually good.

The Hutus had a story: The Tutsi had committed all sorts of atrocities in the past, they greedily hoarded way too much of the wealth, and they were plotting to wipe out the Hutu any minute—so, really, murdering them was simply an act of self-defense. *The Nazis had a story*: The Aryan race was just trying to create good and beautiful things, but the Jews kept tearing it all down. Jews enslaved the poor Aryans by lending them money and jacking up the interest rates, and they had nefariously worked to cause the devastating November Revolution of 1918 while the German men were out risking their lives in the war. *The slaveholders had a story*: The Africans were subhuman; the owners were, in fact, doing them a favor by exposing them to civilized culture and supplying them with food and shelter.

And, of course, Rayburne had a story. He hadn't stolen that old man's life savings for personal purposes. He simply got Mr. Jaworski to *invest* it, and perhaps he had made a mistake or two in the formation of his business.

There was always a story—a lie. Every time.

In that instant my Good Person armor fizzled away like droplets on a hot stove, and I was left exposed against the awareness that there was no ontological difference between me and the genocidal Hutus or the Nazis or the slaveholders; the difference between me and them was merely the difference between truth and lies. Whether or not any one of us is a Good Person or a Bad Person can fluctuate from day to day, from moment to moment, depending on the number of lies we allow ourselves to believe.

I felt vulnerable standing in the empty parking lot, suddenly aware that evil was closer to me—had always been closer to me—than I had ever understood.

21

Aches lingered in my body for the rest of the day, as if I'd been exposed to toxic fumes and had to wait for the poison to get out of my system. Aside from that, I was happier than I'd been in weeks. As I drove home from the deposition, I was high on the certainty that this was the answer I'd been looking for when I stumbled across that passage in *Mere Christianity* that night next to Donald's crib.

C.S. Lewis said that you need to "dust off your mirror" to come to know God. I had memorized the quote by now and could hear the words as if Lewis were standing next to me, speaking them in his British accent: "[God] shows himself to some people more than others. Not because He has favourites, but because it is impossible for him to show Himself to a man whose whole mind and character are in the wrong condition." I'd been puzzling over that statement, trying to imagine how one would go about dusting off one's mirror in order to encounter God. Now, I had the answer.

If it were true that God is the source of good, then to seek God is to seek the good. When I puzzled over why I'd had zero experiences with the divine, the situation wasn't so confusing when I replaced the word "God" with "the source of all goodness". I might find myself sitting at the kitchen table, a cheeseburger from a fast-food chain in one hand, a magazine ridiculing celebrities with cellulite in another, using most of my mental energy to stew about why I deserved to live in Tarrytown, and at some point I'd think, "I can't imagine why I haven't had any experiences of God!" Then I'd decide with a shrug that the problem must be that God doesn't exist. When I imagined that same scene with me shouting, "I can't imagine why I haven't had any experiences of the source of all goodness!" the problem became clearer.

To get my spiritual "mirror" in the right condition, per Lewis' advice, I had to seek goodness. I had to try to *be* good. And, as I had just learned in that horrible, airless room, doing whatever feels nice and labeling yourself "good" doesn't cut it. To be truly good, you have to shut down the infinite human capacity to rationalize away evil. And I had an idea for how I could go about doing just that, but it would involve getting deeper into Catholicism.

My blog readers often mentioned the *Catechism of the Catholic Church*, which takes the mountain of teachings that the Church has developed over the past two thousand years and organizes it by topic. They explained that the Church, led by Peter and the other apostles and their successors, were given the authority to teach, explain, and carry on the mission of Jesus. Part of that was designating which of the many letters and documents that were circulating at the time were worthy of being collected in the official Christian library, or Bible. So the *Catechism* was not supposed to be read instead of the Bible, but since I'd had already read the New Testament cover to cover, my readers suggested that the *Catechism* would give me the clarity I was looking for when it came to the details of the Christian moral code. I still had fundamental problems with the Catholic Church, but it was my best bet for cleaning my spiritual lens, so to speak.

I'd come to see that the only way for people to shut down the power of rationalization is to adhere to an external moral code, one that they don't have the power to change on the fly when it gets inconvenient. If God did become a man and did personally found a religion that he continued to guide in its doctrines, one mark it would surely bear is a clear view of right and wrong that did not change over the centuries. This moral code would not vary by region, and it would not flit around like a weathervane as the winds of popular opinion changed. Within Christianity, the only organization that fit that bill was the Catholic Church.

And so I'd come up with an idea: I would try out this Church's moral code. I would do whatever it told me to do and live the way it told me to live. I would even try to put my heart into it and not just go through the motions.

Part of me was skeptical that anything would come of it. I wasn't sure that all of this Church's teachings were perfectly good, case in point being the nonsensical stance against abortion and contraception. I decided to revisit that after the experiment, though, since neither of those issues impacted me right now. In the meantime, I didn't have any better ideas for where to turn, and I figured that conforming to this ancient moral code would be a good exercise in defeating rationalization, even if the Church didn't turn out to be what it claimed to be.

When I got back to the house that evening, I snuck into my office before Irma and Donald discovered that I was home. Without sitting down, I dashed out an order on the computer for *The Catechism of the Catholic Church*. I clicked on the option for rush shipping.

* * *

The UPS delivery man tossed the cardboard box onto the front porch two days later, which was perfect timing. A searing pain behind my right knee left me unable to walk easily or even sit comfortably, and I had taken the day off from work to lie in bed. I was doing some reading on my laptop, rap music blasting through my headphones, when Irma knocked on the bedroom door and brought me the package.

I ripped open the brown box and stared at the book it contained. I chortled under my breath to imagine how horrified I would have been if I could have seen this moment through a crystal ball when I was younger. Actually, I was slightly horrified now.

Just as I was about to turn off the music to focus on reading, a new song began. As soon as I heard piano chords over tinny beats, I grabbed the player. I always skipped this one. Even though it was one of my favorite songs, I hadn't heard any more than the first three seconds—just long enough for me to hit the NEXT button—in years. It was Tupac Shakur's *Changes*, and the lyrics told the tale of his own life. For the first time in as long as I could remember, I let it play.

Wake up in the morning and I ask myself if life's worth living. Should I blast myself? Tupac began.

There were plenty of rappers who included the occasional social justice screeds about ghetto life in their albums, but Tupac was different. To listen to his music was to know that he saw reality with a clarity that most people did not. He had seen evil; so had others. The difference was that he couldn't get over it. Occasionally he would veer into the territory of popular club music, but he never strayed far from the topic of evil. His most impassioned songs angrily recounted the cesspool of the human experience that he'd seen in his life in the ghetto, stories of babies abandoned in dumpsters, young lives snuffed out through pointless violence. His lyrics offered no solutions. There was simply a question that roiled under the surface: "How, how could this be?"

In that sense, he reminded me of C. S. Lewis. Both men were gripped by the problem of evil, and both men had encountered it firsthand: Tupac on the streets of the ghetto, Lewis in the trenches of World War I. I ached to think of what could have been if Tupac had come across Lewis' writings. He might have recognized someone who shared his burden, who also spent his whole life wrestling with what we're supposed to do about the atrocities that take place in the world every day.

When referring to starry-eyed people who bleat about how God is a part of everything, even cancer and slums, Lewis said, "The Christian replies, 'Don't talk damned nonsense.' For Christianity is a fighting religion. It thinks God made the world ... But it also thinks that a great many things have gone wrong with the world and that God insists, and insists very loudly, on our putting them right again." Tupac's lyrics throbbed with the pain of someone who was aching to join the fight but was never sure where to enlist. He wondered aloud if there would be ghettos in heaven and spoke of how his anguish made it difficult to pray sometimes. In "Hold on Be Strong" he cried that even God had turned his back on the ghetto youth, but quickly added, *I know that ain't the truth.*

I looked down at the open *Catechism.* I didn't know exactly what was in these pages, but I was pretty sure that whatever rules it contained, Tupac had broken every one of them. Before he died in a rain of bullets in front of a Las Vegas casino, Tupac used his music to glorify drugs, objectify women, insult cops, and glamorize violence. He'd gone to jail for sexual assault charges, which he'd denied, and many believed that he was at least tangentially involved in the murder of rapper Biggie Smalls.

But I could not believe that he was in hell.

One of Joe's best friends and fraternity brothers from Yale was Tupac's lawyer, and he once told me a story about something that happened shortly after he'd gotten the infamous rapper out of jail. His secretary announced that Tupac was here to see him, which caught him off guard because they didn't have an appointment. He nervously wondered what he was doing there, since they had no further business to take care of now that Tupac was free. Paralegals froze and attorneys stared when they saw the world-famous celebrity and his entourage swagger through the office, their chains and rings gleaming. Our friend braced himself as he heard the group getting closer.

A group of beefy men entered. They parted, and Mr. Shakur walked through the middle, pausing before the lawyer's desk, his posse of stone-faced friends arrayed behind him. He extended his hand and said he'd only come by to say thank you for visiting him in prison. He died a few weeks later.

Like most people who struggle with evil, Tupac also sought beauty. He studied jazz, poetry, and ballet. He had an extensive library that one man described as a "sea of books" upon seeing the collection after Tupac's death. And even as he immersed himself in a life of violence and anger, he still turned to God. He once told an interviewer that "I try to pray to God every night unless I pass out." Most people in his position would have drifted into functional atheism, pretending that they didn't believe in God so that they could live as they pleased without guilt.

If even I could see this, surely God would, too. I weighed the *Catechism* in my hands. The idea was that this Church's teaching was divinely inspired. If it tried to tell me that Tupac Shakur was in hell, that God didn't factor in his upbringing amidst violent radicals and his life amidst poverty and street warfare, that was going to be a problem. Even I, as someone who only knew him through his art, saw *some* goodness in him—a goodness that counted for something—despite all of the horrible things he did. And if this book told me that there was no hope for him at all, I didn't think I could believe that its ideas came from God.

* * *

I dug through the *Catechism* for hours, flipping pages in my bed as the bricks on the neighbor's house lost their cream-colored glow, becoming a dusky gray in the setting sun.

At first it didn't look good. "Outside the Church there is no salvation", said paragraph 846. God didn't become a man, let himself be tortured to death, and found a Church for nothing. So, yeah, you can't get to heaven without all of that, it explained.

However, the next paragraph said that people who "through no fault of their own, do not know the Gospel of Christ or his Church", but who still seek the One who is the source of all good, "may achieve eternal salvation". What it seemed to be saying is that the woman in rural China who lives a life filled with love for others has encountered Jesus, even though she may not know his name. It's the person of Jesus who does the saving, not some magical properties of the vowel sounds in his name.

But what about Tupac? That "through no fault of their own" part might be a little problematic in his case. He'd certainly heard of Jesus—he had a cross tattoo on his back—but he wasn't exactly the epitome of a person whose every action was calibrated to achieve the greatest good.

His situation posed the question: What does God do with believers who are jerks? They really do believe and in their own way try to be good, but they also do a lot of bad stuff, too. Are they assured of a place in heaven?

The *Catechism* basically said: If you're a believer and a jerk, you don't walk right in to heaven after you die. "All who die in God's grace and friendship, but still imperfectly purified, are indeed assured of their eternal salvation; but after death they undergo purification, so as to achieve the holiness necessary to enter the joy of heaven." Heaven is the place of perfect good and perfect love. To enter it while in a disposition of selfishness or hatefulness or unkindness would be like entering into a gleaming clean house with muddy boots; the house would not be clean anymore.

So the question with Tupac was, was he "in God's friendship" in some way? He encouraged listeners of his music to do drugs, but railed against drug dealers selling crack to kids. He referred to his sexual escapades with women in the most vulgar of terms, yet penned a touching ode to his mother in which he said it was his honor to be able to pay her bills for her.

The *Catechism* emphasized the fact that sin was no joke. If Tupac committed even half the offenses against the natural law that he said he did in his lyrics, it wasn't looking good for him. To sin was to turn your back on God, the very source of all goodness. By living the life that he lived, Tupac had cooperated with the same force that was responsible for the babies abandoned in dumpsters. He was aiding and abetting the very enemy that he so deeply hated.

In a move that was both frustrating and respectable, the Church didn't make final proclamations about who goes to hell. It simply said that people who choose to turn their backs on God completely, in their hearts or in their actions, can expect to end up there; God respects our free will and won't make us hang out with him forever if we don't want to.

I would never know which category Tupac fell into. I could only hope that in his final moments he had turned to God one last time and cried out for forgiveness.

And I could pray.

The *Catechism* explained that praying for the souls of the dead is a tradition going back to the first Christians and to the Jews before them. On the walls of the catacombs, where the earliest Christians worshipped, there were scrawled prayers for friends who'd died during persecutions. The living sent their love for the deceased into the spiritual world, like adding water to a stream that would eventually float their lost friends home.

My music player had been shuffling on all Tupac's songs, and *Changes* began again. Once again I heard the voice that had an intimate knowledge of poverty and loss. I heard the words of a person who despised the evil he saw all around him, even as he participated in it himself. As the song neared the close, I recognized that his voice carried the unmistakable tones of a man who knew he did not have much longer to live.

I slid off the bed and dropped to my knees. I pressed my eyes shut as I waited for a wave of pain to pass through my leg. When it had gone, I folded my hands, leaned my head forward, and poured out the most sincere prayer I had ever said, for the soul of Tupac Shakur.

22

My experiment of living by the Church's moral code was going amazingly well. An entire week had passed, and I had not murdered anyone or started a single unjust war. I hadn't even gossiped (though, truth be told, that one probably had less to do with virtue and more to do with the fact that I didn't have enough of a social life to hear anything worth gossiping about). So far, the main result of the experiment was that I felt like a pretty great person.

On a Friday afternoon, ten days into the experiment, I slid into my bed to take a much-needed nap. For one thing, I had to get off my feet: That pain in my right leg was back and had gotten so bad that I now had a limp when I walked. The main problem, though, was that I was tired—terribly, terribly tired.

At almost eighteen months old, Donald was still waking up at least twice, sometimes more, every night. It was as if he was just so thrilled to be alive that he resented the entire concept of being unconscious for hours at a time. Joe was willing to help, but we both agreed that getting sued for malpractice because he made a mistake from being tired wasn't worth my having a little extra rest. The result was that I rarely got more than four consecutive hours of sleep.

The night before had been particularly abysmal. Irma called in sick on Thursday morning, and that afternoon I'd let Donald drink an entire bottle of a lemon–lime soda while I finished a new contact form for the law firm website. I was in the middle of typing out the last lines of code when a horrifying thought occurred to me. With great trepidation, I picked up the empty bottle from the floor and turned it in my hand until I found the ingredients list. My face probably looked like the woman's from the shower scene in *Psycho* when my eyes set on the third ingredient: CAFFEINE.

The evening played out exactly as I feared it would. Donald's eyes flashed open at two o'clock in the morning, and he didn't shut them again until five-thirty. I spent the hours in between sitting with him on the couch while he excitedly inventoried the entire living room, thrusting his chubby index finger in various directions as he exclaimed, "Chair! Table! Sink! Figh-oh place!"

I somehow managed to make it through the morning and past lunch-time, wondering all the while if I might be the first mother who actually died from sleep deprivation, and now I needed a nap like I had never needed a nap in my life. It was two o'clock in the afternoon, and I fig-ured I could count on Donald sleeping until five-thirty. As I settled into bed, my pillow felt twice as soft as it normally did, and our cheap sheets had somehow transformed into a substance as soft as warm butter. That pain in my leg that had plagued me all day faded away now that I was lying down. If heaven did exist, I was sure that it must feel something like this.

As an extra treat, I pulled a printout off my bedside table. Normally I didn't have time for reading when I was trying to sneak in an afternoon nap, but since Donald would sleep for a long time today, I could indulge myself this time.

The three sheets of stapled paper were from a blog post about a nine-teenth-century American slave named Augustine Tolton, who had gone on to become a Catholic priest. I'd begun reading Catholic blogs, and they were all buzzing about this man's story because his biography was being released soon. Everyone said he was a model of Christlike love—specifically, he was a shining example of what true humility looks like. There were whispers that he might be declared a saint one day.

I was finding that reading about the lives of the saints—as well as saintly people who might not have been canonized yet, like Father Augustine—was far more helpful in my quest to seek goodness than reading the *Catechism* alone. The *Catechism* might tell me to put others before myself, and I'd make a mental note to try to do that at some point. Then I would read of Maximilian Kolbe volunteering to die in place of a young father when they were both prisoners at Auschwitz, and I would realize just how feeble my recent efforts at selfless love had been. My heart would be aflame with a desire to serve others, in a deeper and more vibrant way than when I was simply reading theology. Instead of an intellectual decision, it would be more of a movement of the soul, something powerful within me yearning for more of the pure goodness that had touched me through Maximilian's story. And so I turned to

Father Augustine, eager to see what he might be able to tell me about being good. I pressed my papers flat on the bed and began reading.

Father Augustine was freed from slavery when he was a child and then attended a Catholic school in Illinois at the invitation of a priest. This was the 1860s, and some parishioners became apoplectic when they saw a black child in their school, but the priest didn't back down. After high school, Augustine was not allowed to attend his local American seminary, so he went to Rome, where he became fluent in Italian, studied Latin and Greek, and earned respect among the hierarchy.

After he was ordained a priest in Rome, he went back to the United States to begin his ministry. He was returning to the place where he'd been enslaved, the country where he had been listed among another man's possessions, alongside furniture and cattle.

A noise interrupted my reading. I tried to tell myself that it was a cat mewling in the neighbor's yard, but I knew better. It wasn't coming from outside the window. It was coming from the wall in front of me. And it was getting louder.

That was no cat. It was Donald. He was awake.

I hobbled over to his room, the discomfort in my leg returning as soon as I stood. By the time I opened the door, he'd ratcheted up to a full-scale scream. The poor kid was so wired from our crazy night that he couldn't nap. I felt bad for him, but I felt worse for me. In a more clear-headed state, I would have realized that this wasn't the catastrophe it seemed to be. Even Donald had to sleep at some point, so it would only be a matter of rocking him for another hour to get him to drift off. Unfortunately, I was not in a clear-headed state. My assessment of the situation was that he was never going back to sleep—not today, not ever —and that not just my day but my entire life was now ruined.

His crying was like a flame under the pressure-cooker of my frustration—the louder it got, the closer I got to exploding. The eardrum-rattling noise made adrenaline pour into my bloodstream. I yanked him out of the crib and begged him to *please* stop yelling as I carried him into the kitchen. Did he want a cracker? No. Did he want some *galletitas* (the word for *cookies* that he'd learned from Irma)? No. I pulled a box of cereal from the pantry as an offering. He arched his back and began to flail in protest of my terrible idea, and accidentally knocked the container out of my hand. I looked down to see the mess that resulted. It was as if the box had vomited corn flakes all over my shoes.

I managed to swallow the volcanic rage the resulted from crunching across the floor to get the broom, and by the time I dumped the last dustpan of cereal into the trash can Donald had finally quieted down. I could tell by his red, glassy eyes that the reprieve from his tantrum was only temporary, and I braced myself for the next outburst. In my mind was a chorus of self-pity that got worse by the minute. When Donald first woke up it was, *I never get to nap.* Now it had become, *I HATE EVERYTHING ABOUT MY LIFE!*

My mom breezed in through the garage door, back from having lunch with a friend. I didn't say hello, but threw the broom into a corner instead. My body language evidently hadn't sent the signal that trying to interact with me right now was the worst idea in the world, and my mom made the mistake of talking to me.

"Hey, I've been meaning to tell you—you put my bowl in the bottom rack again", she said. She walked over to the dishwasher to pull out the evidence, a teal plastic bowl that was a favorite for storing leftovers.

"That wasn't me", I said as I kicked the dustpan back into the pantry.

"You did the dishes last night", she said. Now I remembered: I'd been trying to load the dishwasher while a caffeine-crazy Donald went about removing everything I'd just put in. Joe was working late and my mom was out, so I had no help. It was a wonder that I stuck with the task at all, considering that I was fantasizing about ripping the thing out of the cabinet and throwing it through the window.

"I've told you about this before", Mom continued. "This is not the kind of plastic that can stand up to the bottom rack . . ."

I stopped listening. My eyeballs actually ached from lack of sleep. Even thinking felt painful, as if some lubricant had evaporated from my brain and now the gears were grinding together. My mom kept talking about that bowl. Finally, I exploded. "Stop! Just stop!" I shouted. "I don't care about your stupid bowl! Leave me alone!"

I grabbed Donald, went back into my room, and slammed the door. My leg now felt like it had been injected with molten lava, so I flopped down on top of the covers. To my great relief, Donald agreed to lie next to me. I stared at the wall in front of us, ready to fume about my plight. No sooner had I revved up my self-pity engine than a reminder about my stupid moral code experiment popped into my mind instead: *Am I trying to be good?*

I huffed. I didn't need the *Catechism* to tell me the answer to that one. Obviously, you weren't supposed to yell at your mom. However, the "buts" started rolling in immediately: *But she shouldn't have gotten on my case about a stupid bowl! But she didn't appreciate my loading the dishwasher! But I was tired!* I was a font of rationalizations, and if it weren't for this experiment of doing what the Church says, it would have taken me about five and a half seconds to think my way out of any inconvenient convictions. As it was, I found that all my excuses splattered against the immovable brick wall of a moral code external to myself.

Once I began to admit that I had disrespected my mother, other convictions pushed in behind it. Not only had I been rude, but my rudeness was particularly undeserved by her. We had promised her that we would pay her rent when we first moved in, but we hadn't been able to for months. This Jaworski case had been sucking the firm's resources, and Joe was only able to pull out enough to make his student loan payments. My mom had allowed us to take over her three extra bedrooms, leaving only the master for herself. We'd scratched up her walls with our decorations, Donald had added countless stains to her carpet, and we regularly borrowed her car. When we wanted to watch a different TV show than she did, she always volunteered to go back to her room so that we could use the big television in the living room. She even let us choose the heat and air conditioner settings, even though it made her electricity bill 40 percent higher than it used to be.

My gaze drifted from the wall down to my bedside table, where the printout about Father Augustine lay. At the top of the page, in the grainy rendering of my printer, there was a picture of him. Something about it caught my attention. I picked up the papers to look more closely. In his eyes there was a certain essence, something so strong and captivating that it almost seemed as if the picture was not a collection of pixels, but a living thing.

In addition to the virulent racism that was a part of his daily life, Father Augustine also faced anti-Catholic prejudices. And yet he never reacted with anger. He never expressed hatred for his enemies, or even condemned them at all.

When I first came across his story, I thought of the priest as a saintly robot who didn't have the same emotions the rest of us did. In the back of my mind, I assumed that he found forgiving enemies to be a pleasant experience. It was easier that way, to imagine that it came naturally to him to meet scorn with peace. Looking at his picture made me realize how wrong I was.

He had been hurt. Of course he had. And every time he chose forgiveness instead of bitterness, it was a moment of chipping away at his own ego—and it's only when our egos are out of the way that we're truly able to love. What I saw in Father Augustine's eyes was a glow—a glow of something supernatural, the source of goodness itself—which can only come through when our egos don't get in the way. Gazing at his picture, it occurred to me that the secret to being good is to be humble. And the secret to being humble is to be so focused on how you can make other people's lives better that you don't care who's right or wrong.

Still holding the paper, I drifted to sleep, the image of the priest who grew up a slave floating in my dreams like a hologram. I woke an hour later. My exhaustion had abated, and my brain was no longer stuck in frustration overdrive. Donald was sleeping next to me, flat on his back, his mouth wide open, as if he'd been standing on the bed and passed out.

I eased onto my feet and moved silently into the living area. My mom was on a phone call in her office, and I went into the kitchen to look for something sugary to help me wake up. On the counter next to the sink was her bowl, its lid lying next to it. She was right. The bowl was ruined. Its once-circular shape was now like an oval drawn by a young child. The lid no longer sat flat, one of its edges twisted upward by the heat. I tried to place it atop the bowl, but it wouldn't fit.

It was just a bowl—plastic, at that—but my mom loved it. My mom treasured even her smallest possessions, especially those that were given as gifts. My aunt once bought her a coaster on a beach vacation that occurred before I was born; my mom still had it and knew exactly where it was at any given moment. Perhaps because she moved around so much with my dad's job, her possessions were a source of stability when the world outside her home was ever-changing. This plastic bowl had been a gift, given to her by a dear friend with whom she'd long since lost touch.

I walked back to my office, ignoring the pulsing heat in my leg, and logged in to my computer. I clicked around a few times, printed a page, and carried it back into the main part of the house. My mom got off her phone call just as I reached her office.

"Did you need something?" she asked. Her tone was pleasant, as if she'd already forgotten about my behavior.

"Yeah. I just . . . I wanted to say . . ." I hated apologizing. I'd always noticed that it caused me terrible internal pain, almost to the point of being agony. And now I realized: It was the pain of my ego colliding with an attempt at love.

I thrust the paper toward her. "I bought you a new bowl, and it'll arrive in a few days. Here's the description of it. It looks really nice." I'd done some research to find the one that got the best customer reviews. It seemed expensive for a plastic container, but I got it anyway.

"This looks just great." My mom looked at the paper with delight. "You really didn't have to do that. It was just a bowl."

It was clear that she'd already forgiven me for my outburst. Technically, I didn't need to apologize. Part of me wanted to tell her to have a nice day and run back to the room like the coward I was. But as soon as I considered that option, Father Augustine's face appeared before me. More than the details of his features, I saw that haunting glow of the kind of love that can only be bought with great self-sacrifice. I might not be the saint that he was, but I could at least do this one small thing.

I looked my mother in the eyes and forced the words: "I'm sorry." I took a breath and continued, "I'm sorry about the bowl. I'm even more sorry about how I reacted when you brought it up. I've been really ungrateful—not just with that, but since we've lived here—and I'm going to start working on that."

She accepted my apology, but assured me that she was happy to have us living with her. Normally, apologizing exhausted me. On the (all-too-rare) occasions that I forced myself to admit wrongdoing, I felt lingering irritation mixed with only mild relief afterward. This time, everything was different. I was filled with something—something good, and pure, and warm. It was love, certainly, but it didn't come from me. It was as if it had been poured into me by someone else.

23

My mom knocked on the bedroom door as she cracked it open. "Can I come in?"

"Sure." I had already gotten in bed and was waiting for Joe to finish putting Donald to sleep for the night. Donald was still battling his caffeine hangover, so it was taking longer than usual to get him settled down.

She handed me a small hardcover book with a dark green dust jacket, G. K. Chesterton's *Orthodoxy*. "You left this in the living room."

"Thanks", I said. I instinctively set it down facedown on the night table.

"I got something from Kevin today", she said, referring to one of her siblings. "It's a copy of an old letter that was sent to our family, from someone who served with Pop Pop in World War II." She held out an envelope with a postmark from my Uncle Kevin's city.

My grandfather died when I was in the second grade, two years after my grandmother. He'd had a stroke before I was born and so was never able to communicate with me verbally. One of my few memories of him was of the time he visited my Montessori preschool when he was in town to stay with us. When he first ambled in, unable to speak clearly and missing multiple fingers due to an accident, the other children backed away in fear. Yet after only a few minutes, they recognized the unconditional love and acceptance that exuded from him and saw his unmistakable delight at spending a few moments with his granddaughter. By the time my mom helped him back to the car, the kids were following him and asking him to stay.

My mom slid the letter out of the envelope and placed it in my hands. It was written after my grandfather received the Bronze Star Medal, the author identifying himself as a Private First Class who wanted to make sure that the full story about Lieutenant Tom Geraghty was known.

"On a bitter night, a number of men were pinned down by German fire at the turbulent Isar River", the private wrote. "Among them were men who were wounded and dying there on the German side of the river. Some were bleeding and helpless in midstream."

My grandfather volunteered to get them, the private explained. Everyone said it was a suicide mission. He went anyway, crossing the river under heavy fire, and brought the wounded men back.

"Wow", I said under my breath as I flipped to the last page.

"I wanted you to see that", my mom said. She seemed to be about to get up, then she stopped. "I also wanted to say ... you remember that he was Catholic, right?"

"Oh, yeah", I said. Though I knew that my mom had been raised Catholic, it rarely came to mind. My grandparents lived thousands of miles away from us in the few short years that our lives overlapped, so I hadn't been around them enough to see them practice their faith. I had no memories of them going to church or doing anything spiritual, but their religion was a fact that I'd had filed away in the archives of my mind.

"I just wanted you to know—" she hesitated, religion not being a subject that either of us ever enjoyed talking about. "With these books you're reading, going to Mass and everything. I wanted you to know that he would be proud of you."

The thought of my Catholic grandparents whom I never had the chance to get to know unleashed a surprising burst of emotion within me. I only nodded in response.

There seemed to be something else she wanted to say. We sat in silence for another moment before she added, "You remember that you were baptized Catholic, right?"

"What?" I said, more loudly than I'd meant to. The news struck me like finding a fascinating memento that had long been buried in a box in the attic. It wasn't news to me, but it was not something we ever discussed. It hadn't even come to mind since Joe and I had been researching Catholicism. What significance did it have that I was carried into a Catholic church to have water poured on my head when I was six months old, when I had no recollection of it and had nothing to do with this belief system for decades afterward? I lived my life so far removed from this religion that when I asked someone a dumb question in high school and she answered sarcastically, "Is the pope Catholic?" I had to ask her, "*Is* the pope Catholic?" I didn't know if it was a rhetorical yes or no.

"My parents were there, of course, when you were baptized", my mom said. "It was important to them that we do that."

I looked down at the letter in her hand, which she'd refolded and now held on top of the envelope. I thought of my grandfather, the war hero who could never speak to me, yet whose blue eyes expressed a strength that hinted at the man he once was. Normally my memory of him was two-dimensional and incomplete; when I brought him to mind it was like trying to piece together a ripped photograph from its fragments. But as I sat on the bed next to my mom, my image of him was more vivid than ever before. It wasn't that I could remember any more details about him, but, rather, that in some strange way he felt more real than other times I'd thought about him, as if he were present in the room.

In my recent reading I'd learned that Catholics believe that super-natural forces act in a real way in our world and that the Church has never wavered on ancient, mystical beliefs that would be sure to get you laughed out of enlightened social circles today. Catholics say that the Communion hosts they receive at church are literally the flesh of Christ, that when they go to confession a profound reconciliation occurs between man and God, far beyond just a cathartic venting session. They believe that people in heaven are aware of what goes on here on earth, and that they pray for us. And—a fact that I'd known for days but whose relevance was just occurring to me now—they believe that the process of baptism contains real power.

A tingling sensation rippled under my skin. I suddenly wondered if my deceased grandfather might be very much alive, even *present* in a certain sense. I wondered if the baptism that he and my grandmother encouraged to happen would be of some assistance to me, though I couldn't imagine how. I wondered if he had been praying for me all this time—if he was perhaps praying for me right now.

My mom said she was glad we talked, and she stood to leave. I was so dazed, I barely muttered a goodbye. I sat alone in the room for a while longer, trying to wrap my mind around the idea that there could be powerful, unseen forces at work in my life that I'd never known were there.

24

Joe and Donald sat in the chairs that lined the wall in the darkened room, their eyes on the swirl of blacks and grays that washed around on the screen above our heads. The colors came together in the form of a baby.

After another swirl of monochrome, the ultrasound tech announced, "It's a girl!"

I rolled my head over and looked at Joe, and we grinned at one another. A daughter. I couldn't wait to go shopping with my mom and pick out ridiculously frilly dresses and pink patent leather shoes that could fit into the palm of my hand. I studied her profile on the screen, remembering that I had recognized Donald's profile from his twenty-week ultrasound when he was born. Joe laughed as he reminded me that at that ultrasound we'd seen Donald pee in utero.

I thought back to that appointment and remembered that I had had an uncomfortable feeling back then that I never did identify. It was here now, too, and it didn't take much analysis to identify what it was: the specter of abortion.

In the first two trimesters of my pregnancy with Donald, I felt a pang of guilt when I used the term "baby" to describe the new pregnancy; I worried that I was buying in to sentimental anti-abortion propaganda. If I were carrying a "baby" when I was nine weeks pregnant, then an abortion at that same stage of pregnancy would be murder. It's never okay to kill a *baby*, but I saw nothing wrong with ending the growth process of a fetus, which was not fully human until it was old enough to live outside the womb. And so I always wondered if I should speak of "the pregnancy" instead, saving the humanizing term "baby" for the third trimester.

Joe was staring at me, and the ultrasound tech might have been asking me a question, but I couldn't pretend that I was basking in the glow of the great news. I was consumed by a thought that I recognized both as true and horrific: that, by my own worldview, I did not believe that the little girl on the screen was fully human.

* * *

The car ride back to my mom's house started in silence. Joe drove, Donald slept in the back seat, and I looked at the glossy series of ultrasound printouts in my hands.

Joe must have read my mind. "I don't know if I consider myself pro-choice anymore, even aside from what the Catholic Church thinks", he said when we stopped at a light.

Last time he said anything against pro-choice beliefs I had exploded in anger; this time, I remained silent. He didn't seem surprised.

"I read something the other day, and it almost made me sick. I mean literally—I almost puked on my desk", he said. He'd been doing some legal research and happened upon the documents for a Supreme Court case called *Stenberg v. Carhart*. There was a Nebraska law that made the so-called partial-birth abortion procedure illegal, and it ended up getting appealed all the way to the top.

"I've never seen anything like it", he said. He got quiet and looked straight ahead, shaking his head slightly.

He started to elaborate on how it had influenced him, but I held up my hand. I'd just felt the baby kick and wasn't in the mood for a conversation about partial-birth abortion. "Let's talk about something else", I said and looked out the window.

* * *

When I woke up, I knew something was different. I reached for Joe behind me, but felt only a wrinkled mound of covers. I looked at the clock. 11:43 P.M.

Something told me that he wasn't just in the bathroom. I got out of bed and waited for the pain in my leg to hit. It was always worst when I first stood. When it subsided, I shuffled into the living room to see Joe reading under my mom's old brass lamp.

"Hey, what are you doing?" I croaked in a sleepy voice.

He hesitated. "Reading."

"Reading what?"

157

"I don't think you want to see it."

I settled into the couch next to him and saw the title of the page: *Report of the South Dakota Task Force to Study Abortion*. "I don't. But I feel like I have to."

"Okay. But it's troubling."

He handed me the report. I flipped through it, stopping to read where I saw his brackets or underlines. There were 819 abortions in South Dakota in 2003, the report said, and 814 of the women undergoing the procedure were given no information about the fetus other than its developmental age. By the abortion facility's own admission, women were asked to sign a form consenting to the procedure before speaking to a doctor. In 813 of the cases, women got their information about what was about to happen from a prerecorded video.

The task force watched the video and noted that not once did it mention that a fetus or embryo was even present in the womb. The language implied that something was there, but referred to it only in the vaguest terms.

"The uterus is then emptied by a gentle suction", the voice on the video told the woman considering ending her pregnancy. "Occasionally, the contents of the uterus may not be completely emptied", it said at another point. "To remove the tissue it may be necessary to repeat the vacuum aspiration" because, occasionally, "the early abortion procedure will not end the pregnancy."

An angry heat pulsed within me. I flipped faster until I reached the end, then started back at the beginning, this time reading more than just Joe's highlights. By the time I finished the last page of the report, my face had broken out into hot red splotches.

"'Tissue?' The 'contents of the uterus'? What is this, Victorian England?" This kind of thing would have driven me crazy even at the height of my days as a pro-choice atheist. These abortion clinics' practices smacked of the view that we women must be sheltered from hard data lest we get all flustered and make the wrong decision. "Don't upset the little lady by telling her that the eleven-week-old fetus has a heartbeat and can make a fist", I imagined the producer of the video saying. "She might get all emotional about it—you know how flighty women can be!"

"I know", Joe said. He glanced at another, larger stack of papers on the coffee table, then turned his attention back to me. "It's really troubling."

"What's that?" I asked, motioning to the papers.

"Just more of this stuff. Trust me. You don't want to get into this."

"I want to see it."

I reached for it on the table, but before I could pick it up he pressed his hand on it to hold it down. "I know. You should read it. I just don't think now is the right time."

"What's the big—"

"It's one of the most disturbing things I've ever read." He released his hand and assumed an uneasy posture.

I flipped it over to see the cover page: *Stenberg v. Carhart*.

Dr. Leroy Carhart, a doctor who specialized in late-term abortions, was willing to end pregnancies up until the day before a woman's due date. He brought a suit against Nebraska Attorney General Don Stenberg in the hopes of showing that a state law banning certain types of late abortions would be ruled unconstitutional. The case went to the Supreme Court, and what I held were Joe's printouts of the court's opinion.

I began reading.

Dr. Leroy Carhart analogized the type of abortion procedures he performed to "pulling the cat's tail", where he'd grab on to an arm or leg with one of his tools and drag the fetus around. The cause of death would be blood loss, just like for any other person who was dismembered.

I turned away, hoping the sights of my mother's quiet living room would erase the picture that had just taken over my mind. My lungs couldn't seem to get enough air, like the day in the Jaworski deposition room.

"See? Let's go to bed", Joe said.

"No." I wanted to finish this. I didn't want to hide from the truth, whatever it was. Also, that must have been the worst of it. I'd come across the disturbing part that Joe had warned me about, and now surely it wouldn't be so bad.

I returned to the case. After a few more minutes of reading, I realized that it had just been getting started. My stomach bubbled; a deep, sickly feeling crept closer and closer to my throat.

Dr. Carhart regularly aborted babies older than my daughter, weeks older than Donald's age when I'd seen him urinate on the ultrasound screen. And when describing the procedure—for which he was paid handsomely—he testified that he sometimes saw on the ultrasound that the child's heart was still beating, even after "extensive parts of the fetus had been removed". He said he knew of one physician who tore off the arm of a fetus during in abortion, but the fetus didn't die; it was just, in his own words, "a living child with one arm".

Air suddenly seemed scarce and my heart raced, but I kept reading. When I got to the part where a nurse named Brenda Pratt Shafer described watching the death of a twenty-six-week-old baby, I couldn't read anymore. I tossed the papers down so hastily that they fanned out across the tabletop.

"Either I have gone insane, or everyone else has", I said. Was I crazy for thinking that this was an atrocity? It seemed so clear, yet respected leaders of our country were totally cool with it.

"I know", Joe said, his voice almost a whisper.

"I saw a twenty-five-week-old baby once", I said, as much to myself as to Joe. "My college roommate went into labor just a few weeks after she announced her pregnancy. I visited her son in the Neonatal Intensive Care Unit." I remembered walking through the hospital room full of glass cribs. As she led me through the NICU, I saw the tiniest little bodies in incubators, hooked up to tubes and monitors. The babies looked so peaceful as they slept, their eyes closed, their chests moving rhythmically. Taped to the Plexiglas walls of their cribs were tender proclamations like *Mommy's Little Man* or *Our Super Girl!* When I reached my friend's son's bed and saw his perfect body, I was caught off guard by an overwhelming urge to protect this child.

When I considered that he was the same age as the babies that Dr. Carhart talked about, I thought I might vomit. "So I guess the law needs to say that moms of those NICU babies can kill them, as long as they haven't reached their due date yet", I sneered. "That's only fair, right? Why should a woman have to raise a baby just because she went into pre-term labor? What's the difference between *where* you kill them? Inside or outside of the womb, it doesn't matter."

Joe finally spoke. "What I can't get my head around is that the debate in this case is not about whether killing these kids is wrong; it's just about how to do it." He said that the American College of Obstetricians and Gynecologists (ACOG) wrote an amicus brief opposing the partial-birth abortion ban—not because they had any problem with killing these babies, but because "sharp fetal bone fragments can injure the uterus and cervix". It was preferable to kill NICU-aged children after they'd been delivered, the organization said, because that procedure "reduces the incidence of a free-floating fetal head" that can be hard for the doctor to grasp.

"Wait. Doesn't the ACOG oppose homebirth because it's supposedly too risky for babies' health?" I asked.

"Yeah. I think that's what the midwife who delivered Donald told us."

"*But being decapitated isn't?*" Now I was shouting. "Are we really having a national debate about the inconvenience of *free-floating baby heads*?"

"Keep in mind that these procedures are rare", Joe said. His voice was without conviction, like he was just saying it to help me.

I scoffed. "Chainsaw massacres are rare. That doesn't mean it's okay to support them."

I could hardly believe that intelligent, otherwise respectable people were fine with this. Even if it were *never* done and they were speaking only of theoretical situations, there would still be a big problem with Supreme Court justices and leaders of the ACOG saying that there's nothing wrong with infanticide in its most grisly form. They couldn't even justify themselves by pleading the health of the mother, since they were discussing babies who were old enough to live outside the womb if the pregnancy needed to end.

I wanted to hit something. I eyed a stuffed pig in Donald's toy pile that always did seem to have a smug look on its face, and I thought of how cathartic it would be to grab it and punch it a few times.

I was officially disgusted with the pro-choice movement. The average pro-choice people on the street would probably oppose the procedures described in *Stenberg*, yet they'd never do anything to stop it. In all my years of running in social circles where everyone supported abortion rights, I never once heard anyone draw the line and say, "Okay, that's murder, and we need to protect those babies." I certainly never said anything like that. Protecting any unborn life under any circumstances was just not part of the culture. Meanwhile, the movement's leaders vocally supported killing children old enough to live outside of the womb in procedures that were like something out of a horror-movie director's imagination.

I leaned my head into Joe's chest. It felt like this should be the moment that, like Joe, I decide that I was no longer pro-choice. But I couldn't. I wasn't ready to jump on the anti-abortion side with the Catholics— not even close. As much as what I just read called into question the moral footing of the pro-choice position, there remained within me an unmovable resentment toward Catholicism for opposing abortion and therefore making women slaves to their bodies.

My mind was split in two by the increasing disconnect between my intellect, which said that something terrible was happening to women and their children, and my emotions, which said that I'd still fight and die to defend it. Within me there was a conviction with roots a mile deep that said that to oppose abortion would be unfair to women in the direst sense of the word.

Normally, I would have stepped through the problem until I could be confident that I was being intellectually honest. But not here. I was fully aware that I was more determined to remain pro-choice than I was to take an honest look at who was and wasn't human. I didn't like it, but I didn't know what to do about it.

25

The midwife's forehead wrinkled in concern. From my vantage point lying back on the table, I watched her lean forward and peer down my right leg. She paused, then pressed her finger into the back of my calf. "Does it hurt there?"

"Nope."

"How about here?" she asked.

"No."

She moved to the end of the exam table. Tension tightened her face as she approached my right foot, then slowly pushed it back toward my body. She looked at me expectantly.

"Doesn't hurt", I reported.

She let out a loud sigh. "Thank God. It's not a DVT." Her face relaxed, though it still showed concern. "I can tell you now, I was really freaked out when you first described your symptoms."

I had called the birthing center that morning because I could no longer walk more than a couple steps at a time. When I told the midwife that it seemed to have something to do with my veins, she told me to come in right away. She wanted to make sure that I didn't have a deep vein thrombosis, a blood clot in a major vein.

"I still think you should go to the ER, just to be safe", she said as she helped me off the exam table.

"Is that really necessary?" I asked. As the working mom of a toddler, the last thing I had time for was sitting in a hospital.

She addressed me as if speaking to a child who'd been caught playing with matches. "I don't think you understand how serious this is. DVTs are a top cause of death for pregnant women. If you have a large clot and it breaks free, it will go to your lungs. At that point you've got less than an hour until you die."

I raised my eyebrows. "Oh."

"That's why we're not going to take a risk here." She grabbed a business card from the counter and wrote down the address of the nearest hospital on the back. "Go to this emergency room and tell them to take an ultrasound of your leg." She paused, then wrote down another number. "This is my cell phone. Call me if they find anything."

The ER was chaos. From behind the drapes that enclosed my makeshift room I heard the squeaking of rubber-soled shoes mingled with hushed conversations. Doctors and nurses called questions like, "Have you checked on the laceration in three?" and whispered in impromptu hallway conferences, where words like "not stabilizing" or "he's upset" filtered out.

A doctor in pale blue scrubs pulled the drapes open and entered the room. We went over my symptoms, he pushed my foot back like the nurse had done, and he told me they'd need to take an ultrasound of my leg. Before he disappeared through the curtains, he warned me that I might be waiting a few hours, because they only had one ultrasound machine and it was already in use.

I'd called my mom on the way to the ER, and she assured me that she could take over with Donald if Irma needed to leave, so I decided to relax and think of this as a mini vacation. I moved my slouchy beige canvas purse from the chair next to me and picked up the stack of papers beneath it. Ever since I'd begun researching Catholicism, I always had a book or a printout on hand. I couldn't stand the thought of missing opportunities to read when I was in the midwife's waiting room or in between jobs at the office, so I kept reading material on me at all times.

Today I had *Salvifici Doloris*, Pope John Paul II's letter about suffering. It was what they called an "apostolic letter", meaning that it fell into the category of statements that God supposedly protected from error. If the pope were at a restaurant and declared that cilantro was the most vile food known to mankind, he would be right, but it would not be considered an infallible statement handed down by God. That only happened when he exercised the authority given to Peter and his successors by Jesus—sort of like how the writers of the Bible were not necessarily inspired by God when writing personal letters to friends.

Since the Church claimed that God made sure that nothing in letters like this one would be wrong, at least when it came to issues of faith and morality, I was eager to see what this pope had to say about the great question of human suffering. For two thousand years, documents like this one had been circulated by popes to the clergy to be read and explained to the people at church services. Now, in a modern turn of events, they were also available on the Vatican website, which is where I'd printed my copy. With the sounds of the downtown emergency room beeping and clattering all around me, I began reading *Salvifici Doloris*, which had been translated into English as, *On the Christian Meaning of Human Suffering.*

Pope John Paul II used the letter to summarize what has been revealed to us about suffering: God doesn't want it and came to fix it; it is ultimately caused by evil; and it is not to be assumed as a punishment for wrongdoing. But then, at the close of the letter, he said, "Suffering is certainly part of the mystery of man ... an especially impenetrable one."

Mystery. Impenetrable. There was a self-assuredness in the statement, an utterly unself-conscious willingness to say, "I'm just taking dictation here, and that's all I was told." If this Church were indeed run by a bunch of power-hungry guys who made up doctrines and wanted to seem omnipotent, I would have expected to see an effort to explain everything with perfect clarity. I could understand the religious sects that gained traction by preaching that suffering was divine punishment for people God didn't like; as abhorrent as the thought was, at least it was a tidy solution. In contrast, this encyclical delivered the message, with hope and peace, that "we have not been given all the answers".

Over and over again, John Paul simply pointed to the cross. He would talk about esoteric concepts like the paradox of weakness and strength and the possibility of channeling suffering, through Christ, to make it a victory over evil. But there were never more than two or three paragraphs of that before he took it back to God as a man who was nailed to a piece of wood.

I plunged my hand into my purse, digging around until I felt hard, pea-sized balls of plastic. I pulled out a pink Rosary, which had been sent to me by a blog reader. I fed the beads through my fingertips until I held only the pewter crucifix. There was the familiar figure of Jesus, bleeding and dying. This image supposedly answered the question of human suffering. I just didn't understand how.

I set the Rosary aside and got back to the encyclical. The ultrasound machine became available just as I finished the last page, and I put the papers back under my purse to focus on the appointment. After a technician moved a wand slowly down my leg, pausing to push it deep into my flesh every few inches, the doctor came in to tell me that I was all clear. There were some clots in superficial veins, but no DVT.

When I got home, I had to call my mom from the driveway to ask her to help me inside. Irma hustled out the door alongside her. I put my right arm across Irma's shoulder, my left arm across my mom's, and together we lumbered into the house. They hoisted me onto the roomy living room couch, where I flopped down with great relief.

Donald bounced over and climbed into my lap, and I tried not to let him see that I was still in pain. "Mommy home!" he exclaimed, his bright blue eyes radiating pure joy. "You go doctor?" he asked, his expression turning to concern.

He was an incredible talker for being four months shy of his second birthday, and it was one of my life's greatest pleasures to be able to hear him express the thoughts that went through his head. "Yes, mommy went to the doctor today. What did you do?"

"I play with Miss Irma! We eat *galletitas*", he said, pronouncing the last word with a flawless Spanish accent.

My mom offered to take Irma home, and Donald scrambled off my lap and announced that he wanted to go with them. "Car goes *vrrrrooooom!*" he said before they walked out the door. His little voice was so innocent it hurt my heart.

When I heard the final screech of the garage door coming to a close, it occurred to me that I should have asked my mom to bring me something: a book, the TV remote control, anything. The ultrasound had caused the pain in my leg to reach a level that I had not previously experienced, and walking more than one step was now out of the question. The only things within my reach were one of Donald's toy tractors and a jumble of months-old gossip rags on the coffee table. I had given up those kinds of magazines as part of the seeking goodness experiment, and I didn't find pushing a tractor across the floor while making loud grumbling noises to be half as entertaining as Donald did. That left me stranded on a couch in a silent living room.

The ER doctor's diagnosis was almost worse than if it had been a deep vein thrombosis. I knew I should have been relieved to hear that there was no DVT, but at least that diagnosis would have given me a plan of attack.

I sank back into the deep couch cushion, dropping my head against a pillow. I tried to reconcile this with what John Paul II said when he remarked that "the mystery of the Redemption of the world is in an amazing way rooted in suffering".

As I did my couch philosophizing, I unconsciously scanned the fireplace mantle in front of me. There was the silver-framed picture of Donald standing in tiny overalls, eagerly pointing at something out of the shot. The hand-painted wooden block that said *Love Is Being a Grandparent*, the empty iron candlesticks, and then a picture of ... no. I really did not want to think about that right now.

I tried to turn my attention elsewhere. I looked around again for the TV remote. I even picked up Donald's tractor, but that only reminded me of the little boy in the picture, so I tossed it across the room.

The picture was a small, black-and-white portrait of my mom's parents and their first child, taken in the 1940s. My grandmother beamed in a stylish dress, standing proudly next to my grandfather, who wore his formal Army uniform. Between them was their son Tommy, his face frozen in a giggle he'd let loose just as the camera snapped. He bore a striking resemblance to Donald and was Donald's age—to the month—when the picture was taken.

The portrait revealed a young couple in love with one another and with their child, a feisty happiness radiating from their images. They could never have imagined what was about to happen to them.

One morning in April of 1945, while my grandfather was off fighting in World War II, my grandmother, her mother, and Tommy drove through their home town of Carteret, New Jersey. It was a Sunday, so maybe they were going to or from church. But none of us ever heard why they were out, because what happened next erased all the moments that had come before it.

The driver of a large truck ran a stop sign and slammed into my grandmother's car. My grandmother was five months pregnant and was thrown from the vehicle. Her mother was killed instantly. Tommy survived, but was trapped in the car, which burst into flames. When they dragged him from the vehicle, he had been burned severely. In the ambulance on the way to the hospital, my grandmother stared at his fingers, whose melted flesh had been webbed together by the flames.

After suffering through the night, Tommy died the next day. My grandmother buried her first child and her mother next to one another, the dates of death on their tombstones one day apart. Her husband was still off at war. She returned to an empty house.

I shook my head violently, as if I could expel the images from my brain if I just put enough effort into it. Everything I had read that day about redemption and victory in the midst of suffering was demolished by my outrage, like trees flattened by the force of a volcano. If God had appeared to me in the flesh, I probably would have slugged him. "You are supposed to be good! You're supposed to be Love itself! And you let kids burn to death? What in the hell is that?" I shouted out loud, my eyes brimming with tears. "You're supposed to be *good!*"

I pushed down on the couch, testing the possibility of getting to my feet. Pushing through the surge of pain, I pulled myself to a standing position, knowing that the brunt of it was yet to come. I was able to take one long step before the usual agony radiated down my leg. I steadied myself on the couch, determined to accomplish this small mission. I wasn't going to be able to take much more, so I lurched forward quickly. Now I was only feet from the fireplace. I could almost reach it.

Three more steps, and I couldn't do it anymore. The pain made me instinctively raise my leg up, which threw me off balance. I knew I was about to fall, but in the final seconds I was able to accomplish my mission. Before I stumbled to the floor, I grabbed the picture and slammed it facedown.

26

"Fis ih ah-HAY-hee!" Joe exclaimed through a mouthful of food. With a gulp, he repeated, "This is amazing! How did I not know about this?"

I looked around the parish hall of this new church we were visiting, worrying that using too loud a tone would trigger the NOT CATHOLIC detectors and get us hauled out of the building. Joe was undaunted. He mashed a handmade tortilla stuffed with eggs and bacon into a mound of freshly prepared refried beans and stuffed it into his mouth. After he'd wiped the last molecules of food off his Styrofoam plate, he stood up to buy another one, but first he leaned down to proclaim solemnly, "I am going to come to Mass here every weekend, just so I can go to these breakfasts."

Donald toddled after him, and I knew they'd reached the serving line when the cooks, part of a women's group called the Guadalupanas, erupted in squeals of delight to hear Donald make his requests in the Spanish that he'd learned from Irma.

A hand touched my shoulder. "Are you new here?" a voice asked. It belonged to a woman who looked to be about fifty, with a soft, feminine face, and the kind of warm eyes so filled with compassion that they immediately gave me a sense of security. I had my right leg propped up in the chair next to me, and she took a seat in the next chair over.

When I said that this was our first visit, she asked how we found Saint William. The truth was that my blog readers had found it for me, one of their many acts of kindness after reading through my various spiritual flounderings. I didn't want to reveal that I was one of those weird internet people, though, so I glossed over all of that and said that friends told me about it. "I just wanted to come by to welcome you", she said, extending her hand, "My name is Janie Castillo."

"Nice to meet you, Mrs. Castillo."

"Oh, no, please call me Janie", she said.

She didn't need to tell me that she was the matriarch of a distinguished Mexican-American family—I'd had the pleasure of knowing many women like her over the years. My dad and his parents lived in Mexico for most of his childhood, thanks to my grandfather's work as a refinery engineer, and to this day our family had many Mexican friends. Janie's dignified presence was familiar, connecting me to a part of my life I hadn't thought about in a long time.

"Are you visiting from another parish?" she asked.

Now I had to find a way to get around saying "until very recently I was a militant atheist who hated all things Christian and Catholic, but now I'm reading about the Catholic Church while occasionally shouting at God". I really needed to change the subject. So I pretended I didn't hear the question and turned it back to her. "How long have you been a member of Saint William?" I asked.

She let out a weightless laugh that sent musical notes bouncing through the air. "Oh, dear, my whole life", she said. She explained that the parish started in 1916, when Mexican workers at the local limestone quarry met in her grandfather's house. An Irish-American priest from Austin would come up once a month to hold Mass with the quarry workers, sleeping at Janie's grandfather's place before returning to town.

As she spoke, it reminded me of what I'd read of the lives of the saints. For as diverse a group of folks as the saints were, the one thing they had in common is that the people around them always remarked on their peace. To know a saint, I'd heard, was to know someone who was so in tune with God that he became a channel of supernatural love. Not necessarily through his way with words or his great deeds, but through mere presence, infused by something not of this earth. I'd always wondered what it would be like to meet someone like that. And now I was pretty sure I knew.

"Oh my, I've been doing too much talking", Janie said. She leaned forward, as if conducting an interview with the most fascinating person in the world. "Now, which parish did you say you were from again?"

"Oh, I, umm", I stammered. "I'm actually not Catholic." I motioned to Joe, who was gesticulating wildly over in the serving line. "We're working on that."

She closed her eyes, as if I'd delivered amazing news. "Oh, that is just so great, Jennifer. I am so blessed to hear that." Then she added: "Are you in RCIA?"

My blog readers had used that acronym before, but I never knew what it meant. "I'm sorry, what is RCIA?"

"Oh, of course. The Rite of Christian Initiation for Adults. It's an old, old tradition of the Church, going back to the very beginning, where people who are interested in coming into communion with the Church go through a formation process—so they know what they're getting into."

I'd read about the rites that potential Christians underwent in ancient times. They would meet by candlelight deep within the catacombs, using assumed names. They faced several "scrutinies" from the congregation, in part to see if anyone recognized an agent of the state who might be trying to infiltrate. It was fascinating to think that the ritual continued still today. It struck me that this Church was built for battle.

"Conversion can be so difficult", she added. "God doesn't want you to go through the process alone, you know."

She pulled over a napkin and fished a pen from her purse. "Oh, I think it would be so good for you to be in our RCIA program. We're getting a new director—just a wonderful, holy man. His name is Noe, and he'll arrive in the fall." She slid the napkin over to me. "This is the main church number. Do give them a call about RCIA when you're ready."

Joe and Donald returned with new, overflowing plates, and we all chatted for the two minutes it took Joe to finish his food. We said our goodbyes to Janie, and I hobbled to the parish hall exit, leaning on Joe to keep my balance. We paused before going outside, and I noticed a laminated poster on the wall.

"You know, I almost told Janie to sign me up for that RCIA thing right now", I said as I crouched to process the pain that walking had triggered.

Joe grabbed my arm to help me balance. "Why didn't you?"

I jerked my finger toward the poster. "Because of that."

It was an illustration that showed side-by-side cross-sections of two plants in the dirt: On the left was a decaying weed, one of those raggedy dandelion plants with jagged leaves that takes over your entire yard, sucking all the resources away from other living things. On the right was a vibrant, blooming rose bush. Written along the root of the weed was the word CONTRACEPTION. The rose's root was CHASTITY.

I hobbled closer to read the words near the top, which indicated the supposed fruits of the pro-contraception worldview: I wasn't surprised to see that they'd put *Abortion* and *Marital Infidelity* on there. It was a stretch, but at least both of those things involve sex. But the poster also included words like *Euthanasia* and *Lethal Experimentation*.

"Yeah. That's a bit much", Joe said.

"I don't get it. I don't get how this Church can have so much other stuff figured out, but then . . ." I let my words fade away. For the first time, I internalized the fact that this Church really could be guided by God in its teachings. I'd said it, I'd thought about it, but this was the first time I let the idea seep in. And it occurred to me that if it did turn out to be true, then to say that I knew better than the Church on this or any other issue was to say that I knew better than God.

"I don't know what's up with that", Joe said, holding out his arm for me to lean on. "But I feel like there's something we're missing."

* * *

Back at home, I was confined to bed yet again because of the leg pain. I passed the afternoon reading through another inches-high stack of printouts from the internet, this time concerning Catholic teaching on contraception.

In 1968, Pope Paul VI triggered a worldwide hissy fit when he announced in an encyclical called *Humanae Vitae*, or *On Human Life*, that the Catholic Church still did not believe in contraception. Though nobody argued about the fact that this had been a key Christian teaching from the very beginning, every other denomination had reversed its stance on the issue after public opinion changed in the early twentieth century. The last holdout, the Catholic Church, was expected to do the same. It didn't.

In *Humanae Vitae*, Paul VI reaffirmed the Catholic position on that issue and went on to suggest that contraception, if it did become widely used, would be bad for marriages. Everyone laughed at such a silly idea: After all, surely it would help couples if they were free to enjoy sex without the worry of pregnancy.

The encyclical was written in 1968, just three years after *Griswold v. Connecticut* made contraception legal throughout the United States. At the time, the divorce rate was about 10.5 divorces for every 1,000 women. By 1970, it was 15. Five years later, it was 20. And in 1978, ten years after the Church's predictions, the divorce rate was 23 per 1,000 women. It had more than doubled.

So when I got to the part where Pope Paul also predicted that contraception would result in bad things happening to women, it got my attention.

To the pooh-poohs of society at large, Pope Paul VI warned that contraception would lead men to disrespect women. He said that once men got used to the widespread availability of contraception, they would "forget the reverence due to a woman, and, disregarding her physical and emotional equilibrium, reduce her to being a mere instrument for the satisfaction of his own desires".

A mere instrument for the satisfaction of his own desires.

I looked down at a stack of old magazines lying on the floor next to the bed. I picked up four and tossed them on the bed. Each positioned itself as a source of advice for the modern, empowered woman. One bore the headline:

SEXY AT 70! ONE GRANDMA'S RACY PHOTO SHOOT

I grabbed the magazine and opened it to the promised article about the "sizzling septuagenarian". I could be sexy at seventy, too, the article assured me. There was palpable desperation underneath the author's words as she said over and over again that sexiness does *not* have to end at fifty, or even sixty. She assured the reader that many men like the maturity that comes with women of an advanced age, and she informed older women that they just had to use their years of sexual experience to do things in the bedroom that would blow their partners' minds. The author took it for granted that, for a woman, your value is directly connected to how attractive you are to men.

I looked at the cover again: A twenty-year-old girl cocked her hip seductively, her lips slightly parted, her eyes lowered at the camera. Her breasts bulged against a stretchy sequined top, which was cropped short enough to reveal a stomach like that of a fourteen-year-old boy. One of the other headlines promised in large, neon letters to enlighten readers about the top ten things that men found unattractive. Another was about how to lose weight. I scanned the covers of the other magazines: woman in a bikini, woman in a micro-mini skirt, another woman with large breasts about to flop out of her skin-tight dress. All of them had the word "sexy" or one of its synonyms somewhere on the cover, usually more than once.

I pulled up another stack of glossy rags and pushed them around my bed so that I could see all the covers at once. Something I had always wondered, but had never articulated, came to the forefront of my mind:

When, exactly, did the standard of beauty become a dictate that we must all look like Stripper Barbie?

When I saw pictures of my ancestors, the women always looked beautiful, but in a way that didn't overwhelm the senses with their physical beauty alone. The faded photographs of my grandmothers and their grandmothers showed clothing styles that left some attention for their faces, that didn't detract from the subtleties of their expressions. The draping of the material smoothed over details so that a few extra pounds could be smoothed into graceful curves.

Now, a century and a half later, a woman could hardly consider herself truly beautiful without a tight abdomen, perky breasts, a taut posterior, wrinkle-free face, and even, to quote one of the magazines in front of me, "ultra-sexy upper arms". *Upper arms?* Did our ear canals now have to be sexy, too?

This was not a standard of beauty built on respect for women. In fact, it seemed like an outlook spawned by a society that demanded that women make themselves objects for men's pleasure. And when I considered when the standard of beauty began to change, I realized that it was right around the time that everyone started using contraception. Pope Paul VI wouldn't have been surprised.

Half-buried in magazines, I came to the dizzying realization that the Church was not entirely wrong on this issue. I still didn't know if it was completely correct, but I had to give it credit that it alone predicted that contraception would have unintended consequences, articulated what they would be, and had been proven right. It continued to say, as it had always said, that society urgently needed to take an honest look at whether contraception has really been a good thing for women.

These thoughts swirled in my mind all weekend, and as soon as I woke on Monday morning, I knew what I wanted to do. I snatched the napkin with Janie Castillo's handwriting on it from my nightstand and eased my legs over the bed. I was pleased when the pain was only mild and rushed to my feet to find the phone.

Two seconds later, something grabbed my leg. It felt like a demon's claw had reached from under the bed and attacked my calf, and was squeezing and digging into it with the intent of tearing it off. I dropped to the ground and cried out in such agony that Irma, Donald, and my mom came rushing into the room at the same time, English and Spanish and baby-talk all raining down on me at once.

My mom knelt down next to me. "What happened?"

"I'm not sure." I pulled up the leg of my pajama pants. The calf was swollen, but there was no visible damage on the outside. Then I remembered that thing the midwife and the ER doctor had done. I stretched out my leg, leaned forward, and grabbed my big toe. They said that this was a sure test of whether or not you had a deep vein thrombosis. I pulled my foot back toward my body.

BAM! Bombs went off up and down my calf, and I craned my neck in a silent scream. It was a DVT.

"I need the phone", I gasped.

I was able to breathe again once Irma returned with the phone, and I dialed the midwives. When I told the receptionist I had a likely DVT, she immediately shouted across the room for the owner of the birthing center to get on the phone, now. The owner, who was also a nurse practitioner and the head midwife, asked me to go over my symptoms again. I hadn't even finished describing them when she interrupted me and told me to get to the ER immediately.

"Do you need to go to the hospital?" my mom asked after I got off the phone.

"Yes", I said. "But I need to make a call first."

I unfolded the napkin from the crumbled ball I'd turned it into when the pain first hit, and I dialed the number into the phone. When I got an answer, I said, "Hi, my name is Jennifer Fulwiler. My husband and I need to sign up for RCIA."

27

The emergency room doctor pulled his cell phone out of his pocket and called someone with whom he was on a first-name basis. He threw out a bunch of multisyllabic medical terms, then flipped the phone shut and put it back in his pocket.

He scribbled an address on a prescription pad. "You need to be at this office at eight A.M. tomorrow", he said. He ripped off the paper and handed it to me, and explained that the man he'd just called was a doctor who specializes in the treatment of blood disorders. "Dr. Wolfe is possibly the best hematologist in Texas", he said. "He's booked for weeks, but he'll get you in between appointments tomorrow."

He asked me what pharmacy I used, then picked up a phone on the wall and repeated the information to a nurse. "We can't treat the clot while you're pregnant. All we can do is keep it from getting worse", he explained. "Have someone pick up this prescription for you right away. Dr. Wolfe will give you more details, but you'll take it every day for the rest of your pregnancy. If you promise to start taking it within the hour, I won't hospitalize you."

I nodded in agreement, still trying to process everything.

"This medicine you'll have to take, it's shots—you'll have to inject them into your stomach", he added.

"What?" I had a paralyzing fear and hatred of needles. "There's no way."

He leaned forward, and our eyes met. "Maybe you don't understand how serious this is. These shots will probably save your life."

I mumbled a chagrined response and picked up my purse from the floor. I thought we were done, but then he went back to the pad again. "I never do this, but this is my personal cell phone." He finished writing, then handed me a last piece of paper. "Call me—or have someone else call me—if anything goes wrong."

* * *

By the time my mom and I arrived at the hematologist's office the next morning, my condition had gotten so bad that I could not even take one step on my own. She and I got from the car to the waiting room with me hopping on one foot, occasionally pausing for her to lift my right leg until it was horizontal, which eased the pain of blood flow putting pressure on the clot.

The nurse asked about my last birth, and I knew things were about to get weird.

"Was your son born at Seton or North Austin Medical Center?" she asked.

"Neither."

"Which hospital was it, then?"

"He wasn't born in a hospital. I went to the Austin Area Birthing Center."

She looked up, confused. "Where's that?"

"It's in a strip center off of Loop 1."

"Your son was born in a strip center?" She seemed to think she hadn't heard me correctly. "Who's the doctor there?"

"There isn't one. Actually, I didn't see a doctor at all for that pregnancy."

She had an expression on her face as if I'd said that I gave birth in the woods on the eve of the full moon, with only the woodland creatures as attendants. After an uncomfortable silence, she continued, "Who was your midwife then?"

"Well, I didn't have one in particular. There were a few . . ."

She flipped the page and suggested that maybe we should just move on to the next questions. Fortunately, she didn't tell me that there would be a blood test until the very end, so I didn't have time to agonize about it.

"Is this really necessary?" I asked as she wheeled me into the lab. "I'm sure it's fine. Maybe we could just do another ultrasound on my leg."

She jabbed the needle into my right arm and filled a vial with blood so red it almost looked black. Then she filled another, and another. And another. And—man, was one of their other patients bleeding to death or something?

When she picked the ninth test tube out of a bin, I asked, "Any idea why he needs so much blood?"

177

She pulled out the needle, released the rubber strap from my upper arm, and made eye contact with me for the first time since I'd been there. "Sometimes there are deeper causes for these things."

Two days later, my mom drove me back to the office, and we waited in an exam room for Dr. Wolfe to deliver the blood test results. I thought it was annoying that he didn't just have the nurse call me to let me know everything was fine. Given that I was now an invalid, it seemed like a lot of trouble for a two-second visit.

The door swung open, and Dr. Wolfe breezed in, holding a thin stack of faxed pages. "We got the results", he announced. I noticed that the "... and it's all clear" part of the sentence was missing. He rolled a circular stool underneath himself just in time to sit on it, looked again at the papers, and looked at me. "You have the prothrombin 20210 mutation."

"The what?"

"Prothrombin is a protein your blood uses to clot. You have a quirk in your genetic code that makes your body produce too much of it."

"And that's where the clot came from?"

"Right. And there's something else." He flipped the papers to the last page and lingered over it, as if confirming that he hadn't misread it. "This is incredibly rare, but you're homozygous, which means you inherited the mutation from both parents."

"From me?" my mom said, startled. She hadn't expected to get her own medical diagnosis when she'd signed up to be my chauffeur that morning.

He nodded. "We know more about the risk factors for you, assuming you only have one copy of the mutation", he said, speaking to my mom. "But we don't know as much about your condition", he said to me. "We know that being homozygous probably makes it worse, but we don't know how much worse. It's hard to study it because it's so rare."

I had a million questions (starting with: *So did my parents meet at a family reunion?*), but he'd already folded up the papers and straightened his posture. It looked like he was going to stand up at any second. He was clearly in a hurry to leave, since my last-minute visit had probably thrown off his entire morning schedule, so I tried to keep my questions to the minimum. "Okay. What does this mean?" I asked.

"Who is your obstetrician again?"

"I was seeing a group of midwives—"

"Oh. That's right. You know that's out now, right?"

I nodded. I got an email from the birthing center owner that morning explaining that they could no longer work with me as a patient because of the DVT. I'd been trying not to think about it.

Dr. Wolfe continued, "I'll have the nurse make you an appointment with a high-risk OB I know. You'll need to go to the hospital for the birth, and labor will have to be induced. If you go into labor while you are on the anti-clotting medication, it could cause serious bleeding issues."

I was trying not to hide my visceral horror at the thought of so drastically changing my birth plan when I was eight months pregnant—not to mention the fact that our small business health insurance plan didn't cover pregnancy, so we were now probably looking at at least ten thousand dollars out of pocket. And so at first I didn't hear him when he asked: "What method of contraception were you planning to use after the baby's born?"

All my thoughts stopped like a needle had scratched off a record player. I stalled by acting like I didn't hear the question. So he repeated it.

My mom turned to look at me. Though she was probably thinking about her own surprising diagnosis, at that moment I felt certain that her simple glance in my direction conveyed a worry that I was going to embarrass us both by saying something like, "I'm not going to use contraception because the pope tells me not to!"

I stalled again. "Why do you ask?"

Dr. Wolfe stood and slid his stool back under the desk in the corner of the room. "Your blood disorder is exacerbated by pregnancy. Pregnancy is a high-risk condition for you because of the chance of clotting, and so you should consider sterilization."

I started to ask a question, but he wasn't done with the bad news. "Also, after the baby's born, we'll dissolve the clot with a drug called Coumadin", he continued. "It's an FDA Category X drug, meaning you cannot take any chance of getting pregnant when you're on it."

"How long will I be on it?"

"At least half a year. But we'll want to talk about the possibility of putting you on it for life since you're homozygous." He walked over to my chart that the nurse had left open on the desk. He picked up a pen and poised it over the paper. "So what's the contraception plan?"

I was tempted to tell him whatever he wanted to hear—"I'm going to take the pill and the patch and the shot and put barbed wire around my uterus just for good measure!"—but instead I just stared at his hovering pen. I wondered if it would be weird if I pretended like I hadn't heard him again.

"I understand", he said. "There are a lot of options out there. Why don't you think about it, and we can circle back at the next appointment."

"Right! Of course", I said, loudly and stiffly.

He stood and shook our hands, and before leaving he added, "If you don't get sterilized, you're going to need a backup method of birth control, too. This drug is serious business." And with that, he walked out the door.

28

I met with the new obstetrician in another whirlwind of an appointment. They didn't have a wheelchair handy, so after my visit with the doctor a nurse had to help me to my next stop: the financial administrator's office. The nurse was a petite young woman whose extra-small scrubs hung loosely on her delicate figure. I was a foot taller and, at eight months pregnant, about a hundred pounds heavier, and I had to use her as a sort of human crutch in order to walk. Each time I dug my fingers into her shoulder and leaned onto her to cope with the surges of pain, I worried that I would crush her.

The nurse helped me into the windowless office. The administrator tried to talk to me as soon as I flung myself into the visitor's chair in front of her desk, but I held up my hand to request a pause. I put my foot up on the chair next to me, craned my neck back, and squeezed my eyes shut as if I could somehow wring out all the pain through my eyelids. Finally, after a few seconds, I had it under control enough that I could tell her to go ahead.

She asked if it was correct that our health insurance didn't cover maternity. When I said yes, she wasted no time getting to the point: "Between Dr. Martin's fees and the hospital expenses, you're looking at between ten and fifteen thousand dollars."

I pretended to pat my shorts for my wallet. "Let me see if I have it on me." I forced a laugh.

Her businesslike expression didn't budge. "We can put you on a payment plan, but we do need a two-thousand-dollar deposit. And we'll need that up front."

Joke time was over. I was struck with the overwhelming urge to go home, bury myself under the covers, and go to sleep for a day or five. "We're small business owners. I don't have it", I said.

Her blank expression gave me the perfect opportunity to use her as a canvas on which I could hurl all my colorful neuroses. She thought I was a deadbeat. Irresponsible. Lower than low. Certainly not the type of person who would live in her respectable middle-class neighborhood, where people had money to cover their bills. She had no problems in her own life and saw me as a pathetic, hopeless figure, in an untouchable caste far removed from hers.

"This payment isn't negotiable, Mrs. Fulwiler", she finally said. "If you're sure you can't cover it, we may have to", she pursed her lips as she searched for the right words, "make other arrangements for your care."

My mind went into overdrive, thinking of anything I could pawn to come up with the money. I had a couple of ideas, but none that would get me the cash quickly enough. "There's no way I could get it now, but I might be able to have it by next week", I told her.

That seemed to be an acceptable answer. "That will be fine. You can deliver a check to me or mail it in. But if we don't have it by your next visit, your appointment will be canceled."

We were done. I grabbed my purse off the floor and put my foot down to walk out, but there was no way. I had to ask her for help. "Could you call a nurse? Not sure I can get out by myself."

"Oh, certainly." She hastily pressed a button on her phone and asked the receptionist to send a nurse to her office to help Mrs. Fulwiler. When she assured me that someone would be right here, I noticed pity in her voice. After a moment of painful silence, she asked me what gender the baby was.

"A girl", I said. "We also have a son who's almost two."

"How sweet." She smiled for the first time since I'd been in there. Glancing down at my leg, she added, "So I guess you're done now?"

On her desk sat a gold-framed portrait of two blonde, smartly dressed children, a boy and a girl, probably four years apart in age. They were smiling and healthy, with straight teeth and crisp clothes. My Neurotic ESP kicked into gear again, and I was certain that if I answered her question about being done with anything other than, "hand me that letter opener and I'll sever my own fallopian tubes right now", I would be deemed irresponsible and unworthy of respect. To preserve my dignity, I pretended to have a new surge pain in my leg that prevented me from answering.

The nurse came in and helped me to my feet. It was that same girl, who probably weighed as much as one of my thighs. When I first put my weight on her, I thought I saw her and the financial administrator exchange nervous glances. We made it out into the waiting area, and with each step I let out a deep groan, which completed the "wounded yeti" look nicely. When we walked by the check-in desk, people in line paused cell phone conversations to stare at us.

My mom jumped up from her seat in the waiting room, and the two of them basically carried me out to the car, the pain so bad I thought I might pass out.

Back at home I went straight to bed, as usual. After I had recovered from the pain, I fumbled around on my bedside table for a green note card with a long string of numbers on it. When I found it, I picked up the cordless phone and began dialing slowly, checking each digit to make sure it was right. For a few seconds there was only a crackling sound, then came the sounds that were like the tones you hear on a hearing test. Then, my dad's voice.

"Hey, did I wake you up?" I asked.

My dad had moved to Abu Dhabi the year before to manage the construction of a huge new airport. He had spent decades moving all over the country for work, and most of the jobs that I could remember left him stressed out and frustrated, sometimes bitterly disappointed. Before he left for Abu Dhabi he had been giddy with hope. "This could be the job I've been waiting for all my life!" he said the day before we took him to the airport. But things had already begun to go awry, and his dream job was turning out to be anything but. I knew from emails that his stress level was high, and the last thing I wanted to do was add to it. Unfortunately, I didn't have a choice.

We had been keeping him posted with regular emails about the status of the DVT, and so it wasn't a surprise when I told him that new complications had come up, this time involving finances. "We've been hit with a ton of medical bills this week ..." I began sheepishly. I hated asking for money. I decided to just spit it out. "I, uhh, find myself in need of about two thousand dollars."

"Of course." He didn't hesitate for a millisecond. "I can do an online transfer before I go to bed tonight."

"Here's the thing. I don't think I can pay you back. Certainly not any time soon."

"I don't care, Jen", he said, almost annoyed that I even brought it up. "There's nothing I can do for you guys out here on the other side of the world. It's frustrating. Helping you out with money is the one way I can give back."

I mumbled thanks, so overwhelmed by his generosity that I hardly knew how to respond.

He began to say something else, but the loud sound of a man singing filled the line, as if someone had picked up another phone in my dad's condo and began shouting Arabic tunes into it.

"The call to prayer speaker just came on!" my dad shouted. I could still barely hear him. "Hang on a sec!"

I always snickered at the fact that my atheist father managed to move into the one condo in his part of the building that had a call to prayer speaker installed on the balcony. "God's trying to get your attention!" I said when he could hear me again.

He laughed. "I keep telling my Muslim friends over here that a more authentic way to live their faith would be to have the call to prayer done the old way, with one guy shouting from the minaret."

Though he could have done without the speaker outside his window crackling to life multiple times per day, sometimes before five o'clock in the morning, my dad had developed a deep respect for Muslims since he'd been in Abu Dhabi. He regularly remarked on seeing business-men stop meetings to wash up for prayer time, and he was amazed that nobody ate or drank anything during daylight hours for Ramadan, even in the furnace-like heat.

"So, how is your religious stuff coming along?" he asked.

Though we didn't talk about it often, we'd had a few friendly debates over email, and he knew we were reading up on Catholicism. He thought my conclusions about God and Jesus were incorrect, of course, but he was more concerned about the thought process I used to arrive at them.

I forced a laugh. "Oh, it's great. It's causing a bunch of drama with my doctors and generally kind of messing up my life."

"Well ..." he thought for a moment. "Do you think it's true?"

His voice was distant and muffled by the eight thousand miles that separated us, but his question filled my mind as if it had been shouted by someone standing next to me. I was quiet for so long that he said hello to make sure we hadn't been disconnected.

"I'm here", I said, still thinking. After another second I answered, "I guess that's what I'm trying to figure out."

It's not easy, I almost added. But I stopped myself and wondered: *What am I really looking for? What is easy? Or what is true?*

29

We scheduled labor to be induced on a Monday in July, and the date couldn't arrive fast enough. I now spent most of my time in bed; when I needed to go to the bathroom, someone had to help me. We didn't have a television in our bedroom, so I divided my time between reading and staring at the wall, enumerating everything that could possibly go wrong during labor.

The Friday before the big day, Joe stayed downtown late to finish up a few things at the office. When he came home, he presented me with a bouquet of white and yellow flowers.

"What are these for?" I asked, giving them an obligatory smell.

He set the flowers on my nightstand and sat on the bed next to me. "I have some news that might cheer you up."

I raised my eyebrows. "This has all been a bad dream, and I don't have a DVT and a blood-clotting disorder?"

"You might like this better: I took a look at that Tarrytown house today. They had a contract fall through, and it's back on the market."

"Really? Did the realtor say they've had any interest?"

"I didn't meet with the realtor. I just walked around and checked it out. One of the windows was unlocked, and I tried to get in through there until the woman next door threatened to call the cops. It's a great house!"

I remembered the reality of our situation, and my heart deflated. "I guess it doesn't matter, though. With these medical bills, we're toast."

"Actually, I have good news there too: One of the reasons I stopped by the house is because it looks like we're going to land a big new client."

"Really?"

"Yeah. Right now I'm just doing basic documents for this local business, but they're about to start a complicated lawsuit against a bigger company and will probably ask me to handle that, too."

"Wow!" I said, pulling myself to a sitting position. "But I thought you wanted to get out of litigation because it's so high stress."

"It is, but how else are we going to get that house?" He patted me on the leg, making sure to hit the right one.

"Are you kidding? Wow. Wow!" For the first time in a while, I allowed myself to think about our life in that house. "We'll be right by the lake! And I can finally have all my clothes back. And—oh my gosh, I almost forgot about our bookshelves, those ones we had custom made! I still can't believe I accidentally put Donald's baby book in storage ..."

I would have expected Joe to jump in with me, throwing out his own thoughts on what would be so great about it, but he was silent. He smiled, but his expression was tinged with something else. Maybe he was just too excited to speak.

As I was talking, something clicked. The expression on Joe's face wasn't genuine excitement. It was happiness, but not his own. It was happiness for me.

* * *

The following Monday, baby Elaine was born. She had a full head of bright red hair, which made her quite the celebrity among the hospital staff. The labor induction went fine, and I was even able to get an epidural after the anesthesiologist spent about three hundred million hours going over my entire medical history with Dr. Wolfe.

Two weeks later, it was time to get to work. Now that we had decided to step up the law firm to bring in more money, that meant more work for everyone. Thanks to Coumadin, my leg had healed just enough that I was semi-mobile again, and so I could limp into my office to work, with newborn Elaine propped on a pillow in front of me.

Each morning my clock radio would crackle to life at seven o'clock, and each morning it felt like gravity had doubled overnight. Between the early rising and the baby's night feedings, I rarely got more than five hours of sleep in total. My mom kept asking me if I was okay, saying that I looked awfully pale. I explained that I was just busy, and promised to slow it down one of these days.

As the weeks living this punishing schedule wore on, it caused a problem that I had never seen coming: It made it difficult to learn about Natural Family Planning. Joe and I were kind-of-sort-of-mostly sold on the Catholic anti-contraception stuff. We still had questions, but we thought it was likely enough that the Church was right that we were willing to begin sort of following (or at least learning) its teachings.

Every day I tried to find time to read a book I'd ordered that taught women how to track their fertile symptoms, but my schedule was too packed with the demands that came with having a job and two young children. I had picked up enough to know that I should be tracking my temperature on a chart, but the points on my chart always looked like they had been chosen by a random number generator.

After a few months of this, I emailed a blog reader who had kindly answered a few of my Natural Family Planning questions in the past. I asked her if it was normal that my NFP chart would look like it depicted a Himalayan mountain range at this point postpartum.

She happened to be on email and responded right away. "The baby is only four months old; that's likely normal. Though since you mentioned that you had to supplement nursing with formula, you'll want to watch carefully for ovulation."

I snorted as I read. No kidding. The DVT hadn't completely dissolved yet, not to mention the fact that my doctors strongly recommended that I not have any more kids at all, let alone anytime soon.

Her name popped up in my inbox again. I expected a quick word of goodbye, but instead she asked, "Also, are you under any kind of stress that could contribute to weird readings? I know that my charts are always my first warning sign when I'm pushing myself too hard."

Hmm. I couldn't think of anything. Well, unless you counted the fact that I was waking up early each morning, working furiously for ten hours a day with a baby on my lap, driving my babysitter home, running around with my toddler for a bit, getting him ready for bed, getting the baby ready for bed (often by myself if Joe was still at work), going back to my desk and working until midnight, getting up with the baby three or four times a night—all while dealing with severe leg pain and being consumed with fear about whether or not we'd get this big client before the Tarrytown house sold—and starting it all again the next day. Other than that, I couldn't think of anything stressful that was going on.

She continued: "You can still do NFP if you are under stress, but you may need to check more symptoms to get a complete picture of what's going on."

"Oh come on", I muttered to the computer. That's what I needed. Since contraception was off the table and we hadn't figured out NFP yet, we'd decided to take no risks while I was on Coumadin. Now my last dose would occur in four weeks, meaning that we didn't have much time to figure out what to do about birth control before it would be an issue again. The good news is that it was amazing how quickly the months of being on this drug had gone by, but the bad news was that I had not had time to learn NFP. I thought I'd be able to scan the book a few times and pretty much have it down. Now this woman was telling me that I'd have to waste even more time tracking symptoms.

I closed my email and started work in a huff. I seethed with resentment. Some of it was directed at the hassle of NFP, but most of my anger was directed inwardly, at my own body.

I didn't want my body to have a voice; I didn't think it should get a vote. I wanted it to fall in line with whatever I felt like doing. I preferred to push and push and push myself and pretend like everything was going fine, and I resented this system that made me check in on how my choices were impacting my physical well-being.

I'd occasionally come across flowery hippie-talk about how Natural Family Planning was all about listening to your inner body-goddess as she speaks to you. I laughed every time I heard such nonsense. But, now that I considered it, I realized that my own message to my body was something along the lines of, "FALL IN LINE AND SHUT UP. YOU WILL DO WHAT I SAY OR I WILL FORCE YOU TO!" ... which wasn't all that inspiring either.

30

"There is cold for September", I told Irma on the way to her house. It was my best effort to comment on the unseasonably cool night in Spanish.

"*Sí, hace fresco*", she agreed.

I stepped on the gas to minimize the nightly struggle for conversation. Irma was a fascinating person, but our lives and backgrounds were so different. She had grown up in abject poverty in Mexico; I'd grown up in middle-class suburbs across the United States. She had six siblings; I had none. She was single; I was married. When my bad Spanish came into the mix, it left conversation exceedingly difficult. We had already agreed that Donald had done innumerable cute things that day, established that her family was all fine, and now only the road sounds filled the car.

We approached the bridge over McNeil Drive, and I pointed out her window. "Our new church is that way", I said. "We're taking classes there tonight." After I dropped her off I was going to meet Joe for the first session of the Rite of Christian Initiation for Adults at Saint William.

"My church is that way, too", she said.

I suddenly remembered that she and her family were Catholic. In fact, all my life I'd heard them discuss the goings on at *San Guillermo*, which means ... "Saint William? You go to Saint William? That's where we're going, too!"

At that moment it was as if a piggy bank containing an infinite wealth of topics for conversation was smashed. Its riches poured out in heaps, and now the problem was getting through it all before we got to her house. I eased my foot off the accelerator and moved into the right lane. I asked if she'd seen the stunning new building they were constructing down the street. She had, and we marveled at the priest's vision for creating a beautiful church that was large enough to house his thousands of parishioners. I told her a funny story about one of the deacons; she'd already heard about the incident and told me through bursts of laughter some additional information that made it even funnier. After we caught our breath, she repeated an insight that her aunt in Mexico had called to share about the Gospel reading from last Sunday's Mass. I told her that it reminded me of Pope Benedict's commentary in his homily, and as I spoke I was filled with a comforting sense of connectedness to know that every Catholic in the world heard the same Scriptures that we had that Sunday.

I parked the car along the curb in front of her house and locked the doors so we could finish talking. When I eventually had to cut the conversation short so I wouldn't be late for RCIA, I noticed that we'd been parked in front of the house for fifteen minutes.

* * *

"Does anyone have any questions before we wrap up?" asked Noe Rocha, the new RCIA director at Saint William. This was the man Janie Castillo had told us about the day that Joe discovered the Guadalupanas' breakfasts, and I could see why she'd praised him so highly. There was an aura about him that made you want to be in his presence. He was a Hispanic gentleman of a medium build, a neat white beard framing his tanned face. His movements had the confidence of a man who understood the world, yet contained not a hint of arrogance. He spoke in a direct, no-nonsense tone that was punctuated with frequent smiles.

This first class was the Inquiry, a millennia-old tradition where members of the Christian community would engage in dialogues with people wishing to know more about this religion. Those who wanted to continue would undergo the Rite of Acceptance, in which their ears, eyes, lips, and heart would be marked with the sign of the cross. Then would begin the Catechumenate, which was originally a time when seekers would enter the catacombs, learning the Faith by candlelight, using assumed names for safety. After that was the Rite of Election, when the catechumens would stand before the community and announce their desire to become Christians. After a period of purification during Lent, they would come into communion with the Church at Easter.

After a few announcements, Noe said he would conclude the meeting with his own testimony of what Jesus had done for him. I stretched my legs and snuck a peek at the time on my phone. Thirty minutes left. My mind was slipping further and further into an exhausted fog.

Noe took his place at the front of the room and began his tale. His arms were loose and animated as he spoke, the movements of a seasoned storyteller.

"This life of mine that you see now, it is a life profoundly changed by an encounter with the Lord", he began. He'd mentioned that he grew up along the Texas-Mexico border, and a slight Spanish accent clipped his words. He stepped into the aisle between the two rows of seats and made eye contact with all thirty of us before he continued, slowly: "It is possible for your life to change, once you live under the lordship of Jesus Christ."

Oh, boy. When Noe turned to the other side of the room I snuck a glance at Joe, who was intensely focused on the talk. I twisted to see the clock at the back of the room. Noe seemed like a great guy, but I wished we could skip this. He couldn't possibly have that much of a story to tell. He seemed so grounded and devout, I couldn't imagine that he'd missed church more than a handful of times in his entire life. I might like to hear about his journey one day, but right now I was too tired.

"When I was younger, I messed up", Noe began. There was an almost imperceptible tremor in his voice as he added, "I messed up real bad. I got into drugs. My cousin and I would run around, get thrown in jail, cause trouble, then do more drugs. Then I discovered heroin. I became a dealer. And at the age of twenty-eight, after fifteen years of this lifestyle, I ended up in a mental hospital."

Joe and I exchanged startled glances. Noe walked to the front of the room, and I studied the kind, open face of this man whose reputation for kindness and holiness preceded him even before he moved here. I couldn't attribute the term "border-town heroin dealer" to that face.

"They put me on methadone for five and a half years—five and a half! But it didn't work." A beat of silence as he considered his next sentence. "And one morning I was brought into a counselor's office. The counselor looked at my file, which was about three inches thick, and then he looked right at me, and he said: 'There is no hope for you.'" He delivered each word of the last sentence carefully, capturing the weight they once held. *There. Is. No. Hope. For. You.* His liver had malfunctioned twice, he forgot entire days at a time, and he was still strung out on drugs after five years of methadone. It was a simple fact, the counselor explained, that he would be dead or doing life within a year.

Noe got out of the mental facility only to have two drug deals go bad and to rack up multiple felony charges. While on the run from the law he went back to his parents' home, where he lay in bed, becoming increasingly desperate from the symptoms of withdrawal. Then he remembered that he'd seen a new Catholic church next door. He got out of bed, pulled on his boots, and walked over.

His plan was to con the parish's stubborn Irish priest out of fifteen dollars to buy a half gram. But when he arrived in the chair across from the priest's desk, the words wouldn't come out. Instead, he admitted that he was a drug dealer and a drug addict. With his sunglasses on and his head spinning from the symptoms of withdrawal, the words flooded out so quickly he couldn't stop them. By the end, he'd told the priest every bad thing he'd done that he could remember.

The priest was unflustered. He didn't seem horrified, or even surprised. In a moment that Noe imitated by leaning over an RCIA candidate in the front row, the priest calmly rose from his chair, walked over to Noe, lowered himself until he was inches away from his face, and said: "Noe. I'm not going to tell you that Jesus has all the answers. He is your *only* answer."

Noe stood and resumed his place at the front of the room. "And I thought, *That's just lies. I ain't gonna buy that*", he said. When he spoke in his voice from thirty years before, I got a chill. He flawlessly employed a particular kind of Mexican-American accent, a ghostly whisper where the *s*'s are drawn out like a hiss, that I'd only ever heard on documentaries about maximum-security prisons.

At the priest's suggestion, Noe reluctantly attended a church meeting where people laid hands on him and prayed for him. When he got home, he asked his parents for help, and his father pulled together enough money to rent a motel room for a week—one with bars on the windows so there would be no escape. For three days and three nights Noe didn't eat anything and hardly had a sip to drink. As he suffered through the agony of withdrawal, people came by to pray, and the priest came to anoint him with oil. While he writhed in bed, his dad sat in the kitchen, waiting.

"And on the third night, God called me by name", he said. "And he said, 'Look over there.'" Noe turned his head slowly to reenact the moment. "There was my father, on the floor." His father had gone to sleep on the cold ground in front of the door, so that he'd know if his son tried to escape.

"And the voice said: 'Look at how much that man loves you. I love you a million times more than that man lying on the floor does. Because you're my son.'"

Noe's voice grew quiet. "I cried all night—sobbed. I woke up the next morning. My pillow was wet from tears. And I realized that my cravings—they were gone. It was November 11, 1976. I have never craved heroin again."

Nobody moved. The only sound was the whistle of a train that rumbled by a few blocks away.

Noe said that the moment when God healed him of his addiction ignited within him a desperate desire to find and know this God who said he was his father. At first he was still an unemployed drug dealer, so he would sit in the hallway outside of children's First Communion classes, eavesdropping to soak up whatever he could learn. He eventually dedicated his life to being a missionary and spent the next thirty years proclaiming the same message he was here to deliver to us today:

"Jesus *is* alive", he said, searching each one of us so that we might understand. His voice cracked as he continued. "And he *cares*. And he has the *power* to give new life to everyone who wants it."

A hot tightness gripped my throat. Joe wiped a tear from his eye.

At the end of the evening, Noe walked all of us to the exit where he stood with his arms wide, ready for any hands that needed shaking or backs that needed slapping. We were the last to leave. He had simply said goodbye to everyone else, but as he shook Joe's hand, he looked from him to me and asked, "Joe, Jennifer, how is your journey to the Lord going?" I glanced self-consciously at my leg, wondering if my noticeable limp had prompted him to ask.

"It's going well!" Joe said.

Noe turned to me. "Oh, yeah, it's fine", I said. "Well, I mean, there are some challenges. Sometimes it feels like a lot ..." I could tell that I was about to start crying and talking about how much I was working and how confused I was about this contraception issue and how my doctors said I shouldn't have any more kids. So I shut down that whole line of thinking and forced myself to add, "But I'm sure it'll all work out. Everything is fine." I'd hoped my tone wouldn't make it so obvious that I was lying.

Noe's brown eyes met mine, with no hesitation. He gently patted me on the back and said, "Remember, Jennifer, you're not doing this alone."

31

"Happy thirtieth birthday!" Joe said as he accelerated onto the highway. "How long has it been since we've been to It's Italian? At least six months, right? Before Elaine was born?"

I was silent. I hadn't even remembered that we were going there. I was consumed by one thought and one thought only, and I knew Joe would be also as soon as he heard. The only question was whether I should tell him now or wait until we were in the restaurant.

Joe eased the car to a stop in a parking place in front of the restaurant. As I stepped out onto the sidewalk it occurred to me that there might be a line of people waiting for tables, in which case it would be difficult to have a private conversation until we got seated. I needed to tell him now. I grabbed Joe by the sleeve of his leather jacket just before he got to the restaurant. "There's something we need to talk about tonight."

He stiffened, not sure whether to open the door. He twisted his wrist to look at his watch, then glanced over his shoulder. "Do we have to talk about it now?"

I motioned toward the door, "Let's get inside first."

Joe stopped in front of me, blocking the entrance. "It's really fine. Why don't we just stand out here and chat before we go in?"

I walked around him and reached for the door handle. "No, I want to sit."

He jogged to catch up with me. "I think we should—"

"I'm pregnant", I interrupted.

We both froze. He had a look on his face, but it wasn't the sheer surprise or horror I'd expected. Rather, it was some odd mix of hesitation and confusion. He leaned forward to peer inside the dark interior of the main room, then looked back at me. He started to say something, but I pulled the door the rest of the way open and stepped inside.

A long table directly in front of the door was filled with a large group of people. They were all staring at me. Within a second, they morphed from a group of strangers to people I knew, their faces becoming familiar one by one. Irma and her daughter. Our old neighbor from downtown. My best friend from high school and her husband. Two friends who had been coworkers back in my high-tech days and their boyfriends. An employee from the firm. And a couple we had recently met at Saint William.

They all got to their feet, some throwing their arms in the air, some clapping, and everyone simultaneously exclaimed, "*Surprise!*"

I turned to Joe, because I needed confirmation that this was really happening.

He looked like he was in a daze. "It's a surprise party."

I zombie-walked over to the group, reminding myself to move my facial muscles in a way that resembled a smile, and I settled into an empty chair. I found myself in the middle of a checkerboard of social awkwardness, unable to apply the usual remedy of multiple glasses of wine downed in short succession. Our employee learned from the Saint William couple that we were considering converting to Catholicism. Irma learned from our old neighbor downtown that we were almost arrested following our infamous Hip Hop Karaoke party (and he, unfortunately, spoke Spanish so flawlessly that he knew how to say "forty-ounce malt liquor" and "drinking contest" in her native tongue). And our Saint William friends learned from the gals I used to work with that the f-word could be not only a verb, but also a noun, and, after enough glasses of wine, can even be shouted across a restaurant as an adjective.

Two hours into the dinner, one of our old friends attempted to tell the story of the time Joe punched a French guy while watching a heated soccer match at a pub. It was actually a pretty funny tale that included the exchange of witty barbs and ended with Joe and the guy buying beers for one another, but the way our friend conveyed it made it seem like Joe was an anti-French madman who was out for blood. By the time the story skidded to a halt, everyone was staring at their glasses in silence. Unable to bear the awkwardness for a moment longer, I excused myself to go to the bathroom. The hallway door opened and closed behind me, and I turned to see that Joe had followed me. Neither of us spoke; there were no words that could possibly address this situation, which was like something out of a bad sitcom. We looked at one another in awed silence, then simultaneously burst into laughter.

* * *

We shut down the restaurant, one of our friends carrying a half-full bottle of wine out the door with her, holding it up to wave at Irma and the Saint William couple as she left. Joe and I rushed to the car to get out of the chilly January air. He started the engine but left it in park.

"So ... wow", he said. "Are you sure you're pregnant?"

"I took three tests."

"Are we okay on the Coumadin thing?"

"Yes, thankfully." That was the one bit of good news: My treatment was finished. It was a tremendous relief not to have to worry about the potentially heinous consequences that could have come with a Coumadin pregnancy.

Joe smirked, as if he'd just had an amusing thought. "I guess we might need to actually learn Natural Family Planning now."

I grunted in response, and he reached over and play-punched me in the arm. "Well, congratulations!"

"If I didn't know better, I'd think you were honestly excited."

"I am. A baby. That's great!"

I cocked my head in disbelief. "A baby! ... And no insurance! Another $10K on top of the medical bills that were already killing us! And more shots in the stomach! It's all great!"

"God will work it out", he said.

At first I didn't think I heard him correctly. "Did you just tell me that God is going to work it out?" I did believe that God was real now; I just didn't know that we were going to *act* like God was real.

"Yeah, of course", he said. "I mean, do you think that what the Church teaches is guided by God?"

"I guess I'm starting to think that it could be. Why?"

"Do you think God would hand down a set of rules for people to follow that would be bad for them?"

I held out my arms and pointed back to myself as Exhibit A. "Evidently, yes."

"Yeah, but you've been following the rules as part of an intellectual investigation. Are you seeking God like he's a person, or like he's a concept?"

A concept, of course. Until now it had never occurred to me that there was any other way. "Next you're going to ask if I've made Jesus the lordship of my life", I joked.

196

"The Lord of your life", he clarified. But he didn't seem amused by my comment and instead looked at me without a trace of irony. "So, yeah, where are you on that?"

My husband—Joe Fulwiler—wanted to know if I had made Jesus the Lord of my life. And I had thought that the evening couldn't get any more surreal. Not knowing what else to say, I shot the question back to him. "Have *you*?"

Joe started to respond, but the last of the employees emerged from the darkened restaurant, and we exchanged waves as they passed in front of the car on the way to their vehicles. Then Joe fell into silence. After a full minute, he spoke. "About a week ago I was lying in bed, tossing and turning, sweating, couldn't sleep—that's never happened to me before. I've never been that stressed. I was thinking, *Is Amos Adler going to find a way to get me disbarred in the Jaworski case? Are we going to be broke forever?*"

The car, the restaurant, the parking lot, and everything else receded as I focused only on what Joe was saying.

"I was half-asleep, and I heard this tone that lasted for about five seconds. And you know how dreams don't make sense? Well, somehow I just knew at that moment that the high-pitched tone was my name, being spoken to me by God."

"What?" I said the word as a gasp. Joe never talked like this. Never.

He thought for a moment. The inside of the car was so still, I could hear him breathing. "It's like I was being called. I was in God's presence, like when I was baptized. I knew that God could see everything about me, everything I had ever done. It was terrifying, and there was a moment when I felt like I had a choice. I could run away. But I decided to stay, even though I felt incredibly scared. And then I realized I was awake, and I just lay there like that for an hour or two. I was calm. My problems didn't seem to matter anymore. I felt at peace—truly, deeply at peace."

I felt like a more spiritually mature person would understand the significance of this moment. "So ... did God, you know, tell you anything?"

"No, that was it. Then, when we went to Mass at Saint William's, the priest did that thing where he says 'Peace be with you' and holds out his hands like an offering to the congregation. When he turned toward me, I physically felt a wave hit me in the chest. And I relaxed. I just sort of ... let go."

"That's great. It really is", I said. "And maybe that was God calling out to you that night—I could believe that. But the truth is that people who follow him have crappy lives all the time."

He snapped out of his daze. "Oh, well, if you mean that they'll have a bunch of tough things happen to them, sure. Do you remember what Noe said they do to Inquirers at the Rite of Acceptance?"

"Not really."

"They mark them with the sign of the cross. The sponsors trace a cross over their eyes, their ears, their lips, their heart, their shoulders, and their hands and feet. It's to prepare them that the cross will touch every part of their lives."

"What?" My face contorted into a frown. "Well, that sounds horrible. Where do I sign up to have more misery in my life?"

"No. I said 'suffering', not 'misery'."

"Same thing."

"But it's not!" Joe said, an urgency behind his voice. "That's Christianity's whole message: The more you love, the more you're going to have to give up—you can't hold anything back. And that's going to mean suffering. But it's also going to mean joy and peace."

I stared at my hands. "I've been doing this Christianity thing for months now, and I think I have *less* joy and peace than I used to."

"But are you really putting God first?"

I didn't answer.

"We might go broke, or have to live with your mom for another decade, or whatever. It probably won't be easy. But we'll have peace."

I stared at him, searching his face for the smile that would accompany the punchline to this dry joke, but it didn't come. In his eyes was a gentleness, a bottomless vulnerability that I had never seen before.

32

"Hi, this is Jennifer Fulwiler. Could I get Dr. Wolfe to call in a new round of Lovenox for me? I'm ... well, I'm pregnant."

A rustling sound filled the line as the nurse fumbled with the phone. "Mrs. Fulwiler? I'm sorry, I'm confused, it says here that you already had the baby."

"I did. This is, umm, another one."

She told me to hold while she got my chart, and when she came back she mumbled a few details about my medical history and asked, "You have Factor II, right? Homozygous?"

"Right. Dr. Wolfe said that I should call him right away if I ever became pregnant." Well, technically he told me I shouldn't have more kids at all, but he did mention that in the crazy event that I found myself pregnant, I should call him right away.

"Hang on, please." After another round of light jazz hold music, she came back on the line. "Dr. Wolfe wants to see you right away. Can you come in today?"

I switched a sleepy baby Elaine to my left arm so I could type, and I pulled up my calendar. "I could do anything before noon", I said.

She booked it and told me that he would call in a prescription right now so that I could start giving myself the shots immediately.

I grabbed my purse and headed out for what I thought would be an uneventful visit to the pharmacy. A girl in a white technician's coat rang up the medicine while I worked up some good dread for the trip to Dr. Wolfe's office. She announced the total, and I handed her my card. Just before she grabbed it, the number she had just given me registered in my brain. I pulled back the card.

"Nine hundred and twenty eight dollars? Is that what you said? So my insurance doesn't cover it?"

She glanced nervously at the computer screen in front of her. "No, your insurance does cover it. That's your portion."

"How many shots does that get me?"

"Your doctor called in a thirty-day supply."

I felt dizzy. "I want to make sure I understand you correctly: You are telling me that this medicine I need is going to cost me nine hundred dollars a month for the next nine months?"

"Yes, ma'am."

I told her to put the medicine back and sat down on the bench at the blood pressure station to call Joe. As the phone rang, it occurred to me that I'd probably set off some sort of siren if I were to use it to check my vitals right now.

"Do you have any idea what Lovenox costs?" I hissed as soon as he came to the phone.

"Yeah, I did", he said. "But last time it wasn't so bad because we only needed one month's worth, and they threw in some samples to help with the cost."

"Well, now we're looking at almost a thousand dollars a month for the next nine months, in addition to paying for a high-risk pregnancy and hospital birth out of pocket. What are we going to do about that?" Before he could respond, I jumped in to add, "And don't say God's going to work it out."

He laughed. "Is there any other solution?"

* * *

When Dr. Wolfe glided into the room, I became acutely aware that I looked like a slob. I'd been in such a rush to get to the pharmacy before this appointment that I hadn't brushed my hair or put on makeup. For that matter, I also hadn't changed out of the sweatshirt that had a crusty spit-up stain running down the shoulder.

He sat down on the rolling stool, looking tanned and refreshed, as if he'd just come back from a Caribbean vacation. "Did my nurse take this message right that you're expecting again?"

It seemed like there should be a better answer than just "yes". But that's all I could come up with.

"How old is the last baby?"

"Almost six months."

"Wow, okay", he said, and I tried not to imagine what he might be writing on my chart. "You've started taking the Lovenox, right?"

"No. I can't afford it." I didn't even try not to sound pathetic and defeated.

"There really aren't any reliable alternatives to Lovenox that are any cheaper. Is there something you can do about that?"

"I'm working on it."

"Well, you should have already been taking it. Call me tomorrow if you still haven't gotten it covered." He flipped to the next page and read for a moment. I passed the time by imagining that he might be reading a page titled: How to Ruin Jen's Day.

He turned his attention back to me and said expectantly, "Contraception."

"What's that?" I joked.

He smiled and looked at me with genuine sympathy. "Okay, last time you didn't give an answer about what the plan was. I think it's safe to say that whatever it was isn't effective. Now it's time to get serious."

"Okay, I'll think about it", I said. My arms were folded, and my legs were crossed, my knees pointing to the door. It was the sort of body language usually only seen by prisoners in interrogation rooms.

"After this baby I want to talk about you taking Coumadin on a longer basis, and obviously you'll have to find something reliable before then. There's also the issue of your health—each pregnancy is putting you at risk."

It was tempting to lay out all the details of my failed attempts to learn Natural Family Planning. It would be embarrassing, but not as embarrassing as his current perception that I had evaluated my condition as a broke slob with a pregnancy-exacerbated blood disorder and decided that this would be the perfect time to have another baby.

"I just need a little more time."

Dr. Wolfe fidgeted. "We'll set you up with another appointment for two weeks from now. But you really need to decide by then. I know you have a while before it'll be an issue, but we need to start making plans to keep you healthy over the long term."

"Okay. I'll have an answer in two weeks."

I drove back to the house, numb from anxiety burnout, and when I got home I could hear the baby's cries from out in the driveway. I opened the door to an explosion of sound. Irma paced around the kitchen, whispering and cooing at Elaine. Dr. Wolfe's office had a strict "no children" policy because some patients had compromised immune systems, which made my appointments all the more difficult since I had to arrange child care every time.

Elaine was turning out to be what some parenting experts called a "high needs" baby, meaning that Joe received a lot of phone calls in which I screamed that I was going to be dead by the time he got home if this child did not stop crying all the time. Irma gave me a sympathetic look as I scooped Elaine out of her arms and took her into my office with me.

I laid her on my lap, gave her fluffy red hair a kiss, and implored her to be extra quiet for just a little while. The Jaworski case had finally settled. Because of the blurry lines of the fake business partnership, the con artist Eric Rayburne didn't face jail time; he was ordered to give Mr. Jaworski a monetary repayment, though he had so little money left that everyone knew Jaworski would probably never see a dime of it. It was beyond frustrating to see Rayburne get off so easily, but Mr. Jaworski seemed at peace. He stopped by the office one time when I happened to be there, looked at me with his soft, watery eyes, and told me what a difference it made to him that someone stood up for him. I wiped a tear out of the corner of my eye and wondered how I could have ever questioned whether we should've taken that case.

Unfortunately, now we faced a backlog of work that had been put off over the months we were focused on Mr. Jaworski, in addition to the flood of tasks that came with revamping the firm to bring in more money. The most urgent project was a password-protected area of the website where our clients could upload and retrieve documents. It required intensive coding, and now I was behind deadline. First I said we'd have it at the end of the previous week, then that got pushed to this morning.

Elaine wiggled on her pillow and grunted in displeasure, grabbing my hair and yanking on it as I typed. There was one function in particular that was snagging the whole program. No matter what I did, every time I loaded the page it said, *Error on line 156.* I rewrote the line. *Error on line 156.* I rewrote the lines of code before and after it. *Error on line 156.* I rewrote the entire function. *Error on line 156.* Now I resorted to shouting directly at the monitor, calling my computer a liar and defending the immaculate honor of line 156.

There was only an hour before the end of the business day. More than a few clients were waiting on this feature going live, and these delays were putting me behind deadline on other projects. Feeling panic inflate within me, I cut away a couple dozen lines of code to paste into a backup file and started the section from scratch. I copied in snippets from other pages, but wrote most of it by hand, with Elaine growing more and more discontented with every line.

"Shhhhh, just a second", I soothed, not taking my eyes off the monitor. "Mommy's almost done." She arched her back and grunted in displeasure, becoming an angry, squirming ball of muscle. "Ooooone more second", I cooed, finishing one of the last four lines of code.

I removed my hands from the keyboard to adjust her to a more comfortable position, and at that exact moment her strong, chubby arm slammed onto the keyboard. The code screen disappeared. I stared at my naked computer desktop, not daring to think where my work might have gone.

When I reopened the program, I saw half my work. The code stopped at a line I'd written half an hour before. Elaine had managed to hit just the right place to enter a keyboard shortcut—utterly unnecessary and obviously created by an evildoing madman—that would close your work without saving it.

I went to pull up the backup code I'd cut out earlier, but realized that I'd been so focused on getting to the new program that I'd forgotten to save it. I looked at the clock just as Elaine's cries reached an eardrum-rattling crescendo. End of the day.

I stood up and paced the room with the baby tucked in the crook of my left arm, using my right hand to call Joe. Voicemail.

The baby's cries lessened enough that I was pretty sure I heard the beep. "Joe? If you can hear me, we have a problem. A big problem. I lost the code—" Elaine's crying now ratcheted up to DEFCON 2, and I couldn't even hear myself talk. "I AM CALLING TO SAY THAT WE ARE TOTALLY SCREWED! THERE WILL BE NO DOC UPLOAD FUNCTION ON THE WEBSITE TODAY! MAYBE NOT EVER!!"

I turned off the phone and threw it against the wall, then ran outside with Elaine before she interrupted my mom's work. As I paced the brick-paved front porch, each step triggered a surge of pain in my right leg. The pregnancy had made my blood thicken again, and without the Lovenox I could feel it pooling at the damaged part of the vein.

Elaine finally drifted off in my arms, and I went back inside. As soon as I slid her into her crib, I went back to my desk. I couldn't hit the end-of-business deadline, but I could at least have it ready by the next day.

A tap at the door behind me interrupted my thoughts. I whipped my head around to see what Irma needed; instead of her face, it was Joe's. I checked the clock on my computer screen. "What's going on? It's only five o'clock. What are you doing home?"

"I got your voicemail." He took a seat on the twin bed behind my desk.

"I know. Look. I tried to get it to work, but this stupid line—"

"You can relax", he said. "The firm is doing great. That functionality on the website is not going to make or break us. We've added a bunch of new clients, and I actually have more work than I can handle."

"Oh, wow! That's great!" Hope rose within me. "So you came home early to tell me we can get the house?"

"Well, that's still an option." He leaned forward on his knees and clasped his hands. "But there's another option on the table."

"What do you mean? Another option for what?"

He drew in a long breath, and I could tell he thought that what he was about to say was going to make me mad. "I've been talking to another attorney in the building, who has a family-owned firm that's been around for sixty years. He's a great guy, and he's helped me a lot. He needs another lawyer to work for him, a low-level gig, not a partner or anything."

"One of our guys is going to leave?"

"No", he said, waiting for me to understand. "No, I was thinking . . . I was thinking that I might take it."

"You're not serious, are you?"

He held up his hands. "Hear me out: It wouldn't be a lot of money, but it would be a steady paycheck. I would only have to work fifty hours a week and could probably get it down to forty. And we'd have health insurance."

I recoiled into my desk chair. "It sounds like you've already been talking to him."

"I have. He needs to fill the position soon, and I told him I'd let him know by next week."

I stuttered as I asked for details about the salary and then stuttered again when I heard what it was. "That's less than I used to make as a web designer! We'll never get the house with that!"

"I know. It would mean that the house is out."

The news hit me like it had been delivered by taser. "It would mean that moving anywhere in central Austin is out altogether!"

Joe nodded. "You're right. And we couldn't afford Irma either. But you wouldn't have to keep killing yourself with all this administrative work. His firm has people that are awesome at billing, bookkeeping, all that stuff. I could get home before the kids went to bed each night. I think it would be a lot better for our spiritual lives, too."

"I don't see why we can't own a business. Plenty of religious people own businesses."

"I'm not saying that owning a business is objectively bad. I'm saying that I don't think it's where God wants us right now."

I barely heard him. "But I thought that Fulwiler Law was what you'd been waiting for all your life! I thought this was your big dream!" I said, my voice sounding more pleading than I'd meant for it to.

"It was. It's not now. I don't care about being king of the world anymore." He rolled his eyes at the word *king*. "I no longer see the point in working myself to death so that I can become rich and powerful."

"You just landed a bunch of clients. It's all working. It wouldn't bother you to walk away from what you've always wanted, just when you finally got it?"

"No, it wouldn't", he replied. And I knew by the look on his face that he meant it.

"Is this a done deal?" I asked.

"No. If you really still want us to have the law firm, we can keep it."

"I can't believe we're even having this discussion."

Joe grabbed one of my business cards from the desk, which had been half-hidden under a pile of code printouts. He held it up, and I looked at my name under the glossy veneer, next to the elegant logo that said Fulwiler Law. "Do you think that this is what's going to make you happy?"

"Having business cards? No." Before he could retort, I continued: "I know what you mean, though. And no, I didn't think that owning a business was going to make everything perfect. But moving back to central Austin? Throwing parties with Clifford Antone? Having a house by the lake? When you put all that together with owning a thriving business … yeah. Yeah, I do think that would make us happy."

"So you want me to turn down this other job?"

I massaged my aching forehead. "I don't know. I don't know anything right now. Can I think about it?"

"Sure. But we need to decide by next week."

33

I couldn't sleep. My skin was warm and nausea gnawed at my stomach, though I couldn't tell if it was from morning sickness or actual sickness.

I eased myself out of bed and drifted into my office, searching for answers to ... everything. Dr. Wolfe needed a decision about contraception. Joe needed a decision about shutting down the firm. And I had nothing but a hairy mess of questions. The whole theory with this Church was that following its doctrines was supposed to be a good thing. Supposedly, God gave those rules to us as a prescription for a great life, not as a bunch of happiness-killing restrictions. In fact, if any of the rules were actively bad, then it could safely be said that they must not have come from God in the first place. As I hobbled around, pregnant, my limp growing worse every day I was without Lovenox, I wondered if I had stupidly brought all this on myself by falling for a totally bunk belief system.

I settled into the chair in front of my keyboard and listlessly typed in search terms like *Catholic Coumadin birth control*, only to discover that evidently I was the first person in the history of mankind to struggle with this dilemma. Or maybe the second. Finally, I found one message board where a woman named Linda shared my struggle. She wrote in a medical forum that she was Catholic, she'd been told she had to take Coumadin, and she was struggling with the issue of contraception.

The responses seethed with indignation. Commenters pitied her that she would even consider letting the Catholic hierarchy talk her into such a dangerous and unreasonable move as rejecting contraception while on Coumadin. "I'd like to see what a priest would say about those rules if he was in your situation!" one respondent wrote. He identified himself as an ex-Catholic and briefly shared his own journey of throwing off the ball and chain of the Church's dogma and experiencing the freedom of being able to make his own rules.

Two more people wrote in to echo the first gentleman's thoughts, assuring Linda that there was absolutely nothing wrong with contraception.

One person even expressed an empathy with the well-meaning but ultimately misguided rules of the Church, and explained to Linda that surely even the Vatican would agree that her dire need to avoid pregnancy made her the exception to the rule. "Ultimately, you must be in control of your own body", she said in the conclusion of her note.

Linda thanked them for their advice and implied that she was going to go ahead and use contraception. That was the last post on the screen.

I was jealous of Linda, that things had worked out so easily for her. I re-read the commenters' points: If you absolutely can't have a baby, unless you're a grand wizard of Natural Family Planning, contraception is the only reasonable option. *Ultimately, you must be in control of your own body.* That made sense, right? Yes, surely it did. Yet, oddly, I couldn't get the concept to settle in my mind. Something troubled me about it, even though I couldn't articulate what it was.

At the bottom of the screen, I noticed a link to a second page of the discussion. I clicked on it, and it opened a continuation of the comments, the top note dated a few months after the ones on the first page. Linda was back, this time with a much more urgent tone. "Our contraception failed. I think I'm pregnant. Don't know for sure, but we're freaking out. Begging you for any help you can give me." She copied and pasted some information she'd found about the kind of hideous birth defects Coumadin can cause, asked if anyone knew how soon she could find out if the baby was okay. She ended with a desperate plea for prayers.

In a note dated a week later, the woman who had originally replied and told her she had to be in control of her own body responded again. This time she said she was sorry to hear it and then casually remarked, "You'll probably have to have an abortion." The thread ended there.

I leaned forward, pulled the keyboard close, and searched for a response from Linda. I clicked frantically to see if I could find a way to contact her to offer her words of support, even though whatever decision she made had long since passed. My face grew red as my fingers darted back and forth over the keys. I searched on her username and the word *Coumadin* in case she'd posted in other forums, did an advanced search within this forum to check for her in other threads. Nothing.

Finally I gave up and lifted my hands from the keyboard as if it were covered in toxic waste. I glared into the darkness behind the laptop monitor, aflame with indignation at what I had just witnessed. Something terrible had happened to this woman. I couldn't pinpoint what it was, but I knew that she had been sold a lie.

Memories of my past year pondering the issue of women's reproductive freedom reeled through my mind: shouting about Catholic teaching on abortion on the lawn of that first church we visited; seeing the rose/weed poster at Saint William; avoiding Dr. Wolfe's questions about contraception; reading *Stenberg v. Carhart*; seeing this exchange with Linda and the people in the forum.

And then...

Everything coalesced.

I dashed out some searches to make sure I was remembering something correctly, and I stared in disbelief when I found the data I was looking for: According to the Guttmacher Institute, more than half of women who had abortions had been using contraception when they conceived. Of those, fewer than 15 percent had been using it correctly. Given that there were over a million abortions that year, that meant that an incredibly large number of women had not found their contraception to be effective.

There were only two possible takes: The problem was with women, or the problem was with contraception.

I spent hours researching and thinking, so focused on my work that I became as alert as if it were noon. At some point I stopped, probably not long before sunrise, and I considered what I'd found.

Every society must create two critical moral lists: conditions under which it's acceptable to have sex, and conditions under which it's acceptable to have a baby. And in almost every culture from the beginning of time, the two lists were identical. The details of what rules the lists contained may have varied according to social customs, but the one thing almost every civilization had in common was that its two lists matched.

When contraception became widely used, it caused an unprecedented upheaval in which, for one of the first times in human history, the lists no longer matched. Women—like Linda on the message board—had effectively been told: "Having a baby right now would ruin your life? Go ahead and participate in the act that creates babies anyway." She had been given one set of rules for the conditions under which it was okay to have sex ("you can do that while you're on Coumadin"), and another for when it would be okay to have a baby ("you *cannot* do that while you're on Coumadin"). Then she found out she was pregnant.

But as someone taking an FDA Category X drug, she did not meet the conditions on the list of acceptable conditions to have a baby. Abortion suddenly seemed like a necessity, and she'd been left without a choice.

Having a baby right now would ruin your life? Go ahead and participate in the act that creates babies anyway.

One Guttmacher publication estimated that a woman using contraception with a 1 percent risk of failure over a ten-year period has a 70 percent chance of experiencing an unexpected pregnancy. I read it and re-read it, and as I moved my eyes across the screen, something within me shifted. It was as if, all my life, I'd been jamming puzzle pieces together, noticing that they didn't quite fit, seeing that the image they created was jagged and random, yet I kept them there because I thought that's how you were supposed to do it. And now, for the first time, I took them, pulled them apart, and put them back together a different way. A whole new puzzle came together, and this one looked right.

The two pillars upon which my entire view of reproductive freedom rested were the idea that women must have control over their bodies, and the idea that, through contraception, it is possible to sever sex from its life-giving potential. I still believed in the first pillar—more strongly than ever, in fact. But the second pillar had been shaking, and now it crumbled.

The people of my generation were taught that sex was only about the two people involved, that babies were a completely optional aspect of the act. In fact, the idea of nurturing children had become anathema to the idea of sexuality. The pop culture depictions of sex could not have been further removed from images of diapers and car seats and cribs.

It took my breath away—literally, I gasped for air—when I realized that this was why I had felt like I still had to support abortion, even after I saw our babies kick on the ultrasound screens, even after the sickening madness that was *Stenberg v. Carhart*. As long as I accepted it as axiomatically true that it's possible fully to separate the sexual act from its potential for life-changing consequences, abortion had to be okay. People were assured that they could engage in sex without it being a big deal, as long as they used contraception. Yet the astronomically high actual-use contraception failure rates posed a problem for the "no big deal" promise—after all, having a baby is just about the biggest deal ever. One solution was to get rid of the message that it's fine to have sex when you're absolutely opposed to having a baby, but nobody except

Catholics was interested in that. The only other solution was to get rid of the babies.

I lowered my head, remembering all my friends who'd ended up in abortion clinics. Every single one of them had been using contraception when they'd gotten pregnant. They felt stupid. They blamed themselves. They thought they'd been doing the right thing, being "safe", following all the rules of a society that had assured them that it would be fine to have sex, even if they were in no position to become mothers. And then human error got into the mix—as it always does, especially with something as emotionally fraught as sex—and things didn't go as planned. And they found themselves signing checks made out to an abortion clinic, feeling like they had no other choice.

All that my generation knew about human sexuality had been founded on a lie. They had been told that there was no need to give a second thought to parenthood when they engaged in sex; they were encouraged to think of sex as being primarily about their own pleasure. It was a lie that put women at war not only with their own bodies, but with their children.

I thought of that poster of the rose and the weed that I'd seen that morning back at Saint William. I got it now. Catholicism didn't teach that people had to try to have a baby with each sexual act, but it did say that it's a grave disrespect to both human sexuality and human life to try to sever the connection between the two. It connected contraception not only to abortion but also to homicide and euthanasia because it saw that a society can only respect human life to the extent that it respects the act that creates human life. Once a society determines that inconvenient life that results from sexual activity can be extinguished, it won't stop there. All inconvenient life must go.

The Church had been warning people for decades that they misunderstood this most fundamental human act and predicted this error would be bad news for us all. And the Church was right. Accepting contraception was similar to a society declaring that loaded guns are okay to use as toys as long as you put blanks in the chamber. Maybe not every single person who used loaded guns as playthings would have an accident; it might work out just fine for some folks. But that wouldn't make it true that loaded guns are toys. And if the lie spread widely enough, tragedy on a gigantic scale would result, as it must any time an entire civilization misunderstands the nature of something with tremendous power.

I stood and paced the darkened room, shaking my head and muttering. Then I stopped, freezing in place as I considered what I had just been spared. I had considered using contraception while on Coumadin, which would have made it tempting to believe the lie that we were "safe" from pregnancy. I imagined being in Linda's position, having something go wrong, then, two weeks later, seeing the two blue lines on the test strip, hands shaking as I calculated how long the baby had been exposed to the drug. It could have been me.

And the only reason it wasn't—the only reason I had actually clued in the obvious-sounding but little-known truth that if it really is that dire that you not have a baby, you need to avoid the act that creates babies—was because I'd been living according to the rules of the Catholic Church.

These rules—the moral guidelines that I once railed against—had just saved me from potential disaster.

34

I took the long route to the pharmacy, swinging by the Tarrytown house while I was out. It was only forty minutes the other direction, so it was basically on the way.

I checked to make sure both of the kids were still asleep in the back seat of the car before I stopped in front of the vacant home. When I rolled down my window the pungent scent of lake water blew into the car, carried on a chilly breeze. Wiry weeds had sprouted up in the winter-brown grass, creeping over the edge of the sidewalk.

So there it was. I could still hear the murmuring punctuated with bursts of laughter that would float over the back fence when we held our parties. I could still see the windows illuminated with warm light, Joe and our two—or, now three—kids inside. I never had decided which particular kind of luxury vehicle would be parked in the driveway, but it would have the same taut leather interior as our old Jaguar.

A rush of desire surged through me, my body reacting physically like a starving man beholding a thick cut of freshly grilled steak. I admitted it. I admitted to myself, to God, that I wanted this, and I wanted it more than I wanted anything else. It was stupid and I knew it. If I thought God existed, I should be ambivalent about the house, and desire nothing more than for my soul to be in tune with the source of all goodness, now and forever. But if God came down and gave me the choice right now, the house and the parties, or divine unity and deep inner peace … I'd take the house.

I knew it was the wrong answer. In a way, I did *want* to want God more than all of this. And as I looked at the house and considered what our lives could be like if Joe moved forward with this big client, I was aware that I didn't have the strength to let it go.

You're going to have to help me here, I said silently. I put the car in gear, and before I drove away, I made the sign of the cross.

* * *

My plan at the pharmacy was to talk them out of some of their samples. The kids assisted me by crying and squirming in the cart, which helped me look extra pathetic. I told the pharmacy clerk which prescription I was here to pick up, and before I could begin my soliloquy of woe she disappeared behind a row of shelves. She returned to the checkout counter with the same white bag full of shots that I'd had them put back the other day. Before I could object, she said, "That's a thirty dollar co-pay."

I snorted. "I wish. Unfortunately we've already been through this. My insurance only partially covers it."

She squinted at the screen, her fingers intermittently tapping at her keyboard. "I just double checked. It's thirty."

"Are you positive about that?"

She nodded. I fumbled with my purse, which I'd only brought in as an afterthought since I didn't think I'd be buying anything. I pulled out my wallet and handed my debit card to her, steeling myself for the inevitable moment when she realized it was all a mistake. She gave me the bag and probably told me to have a nice day, but I didn't hear a word she said.

* * *

On the way home from Mass on Sunday, we rounded a corner on the road to my mom's house to see a long stretch of red tail lights up ahead. Yellow construction vehicles kicked up dust on the horizon. Just ahead of us, policemen motioned rhythmically with glowing orange batons. All the cars were being directed to turn into the neighborhood next to my mom's, and we were left to figure out how to navigate the maze of subdivision streets to get through.

Traffic was stopped on the main entrance road into the neighborhood. We'd never driven through this subdivision, so we had no idea which way to go. Apparently, no one else did either. After a painful five minutes in which we only covered an eighth of a mile, Joe pulled out of traffic and took a left on a side street.

We were not the only ones who had that idea, and we ended up stuck behind a line of cars waiting to get past the stop sign at an intersection.

I leaned my head against the window and looked around at the houses while we waited. This neighborhood was connected to my mom's, though it was distinctly different. My mom's subdivision was one of custom-built homes with spacious interiors, marble countertops and rounded edges on all the corners. This neighborhood's houses were about half the size, with no impressive architecture or visible decorator touches.

"Look at that", Joe said, pointing out the window. Just beyond him was a red FOR SALE BY OWNER sign with a handwritten number in the white space below the notice.

I hoped this wouldn't turn into an argument, but I had to point out: "If you shut down the firm, we won't be able to afford any house." Words of woe about how we would be living with my mom forever, doomed to sad lives of penny-pinching misery would have rolled off my tongue effortlessly, but I held them back.

"Probably. But it couldn't hurt to call." He already had his mobile phone out and looked back and forth between the sign and the keypad as he dialed. I could hear the ringing, then a garbled greeting. "Hi, my name is Joe, and my wife and I would like to come look at your house ... Okay, great ... Would now work?"

I tugged his sleeve. "I thought you were just going to get the price!"

He held up his hand and pressed the phone closer to his ear. "Yeah ... okay ... we're actually sitting right in front of your house right now." He jerked the car out of the line of traffic and pulled it into the driveway.

As we walked to the front door, I noticed the stone steps that formed stairs down the sloped yard. The lawn was well manicured, and the porch had been swept recently. The friendly face of a middle-aged man appeared at the front door. "Howdy! Glad you could come by!"

He ushered us in, and I was caught off guard by the simple beauty of the interior. A brand new cream-colored carpet glowed on the floor. Freshly-painted white walls lent a new feel to the seven-year-old house, and an entryway ceiling that stretched all the way up to the second-story roof added space and airiness to the modest home. The picture window in the living room revealed a thriving, unseasonably green back yard. The house wasn't large, but its space was used well. The kitchen was small, but the walk-in pantry was bigger than our current closet. The three bedrooms had barely enough room for beds and dressers, but that allowed for a second family room upstairs.

The owner introduced himself as Allan, and he offered us beers to complement our tour, which Joe happily accepted. When we stepped out onto the back porch, overlooking a half-acre yard with decorative brickwork encircling well-tended trees, I could see us living here. For the first time in months, I could think of our future without thinking of the Tarrytown house. But then I remembered that this wouldn't work either if we gave up the law firm. Between Joe's student loan payments and our debt from starting the business, that new salary he'd been offered wouldn't cover a house. When I combined that with the fact that we'd be out of room at my mom's place once this baby was born, I almost had a panic attack.

"How much are you asking for it?" Joe asked. I braced myself for a rousing round of deep self-pity, to begin as soon as I heard the answer.

Allan finished a sip of his beer. "Look, I got a new job up in Dallas that starts right away, and I need to get out of here." He named a figure, and I gasped.

"Are you kidding? You'd seriously let us have it for that?" I blurted. The look Joe gave me indicated that I was officially out of contention for the Negotiator of the Century award, but I couldn't help it. I knew what houses went for in this area and had never seen one at that price.

"We're interested", Joe said coolly. "Could you give us until Tuesday morning to get back to you?"

"Sure thing." After they finished their beers, Allan walked us to the door, and as we made our way through the living room he told us that he had only put out the For Sale sign that morning, and we were the first people to call.

Allan opened the front door for us. He seemed to be about to say goodbye, but then paused. "I hope y'all don't think I'm crazy for saying this", he said as he took his hands in and out of his jeans pockets self-consciously, "but I really feel like you coming here today was an answered prayer."

* * *

When I faced a new problem with the possibility of getting this house, I decided to give prayer a shot. I did a mental comparison of what we had in our storage facility and what was lacking if we were seriously

215

going to be homeowners, and I came up with a specific list: We'd need a refrigerator, a lawn mower, a washer/dryer, and a bed. A coffee table and a couch for the second family room upstairs would be helpful, too. And we could afford none of those things.

Okay, God, that's what we need. I said after reciting the list. *I assume that if we need them, you'll show us how to get them. If you don't, I'll assume we don't really need them.*

That night at dinner, we told my mom about the house over bowls of spaghetti topped with a meaty sauce she'd simmered all afternoon.

She used her fork to point to the west. "Did you say it was in Oak Brook? The neighborhood right over there?"

"Yeah. It's about twenty blocks from here", I said.

She couldn't conceal the delight on her face. "But I thought you were dead set on moving back to Austin."

Joe and I exchanged glances. "We were", I said, "but we're exploring other options, too."

"I didn't want to say anything, but that would be so great if you stayed close to here." She looked at Donald, who had spaghetti sauce smeared around his mouth. "I would love for you all to be close."

"We haven't made the decision for sure yet. We have some other things we need to work out", Joe said, undoubtedly referring to the law firm decision.

My mom thought for a moment, then looked up from her plate. "You know, if you do get this house, could I give you my refrigerator?"

"What?" I said. I remembered the prayer I'd said just hours before. I'd told nobody about it, not even Joe.

"This house came with black appliances, and I've been wanting to get a matching refrigerator for a while. I just didn't know what to do with this white one. Could you use it?"

It took me a moment to answer. "Yes. Yes, we could."

* * *

The next morning, Joe sent me an email saying that Allan called. Allan said that his new place in Dallas was a master planned neighborhood where the lawn care was taken care of by the homeowners' association. He planned to leave us his lawn mower, weed eater, and leaf blower as gifts if we bought the house.

216

* * *

A few hours later, the phone rang. Nothing showed up on caller ID, and as soon as I heard the low hissing in the background, I knew it was my dad calling from Abu Dhabi.

"Hey, kid, how's it going?" he said, his voice sounding weak over the eight thousand miles that separated us.

"Pretty good", I said.

"Well, I got some good news today", he said. I pressed my ear closer to the phone. It sounded like he was calling from Neptune. "I got offered another job a little closer to home, and I'm going to take it."

"That's great!" I shouted, not sure how well he could hear me. I shut the door to my office so I wouldn't disturb the kids' naps.

"It's an amazing thing: They're sending me to Grand Cayman, in an apartment that's right on the beach!"

"That's great, Dad! When does it begin?"

"In a little over a month. I'll be back home for two weeks to see Papaw and deal with my storage facility, and then I'll head out."

We chatted for a while longer, making jokes about the challenges that he would face while living on Cayman Island, like sunburns and melted piña coladas. And then, just as we were about to end the call, he added, "Oh, by the way, this apartment is furnished, and I have a bunch of stuff in storage that I don't know what to do with." He asked me if I had any use for a series of items, which included a washer/dryer, a couch, a bed, and a coffee table.

35

As soon as Joe walked into the bedroom, he knew something was wrong. "How long have you been sitting on the bed like that?"

"I don't know. A while."

He moved into the closet and hung up his suit jacket. "Are you okay?"

"Not really. I'm stressed. Really stressed."

He had been about to hang up his tie, but came and sat next to me instead. "Is it the house stuff?"

I shook my head no, trying to blink away the stinging feeling in my eyes.

"Is it the decision about the law firm?"

I let out a quick and weak, "No!"

"Oh, the pregnancy? Medical bills and stuff?"

Another negative.

"Then what is it?"

"I think God just answered a whole bunch of my prayers!" I said.

Joe furrowed his brow, confused. "And you're upset about this?"

This time I nodded in the affirmative.

"Well. Okay. That is definitely a problem that only you would have." I was pretty sure Joe was stifling a laugh, but he hid it well. "Is there anything I can do?"

I sniffed and dried my eyes. "No. I'm fine. I don't really want to talk about it. I just need to get some air."

Desperate for privacy, I grabbed my Bible, slipped on my shoes, and headed outside. I noticed that the picture of my grandparents and little Tommy had been righted, and I placed it facedown again.

For the first time in weeks, I felt heat on my skin when I walked in the sun. It was a warm February day, the beginning of Texas spring, and the afternoon was noticeably brighter than it had been in recent weeks. Behind the bank of mailboxes at the center of my mom's street was a small nature preserve, about the size of two house lots, strewn with boulder-sized rocks. I took a seat on one of these jagged nature-chairs, its height making me sit in an awkward half-standing position. I opened my Bible to the page I'd been reading over and over ever since the call from my dad, placing my hand over it so it wouldn't be blown by the breeze.

I read of how the women sent word to Jesus, saying, "Lord, the one you love is sick." By the time he arrived in Bethany, his friend Lazarus was dead; he'd been in the tomb for four days. Everyone was mourning and crying, and Jesus himself was moved to tears.

Jesus went to the tomb and told the dead man's friends and sisters to remove the stone that blocked it. They protested that it was going to smell, but they did it anyway. And Jesus called, "Lazarus, come out!" And the dead man awoke, still wrapped in burial linens.

I closed the book and wondered how I was supposed to believe that any of this ever happened—that *any* answered prayer was an act of God and not just beneficent coincidence—when it was so infuriatingly inconsistent. If God was the one behind the thirty-dollar co-pay and the house and the refrigerator and the furnishings, that was great for me, but what about the woman in Guatemala who didn't have access to the medicine she needed at any price? What about the mother in the Congo who did not have *food*, let alone a refrigerator?

I thought of the moment Lazarus awoke from the dead, and imagined the ecstasy that must have overtaken him when he saw the sunlight begin to filter in as the rock slid away from his tomb. What a beautiful moment it must have been for him to step from the dank cave and realize that he was alive again. I clenched my teeth to control my emotions when I thought: *And wouldn't that have been nice for Tommy, too.*

If Jesus could run up and reverse a friend's death, if he could send me lawn mowers and coffee tables, where was he while my grandmother's first baby, my uncle, was trapped in a burning car?

I jumped off the rock. If there weren't a lady checking her mail just a few yards away, I would have kicked the boulder with frustration. Instead I stood rigid, clutching my Bible in front of my chest, holding it so tightly that my knuckles turned white (which was, hopefully, less weird).

I felt ungrateful for not thanking God for what he'd given me. But the moment I permitted even a whiff of gratitude, I felt like an egomaniacal, spoiled yuppie for assuming that God had nothing better to do than give middle-class families nice things to make their lives a little more cozy. The old atheist in me sneered at the whole thing, saying that God didn't even exist and I'd finally sunk to the level of religious people who attributed coincidences to fairy figures. And my practical side screamed that this was all moot and the real question was what we were going to do about the law firm.

With the decision about whether to shut down the firm growing closer by the minute, it was time for me to figure out what I wanted out of life. I knew that it was intellectually dishonest to say that I believed in God but wanted to spend all my time and energy chasing money and houses. But money and houses were safe. Parties were at least fun, even if they didn't add deep meaning to your life. God was a different story.

I had become convinced that God exists and that he became man as Jesus. I had even started to think of myself as a Christian, and knew that it was more than likely that Joe and I would both become Catholic when we were done with RCIA. And now that thought terrified me, because I realized that I believed in a God who answered some people's prayers but not the prayers of others.

My mom's figure emerged from the house, looked around, and disappeared back inside. Then Joe. They must have been looking for me because it was time to take Irma home. I shoved the Bible into my back pocket and stalked back to the house.

* * *

Irma finished a story about one of the Guadalupanas at Saint William that sounded like something out of a sitcom. She was still laughing and wiping her eyes, when she noticed I wasn't laughing. I flattened my lips in imitation of a smile, but it came off like I was doing an impression of a happy robot.

Even though I was watching the road, I could sense her gaze. "*Qué pasa, Jenny?*" She and her sisters always pronounced my name like *JAY-nee*, and I'd come to associate the sound of my name said that way with tenderness and love.

I glanced over to flash another robot-smile and happened to notice her hands, folded in her lap, which bore the calluses of a life of toil. I remembered the stories I'd heard about her childhood in Mexico. Her father was murdered, which plunged her mother and the seven children into a level of poverty not known in the United States. The children did not have beds; they slept on a dirt floor. Their main source of food was the rotting fruit that the vendors couldn't sell. Every now and then their mother could get a piece of cheese that could fit into the palm of her hand, and she and all the children would split it as a special treat. They owned no toys, other than those they dug out of the local landfill.

"Irma?" I asked, my voice shaking, hoping I could cover this in Spanish. "Was your mother angry at God?"

She seemed shocked and maybe even unsure she'd heard the question correctly. "Oh, no, no. No, my mother loved God", she said, the tone of her voice exuding an unseen light that filled the darkened car. "Every week we went down to the church to clean it, and she loved it so much, being there, making it look nice."

I thought about her story for a moment. Then I asked, "Did she ever think that God didn't answer her prayers?"

"No, because he did answer her prayers!" she said.

"Your mother thought God answered her prayers?" I rewound what she'd just said in case I'd misunderstood the Spanish.

Irma nodded empathically. She recounted a story, through the stops and starts of my interrupting to clarify terms, of a time when none of the children had blankets. They all slept on the floor—no beds, no pillows, nothing to cover themselves. Then one day a local bar owner was re-covering his pool tables, and he gave Irma's mother the scraps of old felt for her children to use as blankets.

"The felt?" Now I was the one who thought we had a misunderstanding. "The felt was the answered prayer?"

"*Sí, Jenny, sí*", she said. "God always provides."

I watched the glowing lane lines shoot under the car as I processed what she had just said. Cobbling together words from my limited vocabulary, I started talking, trying to convey what was troubling me. "God has made life easier for me right now. It's good. But why isn't life easy for everyone?"

She wasn't flustered by the question. "Life is hard. Sometimes things will be good. But often they won't." She chuckled at the last sentence, with a certain amusement at life that carried the protection of cynicism, but had all the vulnerability of hope. "Things are easy now, maybe they won't be tomorrow. We don't know. But it's all okay if you have God."

221

She hadn't understood my question. Or I didn't understand her answer. Or something. I tried again. "If the children were cold, wouldn't thicker blankets be a better answered prayer?"

I turned to her just as a gentle smile warmed her entire face. "It wasn't only for the cold. The answered prayer was that they knew God was there."

36

Once again I couldn't sleep, and this time I'd come out to the living room to listen to a new Rosary CD that my blog readers told me about.

The calming effect of this CD rivaled any drug in the world. A priest began each mystery with a short reflection on the life of Christ. Each word was said slowly, carrying a gravitas that could only come with decades of prayer and hard-earned experience. Then he and a golden-voiced woman alternated saying each Hail Mary and Our Father. Violins and a classical guitar filled the background. The tune was both hopeful and mournful, brimming with the tension that comes from knowing that love is always entwined with sorrow. It was like the theme that would be played at the resolution of a great epic.

I escaped into the gentle tones of his words. I first thought that this must be what the voice of God himself would sound like, but the more I listened the more I understood that that this was the voice of a fellow traveler, a frail human who had known what sorrow life has to offer, whose love of God sustained him.

I positioned the headphones on my ears and leaned back onto the couch. Directly across the dark room, that picture of my grandparents' young family remained facedown on the mantle, like a shrine to an unjust God. I closed my eyes every time I caught sight of it.

"The Third Sorrowful Mystery", the priest announced, not a trace of tension in his words. "The Crowning with Thorns."

He described this moment in which soldiers pressed a wreath of needle-sharp thorns onto the head of the man who had dared to give them hope that he really was a king and savior. In the tradition of the Rosary, the priest then considered the moment from the point of view of Jesus's mom, who surely was aware of the event. The mention of mothers and sons made my eyes dart to the picture on the mantle, but I quickly looked away.

The priest wondered what it must have been for Mary to hear that her son's torturers had not only killed him, but mocked him by placing a fake crown on his head that was specifically designed to cause him pain. "The head that she had held, of the tiny baby. The head of her little boy, that she had caressed." I choked at the words *little boy*, unable to banish the image of the giggling toddler in the black-and-white photo, with a face just like my son's. "The head of her beloved son, whom she had seen healing and preaching, is now filled with wounds."

Without pausing for a breath, he began the Our Father.

The words of the prayer descended on me like a tidal wave. The dirge of the solemn violins broke something in my heart, and raw sorrow poured out. I wrapped my arms across my stomach and leaned forward until my head touched my knees, like someone seeking shelter in a storm that threatened to destroy everything. All the misery of the human experience, all the agony that I usually shut out of my mind, all the heart-wrenching things that I tried to pretend didn't happen while I was living my comfortable suburban existence, it all came crashing in, and this time I did nothing to stop the process. I just listened to the Our Father and let sorrow inch up within me, even though it felt like I might drown.

Each time I thought of a new tragedy, a new cosmic injustice that I'd read about in history books or heard on the news, the image that would come to mind was that of the two graves, my great-grandmother's and Tommy's, their dates of death one day apart. Their slate-gray tombstones were billboards announcing that very bad things do happen to good people sometimes, and God does nothing to stop it. I didn't think I could bear it when I considered what my grandmother must have felt when she stood in front of those two stones and saw the dates of death for her mother and her firstborn child: April 22, 1945, and April 23, 1945.

I had been lost in that moment for an endless string of minutes, when the tide of thoughts ebbed, and a new idea came to mind. It had to do with April 1945. There was something about that date. I had heard of something else happening then—not a distant historical event. Something to which I had a connection. April. 1945. What was it?

A jolt went through me, and I threw off the headphones and raced to our bedroom. I tripped over a pair of shoes, clicked on the lamp on my bedside table, and shoved a stack of books onto the floor. There it was.

The envelope that my mother had given me, with the letter about my grandfather's service during World War II.

Joe turned over and was mumbling incoherent questions at me, but I clicked out the lamp and ran back to the living room. The glare of the overhead lights would have blinded me, so I switched on the single light above the fireplace, half-covered by a casing so that its glow shone down only onto the mantle. I dropped down on the edge of the couch and unfolded the paper.

Lt. Geraghty received the high award of the Bronze Star Medal because one bitter night . . .

No, it was after that.

For my money, Lt. Geraghty is all man.

No, before that.

Men were wounded and dying . . . Some were bleeding and helpless in midstream.

Close. I was close now.

And then I found it. The date that my grandfather miraculously survived his suicide rescue mission: April 30, 1945. Eight days after the accident.

For half an hour I read and re-read the letter, stopping at the date every time. I knew from family history that it had taken some time for the military authorities to find my grandfather to tell him about the accident, and that he'd returned as soon as he got the news. So on the night of the rescue, he had no idea. Of course he didn't. Had he known that his wife was at home in an empty house, the bodies of their child and his mother-in-law resting in a graveyard, he would have never put his own life at risk.

My hand set the letter on the coffee table as if acting on its own, since I was too stunned to will it. My grandfather had been spared. And, now that I thought about it, the family had always considered it a minor miracle that my grandmother herself survived the accident despite being violently thrown from the car. She was five months pregnant, and her baby defied the odds and lived, also. That baby was my mother.

I stood up and walked circles around the coffee table, first clockwise, then counterclockwise, barely aware of my own movements as I retreated into the supernova of thoughts and emotions that filled my head. A primal part of my consciousness, residing some place still like the bottom of the ocean, a place safe from overanalysis, told me that God had saved my grandfather; in those most secluded recesses of my soul, I believed that it was divine intervention that had protected him as he crossed a river in Germany under a downpour of bullets, and that that same divine hand had spared his wife and unborn daughter, too.

I thrilled to consider it. But immediately, it brought me back to the Lazarus problem: Even if God did raise the man from the dead, it begged the question of what he was doing during the other billions of deaths that occurred after Lazarus'. If he could save my grandfather from getting shot in Europe, why couldn't he save a two-year-old little boy in New Jersey?

My usual reaction to a thought like this would be to begin a multi-step process that started with shouting accusatory prayers to the heavens and concluded with questioning God's existence. But this time, within me there was one grain of gratitude, one miniscule part of my soul that felt like I owed something to the God who had protected my mother and grandparents. The least I could do would be to give him the benefit of the doubt.

I had been working from the premise that a loving God could not allow suffering, and so every time I encountered it, it sent me into a tailspin of questioning everything I thought I knew about God. Standing in the middle of the room, I closed my eyes, let myself be in silence for a moment, and then I changed my premise. Out of a sheer sense of duty, I whispered to God, *I will start by assuming you are good. I will begin with the belief that you do love us, all of us.*

The tinny voice of the priest floated up from the headphones on the couch, the *s* sounds of *blessed* and *grace* the only noise in the room. I moved back to the couch, returned the headphones to my ears, and— acting on sheer instinct—slid down on my knees in front of the coffee table. I straightened my back and neck in a signal of attentiveness, I said a prayer for understanding, and I listened for the voice of a good God.

By the time the Sorrowful Mysteries were over, my posture had slouched. When they reached the Glorious Mysteries I was dozing off, his words fading out intermittently, as if someone kept pressing the mute button on the CD player. I was in an almost trance-like state, somewhere between life and the unconscious world.

The words of the ancient prayers became tangled with thought-threads of tombstones and gunfire, little boys photographed in mid-giggle, blackened burnt-out cars, and a man named Lazarus stepping out of a tomb.

This mystery calls us to think of our own eternal destiny, someone said, from a place far away. *The sufferings of this life are not to be compared to the glory that is to come.*

My eyes eased open at the word "suffering". The voice jumped back into the headphones, and my thoughts came together enough to realize that this was the final Glorious Mystery, a meditation on the fact that God gave Mary a place in heaven as the queen of the new creation, as mentioned in the book of Revelation.

"When you say the Rosary, no matter whether you are in joy or sorrow, dreadful fear or in exultation, always turn to this mystery", the old priest said. "Because someday, you and I hope that we will be crowned with grace and glory, in the kingdom of Jesus Christ."

Our Father, who art in heaven . . .

Heaven . . .

Heaven. It had been a subject I'd studiously avoided from the first moment I'd considered that Jesus might exist. Even within Christian theology, very little was known about the place. Not many details had been revealed, and our limited perspective within the material world wouldn't allow us to understand it well anyway. And so, for fear of making up stuff that sounded good but wasn't necessarily true, I had spent very little time pondering the afterlife.

I leaned up. That was a problem. Maybe even a big problem.

I'd read all sorts of theological insights about how there was no suffering, no death, in God's original plan. I understood that the first humans chose it for themselves when they severed their connection with the divine good because they wanted to be gods; I'd seen for myself that the rest of us continue willfully to turn away from God every day. I'd pondered the stunning idea that, rather than letting us languish in the cesspool we'd created, God jumped in with us, suffered with us—and for us—to show us the way home. It all sounded great. Until I pictured my grandmother holding her dying child on her lap in an ambulance, and then the rich theological insights disintegrated into impotent words.

But what I had not been factoring in was heaven.

Starting with that childhood moment at The Creek, I'd always been acutely aware of the fleetingness of human life. Now that I took that same awareness and examined it in light of the existence of heaven, everything changed. I'd always heard the ticking of the clock that counts down the seconds as we all get closer to death; now I should see its

227

ticking as a countdown to the end of unjust suffering. As an atheist I mourned the fact that nothing good would last; now it was time to accept the fact that good did last, and it would last forever. Only suffering would end.

I rose from the couch and approached the mantle. I slid the picture off the shelf and held it in my hands, searching the eyes of my grandmother, my grandfather, and, finally, their son. Their suffering was terrible, and God thought so, too. He hated what was going on down here on earth so much that he allowed himself to be murdered, simply to open up an escape hatch for us to get out. And now, my grandparents and their son had gone through it. They were out of this land of war and fire, bullets and car accidents. They were in a place where everything they had suffered on earth was rewarded with limitless joy.

I thought of Lazarus again, that moment when he was called back from eternity, waking in the tomb to see the rays of light shoot through the darkness. Scripture never did say what happened after that. The author John simply recounted that Jesus raised him from the dead, and then he moved on to the next subject. I had always supplied my own image to round out the story, with Lazarus rushing out and giving Jesus a bear hug, almost knocking him down in his excitement and gratitude.

But as I looked at Tommy, and thought once again of where he was now, the scene of Lazarus was utterly transformed. I rewound back through the images of the celebration and the hugs, back to that moment when he first saw the cracks of light. And for the first time, it occurred to me that maybe Lazarus was disappointed.

37

"*Buenos días, Jenny.*" Irma's face appeared before me, blurry and unstable. She was smiling in amusement. I was in the living room. Wait. Why was I sleeping on the living room couch?

When I sat up I felt a tugging on my ears. I removed the headphones and saw the CD player that contained my Rosary recording. "What time is it?"

"*Nueve y media.*"

"Nine thirty?" I stumbled to my feet. "Did Joe already leave?"

"*Sí.*" She said he was already gone when she arrived at eight.

I spotted the phone on the kitchen table and ran to pick it up. I dialed Joe's number, only to have the receptionist tell me that he was in meetings all morning.

"I need to go down to the office, Irma." I grabbed a granola bar from a box on the counter to keep morning sickness at bay, and told her I'd take the baby so that she and Donald could go to the park.

I pulled on jeans and a fitted, white, button-down shirt, changed Elaine's diaper, and set her in her car seat carrier. I surveyed the living room to make sure there was nothing I'd forgotten, and a flash of brassy-colored metal caught my eye on the floor in front of the couch. The picture. I went to the couch and knelt down, the images of my family gazing up at me from the carpet. I picked up the frame, the smooth felt backing soft in my palm. Before I stood, I looked into the eyes of each one of them, from my grandfather, to Tommy, to my grandmother. I said a prayer for each one of them, then pressed the picture against my chest and asked them to pray for me, too. I stood and returned the picture to the mantle, this time faceup.

* * *

We almost ran into Joe as he dashed through the lobby between meetings. "Hey!" he exclaimed. He gave Elaine a kiss on the cheek and gave me a hug. "What are you doing here?"

"I know today's the day you have to give an answer about joining that other firm, and since we also told Allan we'd get back to him about the house today, I wanted to talk in person."

"Okay, sure." He asked the receptionist to tell his paralegal to start the meeting without him, and we went into his office.

I spread Elaine's baby blanket in front of Joe's desk and set her on the floor with some unsharpened pencils, which she immediately used as teethers. Instead of sitting behind his desk, Joe sat in the client's chair next to Elaine.

"I want you to take the job with the other firm." I was caught off guard by the happiness that welled within me as I said it.

He examined me, as if to discern whether I was just saying this for his sake. "Really? You're honestly okay with it?"

"I am. My only concern is what to do about the employees."

"You don't need to worry about that", Joe said. He explained that he'd mentioned the possibility of closing the firm to them and, in another amazing turn of events, every one of them would be taken care of. The head paralegal and the one attorney who worked full time with Joe would have opportunities at the new firm, another paralegal was leaving to go to law school, and a part-time attorney who'd been contracting with us was moving to another city for his wife's job. "I just worry about Irma", he said at the end.

"Her daughter's housecleaning business is booming, and she needs help. I think Irma was going to have to quit soon anyway."

Those were the final loose ends. We sat for a moment and watched Elaine play, both of us knowing that these were our last few moments as owners of a law firm.

"Do you want to call Allan, or should I?"

"You go ahead", I said.

He went around to his desk, pulled a business card out of his wallet, and dialed the phone. We grinned at each other as we waited for the answer. "Hello, Allan? Hi, it's Joe Fulwiler. We want the house." They committed to the deal in a verbal handshake and made arrangements to meet that night to discuss details. We were now owners of a small suburban home.

I took a deep breath, exhaling nervous anticipation. "Are you sure you're okay with this?"

He leaned forward. "Honestly, I've never been this happy in my life." When he said it, I noticed something. Ever since I'd known Joe, an anxiety had always clung to him. Even when we were on vacation, or when he was relaxing after work, if I observed him closely enough, I could see that he was still possessed by the ghost of the boy who'd never gotten over being poor. But now the ghost was gone.

* * *

I dropped Elaine back at home just in time to make it to my doctor appointment. Dr. Wolfe swept into the room and did his trademarked move of grabbing the stool and sitting in a single motion. "So, what's the contraception decision?"

"Okay", I stared at the floor, trying to remember the script I'd carefully crafted. "There is, there is a—something I've been thinking about ..." Oh gosh. This talking about religion thing was harder than I thought it would be. After more hemming and hawing, during which the tension level in the room doubled as I used up second after second of the busy doctor's time, I finally looked up and spat out the words: "I am converting to Catholicism. In six weeks, actually. I'm going to become Catholic." I hoped all that religious talk didn't make him too uncomfortable.

"Okay ..." he said, that pen still poised.

I had hoped he'd extrapolate what that meant, but evidently I needed to spell it out. So I just had to say it. "I'm not open to using contraception. Can you work with me on this?"

It took him a moment to process what I'd said. "The standard treatment is Coumadin, and in many cases Coumadin for life—"

"But can you work with me on this? Can we put our heads together and figure out a different kind of treatment plan?"

He didn't throw up his hands and cry, "Oh, whatever am I going to do with this religious nut job?" as I had imagined he would. He didn't scoff, or look at me like I had just started drooling on myself. Instead, he simply replied, "Okay. Okay, sure, I think we can come up with something."

He said he'd need some time to think about alternative treatment plans and did a quick exam to check my lungs and examine my legs for DVT symptoms. After we shook hands and said goodbye, he rushed to the door for his next patient. As I was gathering my purse, he poked his head back in the door and said, "Oh, and congratulations."

"The baby?" It seemed like an odd time to congratulate me on that, since he already knew, but okay. "Thanks!"

"No, you mentioned that you were becoming Catholic soon. Congratulations."

After I left I drove out of the parking lot in silence, trying on this new image of myself as "Catholic". Now that I had told Dr. Wolfe, someone else—who was neither Catholic nor immediate family—knew. For most of my life, my identity had been wrapped up in atheism. Now it was as if I'd accidentally slipped on the wrong team's jersey.

Before I went back to the house I stopped by the pharmacy to get one last refill of Lovenox on our current insurance. The insurance that we'd get with Joe's new job would fully cover my shots, but the co-pay was a few dollars higher, so I thought I'd get one more round at thirty dollars before the new plan kicked in.

Next to the counter at the pharmacy was a rounded mirror with a sweeping view of the waiting area. The reflection showed the line of people waiting to pick up prescriptions, their figures stretched and distorted by the mirror's curves. The third woman back had shoulder-length reddish-brown hair, was starting to show a new pregnancy, and she believed in God. That woman was me.

As I looked at the mirror, I tried to internalize this new image of myself. Where was this woman going? What would her life be like tomorrow, next year, ten years hence? Joe and I always had our futures planned out to the last detail, our spreadsheets with our twenty-year goals being linked to the ten-year and five-year spreadsheets, which corresponded to our monthly to-do lists. Now it was all blank. I used to believe that I could control my way into happiness, or at least amass enough distractions that it would feel like something close. Now I had none of my illusions of control, but more happiness than I'd ever known before.

It was my turn at the pharmacy counter. I strolled to the front of the line and spelled my last name. After the young clerk retrieved the white bag, he frowned at his computer. "You know this is like nine hundred dollars, right?"

This again. "I know. I thought it was. It used to be. But now it's only thirty."

He typed some more, ran back to consult with a manager, and returned to the computer. "No, ma'am, I'm sorry. It's always been nine hundred. Do you still want it?"

"Just look up the last order, the one from last month. You'll see that that one was thirty."

He clicked away at the keyboard. Stopped. Clicked some more. Moved the mouse around. Clicked again. "You must have gone to a different pharmacy for that one."

"No, it was here."

He looked from me to the computer screen, then back at me again. "Ma'am, there is no record of that transaction."

38

We were all set to move into our new house on Monday, April 2nd of 2007. It was the day before our first confession, and four days before Easter Vigil, the Mass when we would receive our first Communion.

The soundtrack to the weeks leading up to it was the thundering of empty boxes tossed onto the floor, the crumpling of the gray-white packing paper, and the laughing of Donald and baby Elaine as they ignored their expensive toys to play with the cardboard boxes. Then, the phone started ringing. Frequently. More frequently than it had in the entire two years that we'd lived at my mom's house. The sound of the doorbell was heard more than it had been in the past year. Word had gotten out that we were becoming Catholic, and Catholics were coming out of the woodwork to congratulate us.

Our neighbor two doors down came by to present us with a long, ceramic roof tile that had been hand-painted in rich gold and bronze tones with the face of Our Lady of Guadalupe. The neighbor to the left said that they were Catholics who hadn't been to Mass in years, and they wanted to know where our church was located. A friend of my mom's stopped by to present me with a crucifix necklace. Friends and acquaintances whom we'd had no idea were even religious, let alone Catholic, heard about our conversions through the grapevine and called to say they were praying for us as Easter Vigil approached.

My aunt Claudia, who had recently returned to the Catholicism of her childhood, was so excited for us that she and my uncle flew in from Atlanta to be there for Easter Vigil. Joe's new boss at work turned out to be a devout Catholic, and he occasionally joined Joe for daily Mass. Every day there was a new call or knock at the door or email, all from fellow Catholics congratulating us on our conversions.

And then there was my blog inbox. Every time I checked it there were more bolded notes at the top of the screen, new well wishes from Catholics all over the world who had discovered my site. The subject lines read like a joyful chorus, *Welcome home!* followed by *Congratulations, We're praying for you*, and *God bless you!* Every post I wrote on the blog was flooded with comments cheering us on as we got closer and closer to the Church.

Over at my personal email account, my dad forwarded an email from one of his cousins, whom I'd never met. She had heard about our conversions and wanted us to know that my great-great aunt's grandson was a Benedictine monk and a well-known iconographer. I was floored by the news; I would have been shocked to find any Mass-going Catholic on that side of the family, let alone a monk. She told him about us, and he was as eager to meet us as we were to meet him. "We thought it was very exotic to have a Catholic in the family!" she noted at the bottom of her email.

Two days before we were scheduled to move out, my mom waded through stacks of moving boxes to find me at the back of my office. She sat down on a closed book box and handed me a folded piece of paper. It was a typed note, and when I unfolded it a check slipped out.

"Dad wanted me to write you a check from his account", she said. Even though they were divorced, she still managed my dad's finances while he was overseas. "He wanted you to have some extra money in case you need to buy a new outfit before Easter Vigil."

I smoothed out the note. It said:

Dear Jen,

I'm proud of you for sticking to what you have found to be true, even though it hasn't been easy. I've arranged things with the new job so that I will be there for first communion. I told them I wouldn't miss it. Use this money to buy anything you need, let me know if you need more.

I'm proud of you.

Dad

My mom had something else in her hand, a piece of white fabric. "I wanted you to have this." She handed me a triangular cut of delicate lace with scalloped edges. "It's my chapel veil. From when I was a kid."

"Oh, wow, thank you." I ran it through my fingers, admiring its smooth texture.

She dropped her eyes to the veil in my hands. "I mentioned that Pop Pop would have been proud of you. I wanted to make sure you knew that I am, too."

* * *

Two days later I found myself in the chaos of the new house, trying to unpack while Joe got in a few hours at work. After telling Donald for the third time to please not throw torn packing paper all over the carpet, I stood back and surveyed the scene. I felt certain that the movers had accidentally picked up the stuff from five other storage sheds while they were working on ours. Surely it was not even possible that all of this had fit into our old condo at the Westgate. I wiped my forehead, and considered the option of just giving up and resigning to live among boxes for the rest of our lives.

The sound of the doorbell bounced around the empty walls. I went to the front door, and on my porch was a Catholic woman named Catherine whom I'd recently met. She looked to be about twenty-seven, with happy curls all throughout her hair and a classically beautiful face that seemed more like that of a nineteenth-century authoress than a modern minivan-driving mom. She carried a foil-covered casserole dish, and a canvas grocery sack swung from her arm. At her feet were three young children and a boom box.

She seemed to sense my confusion. "This was the day you said it was okay to stop by, right?"

Oh! Yes. Now I remembered. Word had gotten out through the local Catholic grapevine that Joe and I could use some help. Catherine, whom everyone called Cat, emailed me and asked if she could bring by a dinner for our family.

"Oh, hi—hi, thank you, please come in", I said, smiling at her three girls, who wore colorful dresses paired with vividly patterned sweaters and vests, giving the impression that they'd had a lot of fun getting themselves dressed that morning.

"I brought paper plates and plastic utensils and cups so you won't have too much cleanup", she said as I followed her through the living room and into the kitchen. "I hope you like enchiladas—this is one of our favorite recipes."

She set to work unpacking the food, with as much efficiency and confidence as if she prepared meals in this kitchen every day. She slid the foil pan into the empty refrigerator and produced a smaller, round, foil pan from the bag, this one labeled *Spanish rice*. Another, this one announcing chocolate chip cookies, was scooted to the back of the counter. The last thing she pulled from the bag was a bottle of wine, a Napa cab that happened to be from one of Joe's favorite vineyards.

"Thank you again", I said. "I can't tell you how much this helps."

I readied myself to follow her back to the front door, but she didn't move. She wiped her hands on her jeans to dry them from the condensation on the pans. "So, should we start in the living room?"

"Umm, start . . . what?"

She laughed. "Oh, I thought you'd need help unpacking. But if it would be any trouble, we could get out of your hair."

"Oh, I couldn't . . ." I stopped myself, and took another look at the wreckage of my living room. "Actually, that would help me so much. And yes, the living room would be a great place to start."

"Great!" She picked up the boom box that one of her daughters had carried to the kitchen. "But first, we'll need some music." She cleared off a space on the counter next to an outlet and set down the portable stereo. With the click of a button, a toe-tapping Ella Fitzgerald song filled the kitchen.

Her youngest daughter was only a few months older than Elaine, and the two babies sat next to one another, mesmerized. The older kids had discovered a crafts box that contained both plastic grocery bags and ribbon, and they created impromptu kites by tying the string to the bag handles. It was a blustery spring day, and as soon as they stepped outside their poor-man's kites floated high into the air above them. Before we began working, Cat and I stood at the window for a moment, watching our children as they screamed in awe and delight to watch the wind whip their bags through the air.

We started in the kitchen and quickly developed a system for tackling two large boxes of glasses. She would unwrap each one and set it on the table, and I would take it, rinse it in the sink, and put it in the cabinet. We repeated the process about thirty times.

After putting the last of the tumblers on the shelf, I saw the herd of kids run by in the back yard below. The wind had snatched Donald's bag-kite out of his hand, and the kids shrieked as they chased it around the yard, their hair blowing as wildly as the kites. Over the swingy, happy sound of trombones and string bass that poured from Cat's stereo, I could hear the laughter of the children outside. And I was reminded of Noe Rocha's words from our first night in RCIA: *Remember, Jennifer, you're not doing this alone.*

39

I sauntered through the main doors of the church, yapping on the phone to Joe about what to do with a box of clutter he'd just uncovered in the corner of the garage. I kept talking until I was inches away from the door. I shrugged off my coat and folded it over my arm, feeling pricks of icy water on the coat fabric. A surprise cold front had blown over the city the day before, and I'd ducked under a light sleet to get from the back of the parking lot to the inside of the building.

As soon as I entered the church, I paused in silent wonder. I still hadn't gotten used to the beauty of this place. Saint William had needed to build a bigger church to accommodate the mushrooming crowds, and this one opened only four months ago. This new building was immediately hailed by Catholics and non-Catholics alike as one of the most beautiful churches in Texas. Twelve-foot-tall oak doors guarded the sacred space, and inside a long barrel dome stretched high above the pews, hundreds of hand-painted gold stars shone over the deep blue background. At the front, behind the marble altar, was a stand-alone cherrywood wall with four alcoves for statues of Matthew, Mark, Luke, and John. Each man was posed to appear lost in thought, holding scrolls and writing instruments. The crucifix stood guard between Mark and Luke. A sweeping replica of the Italian Renaissance masterpiece the *Disputation of the Holy Sacrament* rose up behind the four men, covering the entire wall behind the altar.

In contrast to the cold, dead night outside, the church bustled with life. Hundreds of people stood in front of ten confessional booths, the lines wrapping through the pews, tracing the walls, and spilling out into the narthex. Women in designer coats stood next to construction workers wearing mud-caked boots; teens with hands jammed into their blue jean pockets leaned against walls next to elderly folks in wheelchairs; Indian ladies resplendent in richly colored saris bounced babies on their hips next to white guys wearing ID badges from local high-tech companies. To see the crowd was to be reminded that the word *catholic* means "universal".

The inside of the church was laid out like a cross, and I made my way to the southern wing, to the left of the altar. There I found what I was looking for: a paper with the name of our pastor, Father Joel McNeil, printed in bold black letters. Though his line was one of the longest, it's where I wanted to be. He was a quiet, studious man who was as humble as he was intelligent. His homilies had consistently impressed both Joe and me with their insight, and "like Father Joel said on Sunday ..." had become a recurring statement at our dinner table.

His makeshift confessional was set up behind an accordion-style wooden divider. A one-hundred-year-old work of stained glass loomed on the wall above, its colors muted by the night sky. I watched one person after another disappear behind the dividers. When they popped out the other side, most were dabbing their eyes with Kleenex.

I pretty much knew what this would be like: I'd confessed my sins a bunch of times in my head. Confession would be just like that, only with a priest acting as a stand-in for God. If anything, I worried that it would seem redundant to what I'd already done privately.

Now the makeshift wall swallowed the lady in front of me. I heard the murmuring of her voice, then the soothing tones of Father Joel's. About five minutes later, she emerged out the other side. My turn.

The confessional consisted of two plastic chairs and a small table stacked with a Bible, the *Catechism*, and printouts of various prayers. I bounced into the empty chair and greeted Father Joel. He was about forty-five years old, with dark brown hair framing a kind, gentle face. He looked right at me and greeted me in the name of Christ. Then he nodded and prompted me to begin.

"Oh—heh—okay." I forced a laugh. I picked up my confession booklet from the pocket of my purse, but couldn't find the introduction statement. "Okay, sorry, hang on", I mumbled. My fingers raced to find the right page. Here we go. Loudly and clearly, I began: "Bless me, Father, for I have sinned—"

The sound of my own voice startled me. The spoken words were real and heavy. They carried a gravitas that my silent thoughts did not. Disoriented, I started over. "Bless me, Father, for I have—sinned. This is my first confession."

Father Joel nodded and waited.

But where could I possibly begin?

I searched my memory for every offense against love I'd ever committed. I held up the life I had lived and compared it to the life of Christ, and I started talking about whatever came to mind. There were the times I'd lied, of course, moments I hadn't thought about in years. There was the unchecked vanity, the cowardice that kept me silent when I should have taken a stand. And, wow, all the petty vandalism of my youth—I had forgotten about that until now.

My words were horrible things, which oozed out of my mouth like sludge. I paused for a breath and noticed that I'd begun trembling. There was no way I could stop talking now. It was as if I'd inserted a lance into a festering wound, and it was finally draining.

I fought against waves of emotion, fearing that if I gave in to tears, I would end up sobbing too hard to get it all out. It was surreal to hear my innermost thoughts put into words, to articulate things I had never said before and would never need to say again.

Father Joel simply listened as I poured it all out. He seemed neither offended nor surprised. He just listened. Finally, I began to feel a lightness within me, when there wasn't much left to say. But there was one thing. One last thing I had not brought up.

"Is that all?" Father Joel asked gently.

It wasn't. Now I had to confess the fact that, on countless occasions, I'd made fun of Jesus Christ himself. The image of that moment on my childhood friend's bed when I'd stretched out my arms and cocked my head to the side burned in my memory. I started to describe the moment to Father Joel, but was stopped by a hot swelling in my throat. How do you say something like that? I thought of the crucifix at the front of the church, depicting the man who volunteered to undergo a long death of unthinkable torture for people like me. I had so little compassion that, even when I hadn't believed Jesus was divine, I still couldn't muster up a crumb of sympathy for a poor carpenter who was unjustly sent to the worst kind of death. My cries broke into a long sob.

Father Joel leaned forward and handed me a Kleenex. He remained still and relaxed, as if we had all the time in the world. I wiped tears from my eyes with a trembling hand and managed to stammer out the rest of my confession between gasps. Then I looked up at him with a puffy, red face, making eye contact for the first time since we began. I waited to hear what he had to say to someone like me.

His face contained nothing but compassion. "My child, you are forgiven", he said. "The Lord forgives you."

I'd forgotten that this was part of the equation. "Really?" I knew it was true theologically, but it didn't seem real.

"Of course. God loves you, and he forgives you."

In a daze, I read the Act of Contrition. Then I bowed my head, and Father Joel lifted his hand, and he carefully, purposefully, made the sign of the cross over me. "I absolve you of your sins in the name of the Father, the Son, and the Holy Spirit."

The whispered word "Amen" passed over my lips, as if someone had said it for me.

I left the confessional, a Kleenex pressed to my eyes, and slid into a nearby pew. I wasn't sure what just happened; the only thing I knew was that my life would never be the same again. Never could I have imagined the power of speaking the words of my sins, going through the process of assigning words to my deeds, articulating them for another human to hear. And never, ever could I have imagined what it would do for my soul to hear the words, *My child, you are forgiven.*

* * *

I arrived home to a quiet house. Joe had already put the kids to bed; their cribs were the only furniture assembled in the house. I peeked into our new bedroom and saw Joe asleep in his clothes on the mattress, a drill and box cutter lying beside him on the floor.

I crept back downstairs and into the living room, all the walls blank with possibilities. I kept my coat on and stepped out to the back porch. All around me, the world was quiet and shadowy.

I remembered a time in my life when I avoided going outside at night. For years after my existential crisis at The Creek, the darkness of night seemed too real, too familiar, as if it had all leaked out of my soul and shrouded the world around me. Even later, when I regained some balance, standing outside alone at eleven o'clock at night would have involved fighting back an avalanche of thoughts that would have buried me if they'd come. Out of habit I waited for all those familiar sensations of restlessness and fear and discontent to bubble near the surface this time, too. But everything was still.

There on the back porch of my suburban house, for the first time in my life, I was aware without any question that I was in the presence of God. I had been looking for him so long, but my sins were like a black smoke that fills the air and blots out the sun, obscuring it so completely that you sometimes wonder if it still exists. Now, the smoke had been blown away. The air was clear. And, finally, I could see.

40

"It's the Fulwilers!" The hostess and two waitresses descended upon us as soon as we pushed through the swinging doors to Guero's. "What have you been up to?"

Joe and I looked at each other, holding back laughter. "Let's see", Joe said, "We started a business, shut it down, and became hardcore Catholics." He turned to me. "Does that cover it?"

"We also moved to the 'burbs, where we have three kids under age three", I added.

"That's a story I gotta hear", the hostess said, leading us to the waiting area. "But first, margaritas!"

"We can't right now", I said, scanning the tables in front of us. "We're on our way to church, actually."

We were downtown for the Red Mass, a seven-hundred-year-old tradition where bishops hold a special blessing Mass for local attorneys, judges, and other legal professionals. Afterward, the bishop was hosting a reception and dinner at a private club near the cathedral. It happened to be the same day as our fourth wedding anniversary, so we thought it would be the perfect way to celebrate.

But first, I wanted to take a detour to South Congress. There was something I had been meaning to do for a long time now. "Is Clifford Antone around tonight?" I asked. His usual table was empty, and I stood on my toes to scan the bar area. Our party-throwing days were on hold for a while, but for the longest time I'd wanted to touch base with him. I often thought of his own plans to start his life fresh, and I wanted to say hello and see how that was going.

The hostess studied our faces, her brow wrinkling in concern. "You didn't hear? It was all over the local news."

"Hear what?" I eased down from my tiptoes. I knew from her tone that I wasn't going to find him here.

"I'm sorry, honey, but Clifford Antone is dead. He died last year."

"What? When?"

She told me the date, and it was within days of my DVT diagnosis. Things had been so crazy for us that we'd missed the news altogether. I searched the restaurant, my mind unable to process it. Surely she was mistaken, and he was about to saunter through the double doors any second now.

"I'm sorry you didn't know", she said, her voice distant. I hadn't known him well, which somehow made it all the more surreal that he was gone.

We drifted out of the restaurant. Joe held the door for me, and before I stepped out I turned around and looked for him one last time, just in case.

Joe offered to bring the car around so I didn't have to walk, and I stood on the edge of the raised restaurant porch, looking down Congress Avenue as if it were a scene from a long-ago dream. I reached into my purse and slid open the zipper on the interior pocket. Under the change and keys that had accumulated over the years, I could see a glimpse of white. I pulled it out, smoothed it in my hand, and looked at the napkin where Clifford Antone had written his phone number.

He wasn't Catholic, and wasn't a practicing Christian that I knew of, but I took comfort in the possibility that he had made it to purgatory, the great refuge of well-meaning sinners, and if he wasn't in heaven, he was close. And hopefully, one day, I would meet him again.

I closed my eyes and said the Our Father for his soul. The wind rose and fell like respiration as I prayed, the gusts rushing past me like a great exhalation. My hair danced around my face like flames, then settled down as the air stilled. When the wind started building once again, I slid my fingers across the weathered paper one last time. And as a deluge of warm air rushed passed me in a crescendo, I released the napkin, and felt it disappear from my hands.

EPILOGUE

"There are two ways of getting home", G. K. Chesterton wrote in the first line of *The Everlasting Man*. "And one of them is to stay there. The other is to walk round the whole world till we come back to the same place."

Even as life as a Catholic felt less new and more normal, occasionally I'd be overcome with the thundering thought, *How did I GET HERE?* I'd traveled a long, rocky path to end up in this place, and it would have been so easy for me to stray off course at countless points along the way. It gave me chills to consider how often a slight difference in the way events played out would have thrown me onto an entirely different path.

The thought came to mind again as I dashed around the house on a September morning, hours before Donald was to be baptized. I realized that almost my entire wardrobe was black, with a few gray pieces mixed in for color, and I dug feverishly through long-forgotten drawers in hopes of finding something to wear for an occasion whose traditional color is white. All the while, that question lingered in my mind. Not so long ago, I was the atheist girl who worked at a high-tech company and hopped on planes to travel the world with her boyfriend. Was I really now the Catholic mother with three young children, a Miraculous Medal dangling from her neck as she scurried through the house to prepare for her son's baptism?

How did I GET HERE?

I yanked open a drawer that I thought might contain my scarves. There were no scarves inside, but instead, a long, rectangular box slid to the front. Its white color was faded to a dusty pearl, the once-red lines around its edges now a weak orange. It looked familiar, but I couldn't place where I'd seen it before. A long object rattled inside. I opened the small flap at the end of the box and slid its contents into my palm.

A candle landed in my hand. My baptism candle.

I rarely thought about my baptism. It almost never came to mind before Joe and I were Catholic, and even throughout the process of my conversion, I only considered it once or twice. I saw our religious explorations as being a purely intellectual endeavor; it didn't seem relevant that a Catholic priest had poured water over my head at a church in the summer of 1977. Even once I understood that the sacrament of baptism contained real power, I couldn't imagine how it would apply to my life, so I put it out of my mind. It was like a seed planted in the ground: I knew it was there, but since I never did anything to help it flower, it was easy to forget.

Now I thought of the moment of my baptism again. I imagined my grandparents looking on as the priest spoke the sacred words over the water. I pictured my baptism candle flickering to life after being held to the flame of the Easter candle, a symbol of the power of Christ to bring light to the world. I looked down and noticed that the wick on the candle in my hand was still darkened from its encounter with the flame.

The sounds of the bustling house faded away, and I closed my eyes. This, of course, was the answer to my question.

The moment the priest baptized me, I was sealed with the sign of belonging to Christ, an indelible mark on my soul that not even a life as an avowed atheist and unrepentant sinner could wipe away. God and his Church were set as my home base, and something deep within me would never truly be at peace until I returned to it, even as I traveled the whole world trying to find an alternate destination. My entire conversion was less of a journey to a foreign place, and more of a discovery of my long-lost home.